HUMAN JOBS AND COMPUTER INTERFACES

HUMAN JOBS AND COMPUTER INTERFACES

Proceedings of the IFIP WG 9.1 Working Conference on
Human Jobs and Computer Interfaces
Tampere, Finland, 26-28 June,1991

Edited by

MARKKU I. NURMINEN
Department of Computer Science
University of Turku
Turku, Finland

GEORGE R.S. WEIR
Department of Computer Science
University of Strathclyde
Glasgow, UK

1991

NORTH-HOLLAND
AMSTERDAM • LONDON • NEW YORK • TOKYO

ELSEVIER SCIENCE PUBLISHERS B.V.
Sara Burgerhartstraat 25
P.O. Box 211, 1000 AE Amsterdam, The Netherlands

Distributors for the United States and Canada:
ELSEVIER SCIENCE PUBLISHING COMPANY INC.
655 Avenue of the Americas
New York, N.Y. 10010, U.S.A.

004.01
H 9181

ISBN: 0 444 89424 1

Printed in The Netherlands

PREFACE

This volume includes selected contributions from the working conference "Human Jobs and Computer Interface" organised by the working group on "Computers and Work" (WG 9.1), of Technical Committee 9 ("Computers and Society") of the International Federation for Information Processing, (IFIP), together with the Department of Computer Science at the University of Tampere, Finland. The conference was held in Tampere on June 26-28, 1991.

1. THEME

The theme of the material presented here manifests a clear reorientation in overall research strategy and implies a shift from a defensive to an offensive approach to the way that problems in the computer and work context are addressed.

Interest in computers and work was initiated by numerous observations that the implementation of computerized information systems was likely to create unexpected consequences. Some of these effects were positive, whereas many of them were negative. Much research effort was expended to explain this phenomenon. Characteristically for consequence research, its results are inconsistent with replication of empirical studies providing many different outcomes.

Of course, explanation alone (where possible) does not eliminate problems, even if it improves our understanding and gives depth to technology assessment. Explanations can also be used for forecasting: under certain circumstances specific consequences are more likely than others. In practice, this indicates a defensive strategy based upon resistance. If the expected consequences are bad enough, the implementation must be stopped.

In the long term, this view is unsatisfactory. It suggests that future users are passively waiting for the implementation of a new application. This appears to be an embodiment of technological determinism. Yet, user participation has been advocated as the liberating power. Instead of just waiting for the next stage in technological progress (or for action from management), the users (or their representatives) are themselves involved in the development process. In this light, socio-technical thinkers have observed social systems in the organizations which belong to the genuinely human sphere and which cannot be treated by the tools and techniques of computer system development.

In effect, any influence embedded in such approaches focussed on the organization of work. The technical system, i.e. information systems, could continue following the same machine metaphor as before. Thus, the non-social character of information technology could persist. This notion had to be challenged. Such a challenge was one of the messages from the first of our two Berlin conferences (1986) with the topic: System development for human development and productivity: participation and beyond.[1]

One of the constraints on participation is that it carries no guarantees of success. The ability to formulate alternative solutions is possible only if there is sufficient insight and competence. But perhaps more important is the revolutionary spirit, the ability to reject established concepts, beliefs and practices. In the second Berlin conference (1989) the topic was formulated as Information System, Work and Organization Design[2]. This tells us that the very concept of information system has been reformulated. It is not merely a technical issue with consequences for work and its organization. The information system is part and parcel of work and its organization.

Yet we cannot change the world merely through statements of how it should be conceived (even if this is a necessary condition). A truly offensive strategy requires concrete construction in order to be implemented. Technology must be conquered. We must specify what we mean when we say that the information system is nothing more than part of work and organization. Implications must also be implemented to be effective. The juxtaposition of human jobs and computer interfaces, the main theme of this volume, openly declares this program. Critical analysis is important, but it must be followed by practical impact.

2. A CHALLENGE PRESENTED

A number of issues that bear on the offensive strategy toward work and organization arise from a consideration of "Human Jobs and Computer Interfaces".

- For the worker (or the user), the interface is the system; it is everything which can be seen and it includes all parameters whereby the system may be manipulated. How faithfully is this pre-theoretical understanding of the 'virtual system' supported by the interface? And should it be?

- The work is where the worker is. Part of the work material lies in the system, behind the interface. How are these two connected? How does the interface support its users in bridging the divide between the physical interface and the underlying application?

---

[1] P. Docherty, K. Fuchs-Kittowski, P. Kolm and L. Mathiassen (eds.): System Design for Human Development and Productivity: Participation and Beyond. Proceedings of the IFIP TC 9 / WG 9.1 Working Conference, Berlin, GDR, 12-15 May, 1986. North-Holland, Amsterdam, 1987.

[2] P. van den Besselaar, A. Clement and P. Järvinen (eds.): Information System, Work and Organization Design. Proceedings of the IFIP TC 9/WG 9.1 Working Conference, Berlin, GDR, 10-13 July, 1989. North-Holland, Amsterdam, 1991.

• What is behind the interface? The mystical functionality? But what is it all about? Where does it reside? Is it part of an information system or part of the work? Is it merely a set of tasks which can be launched through the interface?

• The interface is a constituent of the work situation. How is the relationship between interface design and job design realized?

• What kind of qualifications does the user need in order to use the system (through the interface)? Does the interface support or diminish his or her qualification?

• Can the users control the application software or are they controlled by that system? Is the 'dialogue' (note the symmetry hidden in the term) determined on the premises of the system or of the user?

3. POSSIBLE RESPONSES

Of course, there are potentially many answers to these questions. They are naturally dependent on the underlying assumptions and values of the respondent. The answers suggested below are inspired by contributions in this volume (or in the conference from which they come), accompanied with some aspects of my own work and by the Zeitgeist and general trends.

• The emerging concept of work is anti-Tayloristic: knowledge cannot be separated from other tasks of the work.

• If knowledge-based work is performed by means of computers, the computer functions have no special status. What is done is more fundamental than the instruments used.

• The computer does not qualify as an actor. Therefore it makes no sense to talk of the division of labour between man and computer. In this issue I can see an opposing view. Look for example at people with interest in Artificial Intelligence or Expert Systems who obviously would like to have machine subjects and colleagues.

• It is misleading to talk about users (as if in the world of drug dealers). The important aspect is not the computer or the system but the worker and the work. It violates the dignity of a person if he or she is defined as a supplement to the instrument they use, unless they are a real expert on that instrument, e.g. a clarinettist.

• The interface is a property of the artifact, not of the worker and should therefore be called Computer interface rather than User interface.

• One important quality of the computer interface is that the worker can concentrate attention on the work task itself (instead of the properties of the instrument). So, the computer interface should reflect work practice rather than some abstract system structure.

• The worker should be able to utilize his or her professional competence with no inferiority complex arising from restricted skills in computer technology. This may be supported by the interface (and associated design principles).

• Taken together many of these issues suggest a need to focus sharply not solely upon the way in which work systems and their interfaces are used, but also upon the way they are designed, both in terms of objectives and overall design philosphy. Arguably, a 'user-centered' approach to design, one that attempts to embrace the needs and capabilities (both cognitive and ergonomic) of the worker, promises dividends, both in system performance and worker satisfaction. This is likely, given that the initiative in such design aims to accommodate the vagaries of the users final work situation. The significance of this theme is evident in several of the papers within this volume.[3]

4. STRUCTURE OF THIS BOOK

The structure of this book follows to a great extent the structure of the conference. Plenary sessions, for example, were bound together by discussants. These units have been retained. The rest of the material has been structured along similar lines.

In Section 1 the very concept of interface is discussed. A three-dimensional redefinition of the concept is presented in order to cover all aspects from technological through conceptual to the actual work process.

Requirements for user interfaces vary according to the user's context. The wide range of interface characteristics, even within industrial applications, is illustrated in Section 2, while Section 3 attends to special needs presented by particular groups at the interface. Such needs may be specific to particular professions or due to characteristics of individual users (e.g., physical disabilities).

The office is an important application area of information technology. In Section 4 we focuss upon computer-supported work as a whole rather than upon interfaces as such. One aspect of meaningful work is feedback on the success or failure and cooperation. The role played by the computer in supporting these tasks is the topic of Section 5.

---

[3] See also G.R.S. Weir: Human-computer interaction and man-machine systems: an intimate relationship, pp. 327-335 in P. van den Besselaar, A. Clement and P. Järvinen (eds.): Information System, Work and Organization Design. Proceedings of the IFIP TC 9/WG 9.1 Working Conference, Berlin, GDR, 10-13 July, 1989. North-Holland, Amsterdam, 1991.

Section 6 extends our understanding of organizational use of information technology towards processes of dynamic change. Each organization is subject to intended and unintended changes. Additionally, organizational cultures are facing dramatic changes. Neither of these two types of change can be beneficial unless the participants follow and lead the change through continuous learning. Information technology may be both the object of learning and a medium for its support. This is illustrated by the contributions in Section 7.

October 1991

Markku I. Nurminen   *George R. S. Weir*

ACKNOWLEGDEMENTS

The International Program Committee
Markku I. Nurminen, Finland, Chairman
David Ackermann, Switzerland; Peter van den Besselaar, The Netherlands; Boris Ivanovich Boiko, Ukraina, USSR; Ulrich Briefs, Germany; Susanne Bødker, Denmark; Andrew Clement, Canada; Pentti Hietala, Finland; Jean-Michel Hoc, France; Pekka Huuhtanen, Finland; Sture Hägglund, Sweden; Pertti Järvinen, Finland; Antti Kasvio, Finland; Juhani Kirjonen, Finland; Oyar Krumberg, Latvia; Pekka Lehtiö, Finland; Bronius Paradauskas, Lithuania; Barbara Pernici, Italy; Catherine Plaisant, U.S.A.; Mike Robinson, The Netherlands; Kevin Ryan, Ireland; Kari-Jouko Räihä, Finland; Fernando Saez Vacas, Spain; Pål Sørgaard, Norway; Jaak Tepandi, Estonia; A Min Tjoa, Austria; Matti Vartiainen, Finland, George R.S. Weir, Scotland U.K.; Leikny Øgrim, Norway

External Reviewers
Timo Alanko, Christer Carlsson, Kari T. Eloranta, Jonathan Grudin, Heikki Halme, Riitta Hellman, Jorma Kuopus, Kari Kuutti, Hans-Erik Nissen, Kent L. Norman, Leena Norros, Matti Pettersson, Janine Rogalski, Heikki Salo, Ben Shneiderman, Risto Suitiala, Jukka Teuhola, Pekka Tyllilä

The Organization Committee
Pertti Järvinen, University of Tampere, Finland, Chairman
Johanna Järvinen, Tero Taubert and numerous co-workers from the Department of Computer Science at the University of Tampere, Finland

TABLE OF CONTENTS

Section 1

Jobs and Interfaces

HUMAN JOBS AND COMPUTER INTERFACES
M.I. Nurminen and G.R.S. Weir
Elsevier Science Publishers B.V. (North-Holland)
© 1991 IFIP. All rights reserved.

Some Confusions at the Interface: Re-conceptualizing the "interface" problem

Kari Kuutti[a] and Liam J. Bannon[b]

[a]Department of Information Processing Science, University of Oulu, Linnanmaa, SF-90570 Oulu, Finland

[b]Center for Innovation & Cooperative Technology, University of Amsterdam, Grote Bickersstraat 72, 1013 KS Amsterdam, The Netherlands

> (the interface is) that part of the program that determines how the user and the computer communicate.
>
> Newman and Sproull, 1979

> Instead of seeing it (the interface) as a part of the program I propose that we view it as a relation between program and use context....It does not make sense to say that a system in isolation has an interface; interfaces "emerge" when the system is used......
>
> P.B. Andersen, 1990

Abstract

Discussions about the nature of the human-computer interface, and how it can be improved, play a leading role in the field of Human-Computer Interaction (HCI). Despite, or perhaps because of this role, there appears to be some confusion over exactly what is meant by the term, and the implications of these different views for the very nature of the HCI field. In this paper we discuss some of these problems and confusions, drawing on a variety of sources. We then outline what we believe is a richer conceptual framework for discussing 'interface' problems, based on abstraction levels, as developed in the information systems research field. Some interesting features of such an approach are mentioned, including clarification of the argument concerning separability of the interface and functionality of an application. The framework is still being developed, and the full implications of taking such an approach seriously in interface and work design have not yet surfaced.

1.INTRODUCTION

This paper explores, and hopefully alleviates, some of the confusions surrounding the meaning and use of the term "interface" in the context of the design, development and use of computing systems. Our approach is not intended to be an exercise in verbal gymnastics, nor a textual exegesis for its own sake, but an attempt to penetrate the fog of verbiage on the interface issue. A central point in our paper is to show how certain apparent arguments about what is and is not an 'interface' problem, or comments about exactly where the boundary of the interface lies, can be dissolved when one understands that the same term is being used quite differently by people. Some confusions can be resolved simply by taking into account the context in which the utterance is embedded and the disciplinary perspective of the person who utters it. Not all confusions are amenable to such an approach however, as there remain other points of disagreement which represent genuinely different positions on the interface and whether it is the proper focus of our study in HCI. We critique some of these positions and present our own in the hope that it might provide some clarification - while accepting that our own position too will necessarily have its limitations.

The paper is organized as follows. In Section 2 we provide an explication of a couple of the distinctions that we can identify in the recent literature concerning the interface, and show how the problems encountered are a mixture of confusion about the meaning of the term, based on differing perspectives, and genuine disagreements about a particular issue. Section 3 studies attempts to provide a multiperspective view on the interface issue, and introduces an 'abstraction levels' framework which we suggest may be useful. Section 4 then elaborates on the use of abstraction levels in interface design and use and argues for a system of interface definitions for different design domains. In Section 5 we study the relationship between information system design and interface design and suggest a new viewpoint, based on the results presented in section 4. Finally, Section 6 contains some conclusions.

2. CONFUSIONS ABOUT HCI

2.1 Terminological Confusions at the Interface
Much of the discipline of human-computer interaction necessarily revolves around the design and use of the human-computer interface. By this is usually meant all aspects of the interaction between the computer system and the person, and not only that part of the computer system that deals with input and output. Indeed, for many people, the whole field of human-computer interaction (HCI) is synonymous with the design and use of interfaces to computing systems. For example, Robinson (1990) notes: "The interface stands as a defining and sustaining boundary for the business of HCI, both conceptually and literally."

Usually the term "human-computer interface" is just abridged to the "interface", or the "user interface" to the computer system. This change is not unproblematic however, as has been recently discussed by Grudin (1990b), where he notes that one might more naturally expect people to talk of the term "computer interface" rather than the "user interface". This is not simply a question of grammar as he notes: "A user's interface to a computer does *not* match or complement a computer's interface to a user. ..Our equation of "the user interface" to software and I/O devices means that "user interface" denotes the computer's interface to the user, not the user's interface to the computer" (Grudin, 1990b).

We certainly agree with the idea that the user's view of the interface to the computer goes well beyond software and I/O devices to include documentation, training, and even colleagues in the work environment (Bannon,1986). However, we would prefer to label what Grudin calls the "computer's interface to the user" as the (traditional) "software engineering view of the interface", to emphasize that this view of the interface is shared among a professional community.[1] We would then agree that focussing on the latter rather than the user's interface to the computer, while understandable at one level, is problematic in terms of understanding how the overall human-computer interface is perceived by a member of the user community, as their view of the interface to the system has this larger compass that goes outside of the computer hardware and software itself. Thus one source of misunderstanding of the term interface has been uncovered, one which is based on different understandings of the inclusiveness of the term and of the perspective from which the 'interface' is viewed, - from that of the software engineer or that of the user.

There have been a number of calls for clarifying confusions surrounding use of "interface" and other terms in HCI, through the development of a common dictionary of concepts, to which all communities must adhere in discussion of computer systems. Such a grand unifying idea is, we believe, fraught with many kinds of problems. The problems cannot be resolved simply by making more exact definitions. This is because the use of the terms is spread across a variety of disciplines, and it is impossible to enforce a single meaning of a term already in use across these quite distinct, even if overlapping communities. The least that we could do would be try to make the contexts for use of the term clearer for all the parties involved, so that they can recognize that use of the same term does *not* imply similar meanings. On the other hand, in practical development work these distinct communities should be able to cooperate, and in order to do that the plain recognition of differences is not enough, but the different contexts should be related and different meanings bridged, at least to some extent.

2.2 The Interface - The proper focus for HCI?

The noun, *interface*, is taken to be a discrete and tangible thing that we can map, draw, design, implement, and attach to an existing bundle of functionality. One of the goals of this book is to explode that notion...(Laurel, 1990)

While the HCI area is acknowledged to be an interdisciplinary one, the loudest voice has usually belonged to psychologists. A line of demarcation between programmers and psychologists in software design is sometimes drawn by focusing on the separation of the 'interface' from the underlying 'functionality'

---

[1] Even within this community, differences can be found, of course, but we believe that it is justifiable to describe the perspective as a disciplinary one.

of the system. As noted by Robinson, 1990, this traditional conceptualization can be described thus: "The interface stands as the boundary between what is the work of HCI and what is the work of the software engineer. The 'true' nature of the system - *what* it does - is defined by the state of the software 'behind' the interface...the neutral and objective functionality of the 'internal' state (of the machine) may be realised by alternative interface designs". Such an approach has had the unfortunate effect of reifying the interface concept for much of the HCI community as the prime object of study. This reification has also tended to result in an undue emphasis on rather 'surface' aspects of interface design, within many of the different interpretations of the interface that are commonly used. Thus studies on how to redesign menus, or make more meaningful command abbreviations become seen as prototypical. Yet, paradoxically, this reification of the interface as the domain of HCI has actually marginalized its impact. For example, Seymour Papert (1990) recently commented: "I think the interface is part of a larger thing. I think that putting the emphasis on the interface somewhat confuses the issues. ....if only the interface (is changed), and what lies behind it and what you can do with the system isn't changed, you're only scratching the surface. *The interface is only the surface*". (our emphasis). Years earlier, in discussing the commercial failure of the path-breaking Xerox Star computer system, despite its highly touted interface, Mike Hammer (1984) put this view more bluntly: "In reality, user interface is a second-order factor. ...a system with better functionality will almost always win over one with a better interface...." (Hammer, 1984).

Over the last few years, a rake of papers and studies have attacked this view of HCI as being only concerned with low level interface issues. They argue that much of the HCI world pays too little attention to the underlying functionality of the computer applications and their usability in everyday work contexts. More recently, voices in the community have begun to speak out about this problem and argue for more concern to be placed on what people are actually using computers for. For example, Don Norman, one of the doyens of the HCI community, comments: "......What's wrong with interfaces? The question for one. The interface is the wrong place to begin. It implies you already have done all the rest and want to patch it up to make it pretty for the user. That attitude is what is wrong with the interface...........In the future I want less emphasis on "interfaces" and more on appropriate tools for the task" (Norman, 1990). Similar concerns can be found elsewhere in recent years, for example, in the paper by Goransson et al. (1987) entitled "The interface is often not the problem", in Thomas and Kellogg (1989), Bannon and Bødker (1991) and in many other articles.

The idea that we can separate out the design of the interface from the design of the functionality of the system, and perhaps also the coding of the interface from the coding of the rest of the application has generated a lot of discussion over the last several years. As we have seen, it can be seen as a possible territorial division of responsibility between software engineers and HCI people, as well as having implications for the software development process, and the modularization of code. The popularity of User Interface Management Systems (UIMS's) significantly contributed to the impression of this separability, despite some warnings about the limitations of such systems, even by their proponents (e.g. see Tanner and Buxton, 1985). Arguments about the desirability of such a separation have continued to rage. In some cases, the focus of the comments is clearly on the actual programming tasks, and the need for modularization of the 'interface' code. Surely most people are in agreement that there should be separability at the *code* level, as otherwise modifications and general maintenance on programs become impossibly difficult. However, at the level of *design*, we have a different picture. In designing a program or system, we obviously must pay attention to the needs of the user and the use situation, and to how the design will meet these needs. The idea that in such situations a neat separation between interface and functionality can be accomplished is open to question.

So far we have discussed some problems with the meaning of "interface" as well as the choice of the 'interface' as the object of study for HCI. The simple interface/functionality separation begs many questions. What we need is some kind of a general framework that provides a better grounded and conceptually coherent set of concepts within which to discuss the design of computer systems which people can use in their daily work. In the next section we introduce one such framework, which has its origins in the information systems design community, and which we believe can provide a useful starting point for developing the required framework.

3. RE-CONCEPTUALIZING THE INTERFACE CONCEPT- THE SEARCH FOR A FRAMEWORK

3.1 Managing diversity -the need for multiple perspectives

One reason for the different use of terms has naturally been the historical evolution of the focus of interface research and development. For example Grudin (1990a) has argued for five phases beginning from "the interface at the hardware" and ending with "the interface at the work setting", each phase having a different viewpoint and emphasis. Given this variety, it is not surprising that the idea of reducing the confusion by looking at the interface from several perspectives or levels has been attractive to many researchers, e. g. Clarke (1986), Gaines and Shaw (1986), Rasmussen (1986), Kammersgaard (1988), Weir (1988), Booth (1989) and Stary (1990). There are some problems with these attempts, however. Although the use of different perspectives may help in clarifying different approaches to the interface, it does not necessarily help in relating them to each other because of the lack of any unifying background. Even in those cases where a hierarchical, layered model has been proposed (e. g. Clarke 1986, Stary 1990), the result is more *ad hoc*. The most appropriate among our limited sample may be the five-level abstraction hierarchy used by Rasmussen (1986), based on general functional properties of a technical system.

However, there is another tradition based on hierarchical models that has a closer relationship to interface issues than the 'technical systems' discussed by Rasmussen and we suggest that it might be beneficial to use the experience collected there in clarifying the interface confusions. This tradition is, of course, the research on design of information systems which, in principle, should include the interface design as an organic part. In practice, the shared knowledge between the 'information systems' and 'interface' research disciplines is minimal. We will return later to possible reasons for this lack of interaction among the research communities, but let us first briefly discuss the information systems (IS) research area.

3.2 Research on information systems development

Although the roots of research on IS date back to the 1960s there is still lively debate about the nature of the object of research (e. g. Nissen et al 1991). It is very interesting to note that in the IS research there are quite similar terminological and conceptual confusions as in the HCI debate described earlier: "It is often difficult to get any agreement on the basic terms and concepts of the field. The concept 'information system' is a good example of this: different authors use different terms to refer to roughly the same concept, the terms possibly reflecting different perspectives applied to the concept 'information system'" (Iivari 1989, p. 323). One of the major reasons for terminological and conceptual difficulties has also been the evolution of the actual object of development. It has expanded far beyond the original technical 'core system', to include also social and organizational aspects, as has been described in the recent historical text by Friedman (1989).

One can make a claim, however, that IS research is more 'mature' than HCI research because it has been able to produce practical advice on how to develop real information systems - an aspect notoriously lacking in much HCI work. This advice has been collected and condensed into a number of Information System Design Methodologies (ISDMs- see, for example, Olle et al., 1982). There are a large number of different ISDMs, and some of them are even used in practice! So it is possible that they actually contain some features which are useful in mastering the complexity of design. One of these features has been the use of different perspectives and layered models both in traditional IS design and in related areas, such as database research, software engineering, and in data communications. Iivari draws the following conclusion: "In fact, there is currently a growing agreement about the need to distinguish three major levels of abstraction for an information system: the organizational level, the conceptual/infological level, and the datalogical/technical level." (Iivari 1989, p. 324). 'Abstraction levels' are a general modelling principle which is believed by Iivari to provide a framework that helps avoid confusion and unifies different approaches: Such a framework would be helpful for interface research, too. Given the general relationship between IS design and interface design and the apparent similarity of the conceptual confusions in both research discussions, we think that the experience gained in IS research and development is worth exploring.

3.3 Abstraction levels

What are abstraction levels? The term refers to a widely accepted principle that in order to master the complexity of IS design it must be divided into several levels or subdomains, which can each be treated relatively independently. These subdomains are not some arbitrarily selected points of view, but they must be derived from the ontology of an IS and they must have pre-determined interrelationships so that they together form a whole. In the research tradition we are referencing these subdomains are called abstraction levels. The reason for the existence of the subdomains or abstraction levels is that an information system is always embedded in several development contexts (Lyytinen 1987) at the same time. Because the system to be designed must be implemented in each of the contexts, the designer has to develop a model for each context - either consciously or implicitly - and implicit design decisions easily lead towards confusion and inconsistent solutions. Thus, it is better to do the design explicitly within separate subdomains, while paying attention to the interrelationships between them.

As noted, the subdomains are relatively independent, each having their own models, concepts, methods and background theories. Although the terms "hierarchical" and "level" are used, the relationships between the subdomains have nothing to do with "levels of detail" or hierarchical decomposition. The relationship is more like a means-ends - relation: the lower levels describe the means used to realize the ends of the next upper level which again contains the means to realize the next level and so on. So there is a certain top-down determinacy, but not vice versa: the same ends can be achieved using different means. Of course, the lower levels form the potential resources for realization and may enable or restrict the achievement of certain upper-level goals.

Note that the links between the domains are not simply formal relationships, either. They consist of different transformation procedures, some of which are even informal in the sense that their execution needs human skills and judgment. The main content of different ISDMs consists of such descriptions of the subdomains and descriptions of transformations between them (see e. g. Olle et al. 1982).

As was mentioned earlier, in IS research three levels of abstraction have seemed sufficient to capture the phenomenon. In the terminology used by Iivari they are named as follows: the organizational level, the conceptual/infological level and the datalogical/technical level. We thus have the following three separate domains:

The organizational domain which consists of a description or model which tries to provide a "rich picture" of actual organizational practice, including the inconsistencies and contradictions that are inevitably a part of the situation. The model is used as the basis for initiating change in the current situation. Some particular areas are selected to be supported by the IS and this support is defined using organizational rather than computer terminology. This includes a fuller understanding of users' work and descriptions of the ways that IS should support this work and the overall functioning of the organization: automation of some routine tasks, satisfying information needs within other tasks, etc. Sometimes the development of this definition is called defining the *requirements* of the system. Traditionally, this work has been done by the systems analyst, but in recent years the demand for more participative forms of system development, especially in the "definition of requirements" phase, has risen considerably (see Greenbaum and Kyng 1991).

The conceptual domain which mediates between the more concrete organizational and technological domains. It contains an abstract, formal model how a hypothetical computer system could realize the requirements (defined in the organizational domain) in a limited,idealized, error-free world. Usually it consists of several submodels, like a model of that part of organizational practice to be supported ("universe of discourse"), a data model explicating the logical content of data items to be included in the system and a process model explicating the logical manipulation of the data items. This domain is central in most ISDMs (see e.g. Olle et al. 1982). Sometimes the definition of the domain has been called the *specification* of the system.

The technological domain. While models in the conceptual domain are idealizations, models of the technological domain relate directly to practice. The domain contains a description of how the hypothetical system described in the conceptual domain is realized in practice using specific technologies that are currently available. Besides the implementation of the basic data and process models (down to the file and program code level), all kind of practical problems - hardware defects and errors, inconsistencies and breakdowns in organizational practice - must be dealt with. Also the fit between the technical system and everyday organizational practices has to be clearly defined.

In the next section we will briefly note how such a structure could be utilized within HCI to clarify some of the interface issues which we have been discussing.

4. RE-DEFINING THE INTERFACE CONCEPT

What can interface design learn from this IS work? The topic has hardly been mentioned in the HCI or IS research literature.[2] What follows should be considered more as the initiation of a discussion than any solution to the problems addressed.

Probably the most liberating aspect of this framework is the observation that in the related IS area a set of independent, dramatically different models are needed for design and that despite the variety of these models they can be used together successfully in practice. It does not matter if it is impossible to discuss topics at the organizational level using the concepts and vocabulary of the technological level and vice versa, so long as we can establish the transformational procedures needed in order to cross the borders.[3] We will return later to these procedures.

Following the IS example of using a series of related, but conceptually different levels of definitions of information systems, we suggest that it might be beneficial to also have several different definitions of interface - one for each level. Note that this layering is fundamentally different from attempts to make a separation between the 'interface' and the 'application'. In our suggestion the demarcation line is not drawn between the interface and application, but between the different design domains of an application, each also containing an inter-

---

[2] An exception has been Iivari & Koskela 1985.

[3] Note that the approach we are borrowing from here is often critiqued for a too-rigid model of both analysis and design procedures. While we support the need for more flexibility in techniques for requirements definition and in prototyping and iterative development methods, we believe that aspects of the IS modelling work can be fruitfully adopted. The modelling can serve as a resource for design, rather than a strict specification of what must be done, as the models will inevitably be only partial.

face as an integral part. The nature of the relationship between what is assumed to belong to the 'interface' and the 'application' parts need not remain the same from level to level.

What, then, are the appropriate definitions of the interface for each level? First, the 'uppermost' level must be redefined. According to our opinion, the term "organization" (e.g. in Malone 1987) is too broad for our purposes. On the other hand, restricting considerations to a single individual may also be too limiting. Thus our terms for the uppermost level should not exclude cooperative work processes.

Interface at *Work process or use situation domain.*

At this level we are quite happy with the definition by Andersen (1990) which is given in the foreword of this paper: "Instead of seeing it (the interface) as a part of the program I propose that we view it as a relation between program and use context....It does not make sense to say that a system in isolation has an interface; interfaces 'emerge' when the system is used...". From the user's viewpoint in the use situation, *the interface is the system.* There is no possibility to separate interface from functionality, but the interface *is* the way user's work is supported by system.

Interface at *Conceptual model domain.*

In the conceptual models of ISDMs the interface is mostly neglected - in fact, there are only a few experimental or theoretical approaches (e. g. Wasserman 1982, Iivari and Koskela 1987, Iivari 1989), which try to address interface issues at all. Iivari and Koskela's approach is based on abstraction levels and contains at the conceptual level a "model of the user interface" as a subpart, separated from "the rest of the system", like the object system model, the information model, the processing model, etc. We would like to expand that interface definition in the following direction:

At the conceptual level, *the interface is that part of a system or application which must be understood and mastered in order to utilize the system meaningfully for some purpose in some definite use situation.*

Interface at *Technological domain.*

In this paper we do not try to plunge deeper into the technological level, but we are ready to accept the definition by Newman and Sproull (1979) as an example of an interface definition at this level: *(the interface is) that part of the program that determines how the user and the computer communicate.* However, this definition can be valid only to the extent that this kind of implementation shall not disturb the achievement of goals stated already at 'upper' levels.

4.1 Implications

Our new, 'layered' definition of interface has several interesting implications:

1) On the use situation level, the interface design is inseparable from the application design, which is inseparable from the work process design. (Today, this kind of work process design is mostly done unconsciously and implicitly.) Thus the traditional separation between 'interface' and 'functionality' becomes irrelevant in this context.

2) The relationship between 'interface' and 'application' can have different and even seemingly contradictory interpretations within different design domains. At the work process level they are unified, at the conceptual level probably partially overlapping, and at the technological level they may be fully separated. This offers a way to deal with the 'separability' confusion we have discussed earlier - by identifying more accurately the actual development contexts and their demands.

3) At the conceptual level the relative portion of the interface varies in different applications. In fact, we have a whole spectrum of applications: On one end we have applications which have no interface whatsoever, e.g. EDI (electronic data interchange)-programs, where there is no human user needed to understand something when the application is running. At the other end of the spectrum we have programs which can be claimed to contain nothing but the interface, e.g. scientific visualization, where visual cues are put into use in the study of natural phenomena. In order to get useful results the researcher must understand the whole chain of transformations included: phenomenon - mathematical model - computer solution - graphical representation, in many cases to the level of individual algorithms. Thus according to our definition the whole application belongs to the interface in this case.

4) The relative independence of different domains can be maintained only when we can establish 'links' - practical transformation procedures - between the domains. Such links are not yet in existence in most cases, partially due to the lack of recognition of different domains and the corresponding lack of a need to establish the links. Some such links can be found, however. Thus we can interpret an UIMS as an attempt to develop automatic transformation procedures between the conceptual and technological level, so that the design and manipulation of (some aspects of) interfaces can happen at a conceptual level and the result is automatically transformed to the technological level (e.g. window managing, menu building, etc.). This is in correspondence with the best traditions of software design and with the general trend in human toolmaking, according to which any stabilized body of knowledge sooner or later will take the form of a tool. Thus we have nothing against it, but the same restriction must be made as was done earlier when discussing the separation of interface and application: from the viewpoint of the whole system a UIMS can be useful only when it does not restrict the attainment of the design goals stated at the work process or conceptual level. Because many UIMSs are grown 'bottom-up' - the main emphasis being the management of code - this may be a potential source of problems.

Why has IS research and design not been able to develop appropriate transformation procedures for interface design - despite their apparent importance? We investigate this issue in the next section.

5. THE RELATIONSHIP BETWEEN IS DESIGN AND INTERFACE DESIGN

5.1 Does IS design really care about interfaces?

Because of the high visibility of HCI issues the importance of the 'interface' in the design of new systems and applications is now accepted. However, when we look at current IS design practice, it is still very difficult to see signs of pressure towards any kind of radical change towards better interfaces. Apparently IS design is not in such a crisis or at least IS people do not think that better interfaces would be the remedy for their difficulties. For example, in a recent survey among the software designers in leading English software houses it was found that: "None of the designers interviewed reported ever having used any HCI design and evaluation technique, some stated that they were unaware of the existence of such techniques" (Bellotti 1988, p. 23).

Because the development of ISDMs has been an attempt to collect practical and theoretical knowledge concerning information system design, they contain elaborate transformation procedures between the design domains, (for example: how to analyze reality -> produce an information model -> create an actual database, or: how to analyze information processing needs -> produce a process model -> proceed towards a structured code). One would expect to find methods for interface design here, too. A closer examination leads to disappointment, however. Iivari has analyzed the content of four prominent ISDMs (CIAM, ISAC, JSD and NIAM) and found that none of them has any conceptual tools for handling interface issues. "Still more strikingly, the total neglect of the area of user interface is really surprising" (Iivari 1989, p. 346). Apparently there has not been need enough to include tools for interface issues into the ISDMs.

We are forced to the conclusion that in the majority of information system development cases interface issues have not been - and perhaps are still not - crucial for successful development.[4] In this light the increased awareness of interface issues seems to be difficult to comprehend. How can this anomaly be explained?

5.2 A tentative answer

We think that our new interface definition can help in finding an explanation. It was found earlier that there is a spectrum - a scale - of applications with different portions of interface. (According to our definition this portion does not mean the portion of code, but the portion of an application, which must be comprehended or made 'visible'). Figure 1 represents that 'scale' - EDI ('zero interface') at one end and scientific visualization ('100% interface') at other end. A tentative position of a couple of other examples is also presented in the figure.

The figure helps to explain the wide difference in opinions concerning interface issues.

The relative proportion of the interface - according to our definition - in routine automation software is low indeed. Routine automation can be seen as an extension of Tayloristic work organization, where the worker has no need to understand the nature of the work but just follows directions. "We found ... a continuation of a very old process - the mechanization and automation of work - using a new tool, the computer" (Kraft 1987). The goal of the interface in this case is simply to help to achieve error-free execution of predetermined action sequences. No matter how bad the interface is, the adaptable user sooner or later memorizes the actions needed and the error rate will fall to an acceptable level. Because the bulk of applications to date involve routine automation, it is

---

4 We realize that the issue is more complex than this, but for the sake of our argument we will not pursue these alternative explanations.

possible to understand why designers do not feel interface issues are important
or why such concepts have not been included into design methodologies.

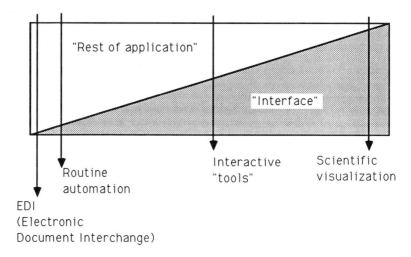

Figure 1. The spectrum of applications with increasing relative proportion of
the system related to the interface.

On the other hand, the situation will change, when we move away from the
'zero-interface' end of our scale. The further we go, the more important will the
role of interface become. Rote memorization does not help any more, because
the user has to understand, what he or she is doing and what kind of tool he or
she is using (see Bannon 1991). If the interface does not help in this understanding, it will have a paralysing effect. So, when we move further, the relative weight of interface design in the overall design will grow and beyond some
point on the scale interface design must have a dominating role in the system
design.

Have we any reason to believe that there will be some shift in the nature of
applications towards the 'more interface' end - and what could then be the
cause?

5.3 Why have HCI issues become important today?

There really is an external factor which is forcing a movement towards the
'more-interface' end of our scale. We believe that this factor is also one of the
background causes behind much of the current usability discussion (Whiteside
et al. 1988) and the high visibility of HCI issues. This is the widely accepted belief that we are living in an era of significant structural change. "In all developed economies, major transformations of market structures, production technologies and production organization are presently going on" (Naschold 1987).

QWL in the 1970s	High Performance of the 1990s
– personnel administration technique	– human resource management strategy
– aimed to reduce costs of absenteeism and labour turnover and increase productivity	– aims to improve organizational flexibility and product quality for competitive advantage
– based on argument that increased autonomy improves quality of work experience and employee job satisfaction	– based on argument that increased flexibility improves skills, decision making, adaptability and use of new technology
– had little impact on the management function beyond first line supervision	– involves change in organization culture and redefinition of management functions at all levels
– 'quick fix' applied to isolated and problematic work groups	– takes two to three years to change attitudes and behaviour throughout the organization

Figure 2. Comparison of two approaches to change Tayloristic work organization (adapted from Buchanan and McCalman 1989).

There has been in socio-economic studies a wide-ranging discussion about the nature of the change. It is not possible to open up that discussion adequately here so we just take one example. The basic message is that Tayloristic work organization is undergoing a significant and irreversible change, and that this change is more fundamental than earlier Quality of Working Life (QWL) attempts. Figure 2 outlines these differences as described by Buchanan and McCalman 1989. They believe that this change is real - not just a cosmetic one like that in the 1970s.

Emphasis is on achieving more efficiency through flexibility, or as another theorist puts it: "The informated organization does move in another direction. It relies on human capacities for teaching and learning, criticism and insight. It implies an approach to business improvement that rests upon the improvement and innovation made possible by the enhanced comprehensibility of the core processes. It reflects a fertile interdependence between the human mind and some of its most sophisticated productions" (Zuboff 1988, p. 414).

Figure 3 (Kuutti 1991) is a condensation of key points from two discussions during recent years: one in leading management journals analyzing the characteristic features of emerging 'new types' of work - another within the IS research community, analyzing the *desiderata* of properties of 'new' information systems.

Routine automation is hopelessly inadequate to deal with this kind of work. Hence the new work organization will need new kinds of applications, where the support for tool-like operation, understanding and communication can be realized. These applications belong far closer to the 'more-interface' - end of our spectrum than routine automation. Contrary to earlier practice, the design of their interfaces must be taken seriously. Of course routine automation applications will not fade away but will stay as a backbone of information systems - there is still a lot to be automated - but a new and important class of applications is emerging. This is already demanding different treatment and thereby causing pressure towards more advanced HCI development.

Features of the 'new work'	Desirable 'new' system properties
– flexibility	– flexibility
– integration	– communication support
– continuously evolving	– craft enhancement
– cooperation	– group work support
– own work planning and control	– personal tools, human scale systems
– theoretical thinking with models, better understanding of work	– understandability, coping ability, visibility as a system attribute
– large and flexible assortment of skills	– skill conservation and development
– new motivation, responsibility covering larger area than just own task	– emancipation of interests, democratization of working life

Figure 3. Comparison between features of 'new' work and the properties needed in 'new' information systems.

We believe that this change in the nature of the work and the growing pressure to develop corresponding applications is one of the major reasons behind the on-going debate in HCI.

6.   CONCLUSION

This paper has taken a critical look at the field of human-computer interaction. It has critiqued the 'interface' concept and how it has been discussed in much of the literature, arguing that it focuses attention at an inappropriate level. Looking at our Conference "Human Jobs and Computer Interfaces", within the perspective that we are developing here, this juxtaposition of terms in the title seems somewhat odd as it reifies a concept which we are at pains to demystify and dissolve. Rather we would prefer to talk about work practices which may be computer-based, and which undoubtedly will have interfaces, but we do not start out with the interface *per se* - certainly not in the traditional usage of the term.

Our initial explorations have hopefully demonstrated that our suggested multilevel framework for discussing interface concepts for different design domains might help in clarifying confusions and concentrating efforts on real problems. The most obvious problem blocking progress is the lack of understanding of the relationship between the 'use situation' and 'conceptual model' domains in our system model of interface. What is needed are conceptual models over both the work process *and* use situation – models rich enough so that the design of the interface, the functionality, and the whole system can be based on them. And, of course we also need methods to analyse situations in practice in order to produce such models. When it comes to background theories, mainstream cognitive psychology has shown itself to be better suited to design 'computer interfaces to users' and not vice versa; richer theories and multidisciplinarity are needed. There has already been a certain shift of emphasis in that direction, but the effort could be expanded and made more systematic. The work in front of us is to make our outline framework more robust and attempt to answer how such a framework can be used in the actual practice of design.

7.REFERENCES

Andersen, P.B. (1990) A Semiotic Approach to Construction and Assessment of Computer Systems. In H.-E. Nissen, H.K. Klein and R. Hirschheim (eds.) Proceedings of ISRA-90 Conference. Univ. Lund.

Bannon, L.J. (1986) Helping Users Help Each Other. In Norman, D.A. and Draper, S.W. (Eds.) *User Centered System Design: New Perspectives on Human-Computer Interaction*

Bannon, L.J. (1991) From Human Factors to Human Actors. In Greenbaum and Kyng (eds.) Design at Work. New Jersey: Erlbaum, 1991.

Bannon, L. J. and Bødker, S. (1991) Beyond the Interface: Encountering Artifacts in Use. In J. Carroll (Ed.) Designing Interaction: Psychology at the Human- Computer Interface. New York: Cambridge University Press.

Bellotti, V. (1988) Implications of Current Design Practice for the Use of HCI Techniques. In D.M. Jones and R. Winder (Eds.) *People and Computers IV*, Cambridge Univ. Press, Cambridge, pp. 13-34.

Booth, P. (1989) *An Introduction to Human-Computer Interaction*. Lawrence Erlbaum, Hove and London.

Buchanan, D. A. and McCalman, J. (1989) *High Performance Work Systems: The Digital Experience*. Routledge, London.

Clarke, A. A. (1986) A three-level human-computer interface model. *Int. J. Man-Machine Studies*, vol 24, pp. 503-517.

Friedman, A. (1989) *Computer Systems Development: History, Organization and Implementation*. John Wiley, Chichester.

Gaines, B. R. and Shaw, M. L. (1986) Foundations of dialog engineering: the development of human-computer interaction. *Int. J. Man-Machine Studies*, vol 24, pp. 101-123.

Goransson , B., Lindt, M., Pettersson, E., Sandblad, B. and Schwalbe, P. (1987) The interface is often not the problem. In J. Carroll and B. Tanner (eds.) *Human Factors in Computer Systems IV*, North-Holland, New York.

Greenbaum, J. and Kyng, M. (Eds.) (1991) *Design at Work: Cooperative Design of Computer Systems*. New Jersey: Erlbaum.

Grudin, J. (1990a) The Computer Reaches Out: The historical continuity of user interface design. In *Proceedings of CHI '90, ACM SIGCHI Conference*, Seattle, Wash., USA, April 1990.

Grudin, J. (1990b) interface. In CSCW'90, Proceedings of Conference on Computer Supported Cooperative Work, Los Angeles, 1990.

Hammer, M. (1984) The OA Mirage. *Datamation*, Feb. 1984, pp. 36-46.

Iivari, J. (1989) Levels of Abstraction as a Conceptual Framework for an Information System. In D. Falkenberg and P. Lindgreen (eds.) *Information System Concepts: An In-depth Analysis*, Elsevier/North-Holland, Amsterdampp. 323-352.

Iivari, J. and Koskela, E. (1985) On the Modelling of Human-Computer Interaction as the Interface between the User's Work Activity and the Information System. In *Proceedings of INTERACT '84*, Elsevier/North-Holland, Amsterdam, pp. 539-546.

Iivari, J. and Koskela, E.(1987) The PIOCO Model for Information Systems Design. *MIS Quarterly*, Sept 1987 pp.401-419.

Kammersgaard, J. (1988) Four different perspectives on human-computer interaction. *Int. J. Man-Machine Studies*, vol 28, pp. 343-362.

Kraft, P. (1987) Computers and the Automation of Work. In Kraut, R. (ed.): *Technology and the Transformation of White-collar work*. Lawrence Erlbaum, New Jersey, pp. 99-111.

Kuutti, K. (1991) Activity Theory, Transformation of Work and Information Systems Design. Manuscript, Univ. Oulu, Dept. Inf. Proc. Science.

Laurel, B. (ed.) (1990) *The Art of Human-Computer Interaction Design*. Addison-Wesley, Reading.

Lyytinen, K. (1987) A taxonomic perspective of information systems development: theoretical constructs and recommendations. In Boland, R. and Hirschheim, R. (eds.): *Critical issues in information systems research*. John Wiley and Sons, Chichester.

Malone, T.W. (1987) Computer Support for Organizations. Toward an Organizational Science. In J. Carroll (ed.) *Interfacing Thought. Cognitive Aspects of Human -Computer Interaction*. MIT Press, Cambridge.

Naschold, F. (1987) Technology and assessment. Developments, controversies and perspectives. In *Future of Work: A Viewpoint of Social Sciences*. Nordic Institute of Advanced Occupational Environment Studies, Helsinki, pp. 31-50.

Newman, W.M. and Sproull, R.F. (1979) *Principles of Interactive Computer Graphics*. McGraw-Hill, New York.

Nissen, H.-E., Klein, H.K. and Hirschheim, R. (eds.) (1991) *Information System Research: Contemporary Approaches & Emergent Traditions*. Proceedings of the IFIP TC 8 Working Conference ISRA'90, North-Holland, Amsterdam.

Norman, D.A. (1990) "An interview with Don Norman" by H. Rheingold. In Laurel (1990), pp.5-10.

Olle, T.W., Sol, H.G. and Verrijn-Stuart, A.A. (eds.) (1982) *Information System Design Methodologies: a comparative review*. North-Holland, Amsterdam.

Papert, S. (1990) Interview in "Byte´s 15th Anniversary Summit", *Byte* September 1990, p. 230.

Rasmussen, J. (1986) *Information Processing and Human-Machine Interaction. An Approach to Cognitive Engineering*. North-Holland/Elsevier, New York.

Robinson, H. (1990) Towards a Sociology of Human-Computer Interaction. In P. Luff, N. Gilbert and D. Frohlich (eds.) *Computers and Conversation*, Academic Press, London, pp. 39-50.

Stary, C. (1990) A Knowledge Representation Scheme for Conceptual Interface Design. In A. Finkelstein, M. J. Tauber and R Traunmuller (Eds.) *Human Factors in Information Systems Analysis and Design*. North-Holland, Amsterdam, pp. 157-171.

Tanner, P. and Buxton, W. (1985) Some Issues in Future User Interface Management Systems (UIMS) Development. In G. Pfaff (ed.) *User Interface Management Systems*, pp. 67-80, Springer, Berlin.

Thomas, J., and Kellogg, W. (1989). Minimizing Ecological Gaps in User Interface Design, *IEEE Software, January*, (pp. 78-86).

Wasserman, A.I. (1982) The user software engineering methodology: An overview. In A.A. Verrijin-Stuart (ed.) *Information System Design Methodologies*, pp. 591-682, North-Holland, Amsterdam.

Weir, G. R. S. (1988) *HCI Perspectives on Man-Machine Systems*. Scottish HCI Centre, Strathclyde University, Report No. AMU3588/01S.

Whiteside, J. Bennett, J., and Holtzblatt, K. (1988). Usability Engineering: Our experience and evolution. In M. Helander, (Ed.), *Handbook of Human-Computer Interaction* (pp. 791-818). Amsterdam: North-Holland.

Zuboff, S. (1988) *In the age of the smart machine: the future of work and power*. Basic Books, New York.

HUMAN JOBS AND COMPUTER INTERFACES
M.I. Nurminen and G.R.S. Weir
Elsevier Science Publishers B.V. (North-Holland)
© 1991 IFIP. All rights reserved.

Jobs and Interfaces : Discussant's Note

Kevin T. Ryan*

*Department of Computer Science and Information Systems, University of Limerick,
Limerick, Ireland

It is a pleasure to be here in Finland and to have the opportunity to contribute to this conference. Before commenting on the paper, a particularly intersting one, I should like to explain why the theme of this conference is of interest to me and to the country I come from, Ireland. There has been a deliberate government policy in Ireland to foster a computer industry over the past 15 years and this policy has been succesful in attracting many major international producers, such as Apple, Digital, Wang, Microsoft and Dell, to name but a few. Natural advantages, including access to the EC, a young educated population and proficiency in English have been supplemented by favourable tax regimes. Universities, not least my own University of Limerick, have played a major role in educating the employees of these firms and in supporting their research activities. On the other hand, such is the pressure to provide jobs in Ireland, so as to reduce our high levels of unemployment, that there is constant danger that the quality of the working environment might be ignored in the process. For this reason, as well as to broaden my own social awareness of the impacts of computer technology, I find both aspects of the conference theme, both Human Jobs and the corresponding Computer Interfaces, are of relevance to me and to my homeland.

The paper by Bannon and Kuutti has a welcome breadth to it, seeking as it does to lift the readers gaze from the minutiae of interface design to the higher reaches of methodology and indeed philosophy. That its ambitions are both broad and deep is without question. What is to be established is the extent to which these ambitions are realised. I will first consider their general approach then try to summarise their main hypotheses and conclude with a few observations and caveats of my own.

The authors seem to have set out to deconstruct not just the title of the conference but practically the entire field of HCI. Pointing out that whereas humans have jobs computers do not really have interfaces they cast doubt on whether the conference title can have any literal meaning. If they are right, and their case is certainly well argued, we must face the possibility that HCI is not even a defined field for proper research. However they do not limit themselves to criticism but, using an admirable cross-disciplinary approach, they offer some quite radical suggestions for reforming the HCI paradigm and putting it on a more consistent and scientifically defensible footing.

Having disposed of some preliminary definitions, primarily by illustrating the profusion of contradictions, the authors attempt to, in their own words, "re-conceptualise" the interface concept. They propose to do this through building a new framework for HCI concerns. Based on the approaches taken in Information Systems (IS) design this provides for a levelled separation of concerns. Working inwards from the user we move from the users world, through the conceptual world to the level of technological implementation. Their second main contribution is propose a spectrum, illustrated in Figure 1, that reflects the varying level of user interface concerns that can arise in different application domains. The implication of this diagram is that the more powerful systems of the future will devote increasing attention to supporting user interaction.

Methodology, the study of methods, is at the heart of this paper. Whereas, in the authors opinion, some other fields of computing endeavour have evolved consistent and workable methods for posing and solving design problems, the field of HCI has not. The field they choose as an example of successful methodology is Information Systems. As one who has been involved with such software engineering methods for over 15 years now I have a keen interest in what they have to say. They are correct in stating that Information Systems Design Methods (ISDMs) provide powers of abstraction that assist in managing complexity and that a levelled approach allows separation of concerns. It is also true that these design methods are "even used in practice". In fact one the major forces behind the spread of Computer Aided Software Engineering (CASE) tools is the desire to follow a more or less rigorous method. I would take issue with a few points however.

Firstly, the division into "Use", "Conceptual" and "Technological" is correct, although there are many other proposed models with more layers. However the use of the term "domain" is unfortunate since within CASE and other communities this term denotes the area of application and not a level in the development process. The alternative word, "level", used in Kuutti's presentation, is preferable. Secondly, I would not agree that most of the methods have nothing to say about user interface concerns. Current research on systems engineering methods, such as that being carried out in the Esprit project ATMOSPHERE, places considerable emphasis on interface design methods and a major section of that project is devoted to "presentation integration" which is essentially the problem of systematic user interface design.

So on a broader front I would like to assert that we software engineers are widening our concerns. The demands of the 'new work' as cited in the paper, are definitely part of the driving force behind this, but so is the realisation that interfaces to potential users constitute a crucial factor in most modern systems. The object oriented approach, ironically most often illustrated by window management, is gaining ground in the information systems and systems engineering communities. The trend towards open systems, now seemingly irresistable, is also most visible, in every sense, in the windowing domain.

Finally, while the authors concern to found a methodology for HCI is admirable and worthy of support, it would be foolhardy to expect too much too soon. The ISDMs have been developing for over twenty years now but, although they have contributed to the codification of design approaches, they have not been the only influence at work. My own experience is that more benefits are attributed to the methods than they warrant since it is often the very process of introspection that leads to more systematic and more thorough design.

However, these are minor criticisms. Overall, the paper is original and very thought provoking. It deserves to be widely read and studied. Its suggestions about layered design ought to be tested in practical applications as soon as possible while its definition of the "user interface spectrum" may prove to be one of the most copied diagrams from this, or many other, conferences.

Section 2

Industrial Interface Design

HUMAN JOBS AND COMPUTER INTERFACES
M.I. Nurminen and G.R.S. Weir
Elsevier Science Publishers B.V. (North-Holland)
© 1991 IFIP. All rights reserved.

Human-computer interface in computer-aided control system design

Monika Oit

Institute of Cybernetics, Estonian Academy of Sciences,
Akadeemia tee 21, 200108 Tallinn, Estonia

Abstract
Interface problems of one class of human-computer systems – computer-aided control system design systems are discussed. Using the concept of the state of dialogue the quality of dialogue is studied. Advances and shortcomings of menu-driven dialogue are examined.

1. INTRODUCTION

The human-computer interface is an organized exchange of information between two different active components, a human and a system. The main difference between them is a different level of information processing – a human works on a conceptual level, whereas a computer works on a manipulative level. Both a human and a computer have their own strengths as well as their own weaknesses, and the main function of the interface is to make it possible to use all the advantages of both, and to compensate for their shortcomings.

The design of a suitable interface is an important problem to be addressed in most contemporary human-computer systems. There are a lot of such systems nowadays, and the computer-aided control system design (CADSD) is one of the most computerized areas. Control systems were one of the first areas to which computers were applied, as it is next to impossible to solve mathematically complex and labour-consuming control problems without them. Specific to control systems design is an ill-defined control problem specification. It is often difficult to determine all the parameters of a control object and thus it is rather complicated to fix the requirements for the control system. Also, it is not easy to estimate directly all the results of the design process. This is judged principally by the quality of the functioning of the control system.

The results of the design process depend on several factors, and for that reason the design of a control system is usually an iterative process in an interactive mode. An iterative process is encouraged by the fact that there need not be any too exact solution for the control problem at given conditions. The solution can be found by checking the problem with changing requirements and conditions. An interactive mode means that after passing one iterative step the user makes a decision about the computing results, and gives corresponding information to the computer. As the result of the whole design process depends on the correctness of decisions, both the presentation of the computing process results as well as the contents, and the formalization of the user's commands are important. Each of these depends upon the possibilities of the interface.

2. APPLICATION AREA OF CACSD SYSTEMS

CACSD systems are mainly meant for control systems design, but they often serve as teaching aids as well. CACSD systems are successfully used to support several theoretical courses on control theory, control systems design and CAD of control systems. Using such design systems for wider application results in the need for more diverse possibilities in a user interface. This means that CACSD systems, like all contemporary human-computer systems, need a user-friendly interface. This is mentioned in [1] as one of three major areas that have emerged in the last five years, namely advanced user interfaces, data-base management, and expert aiding.

Characteristic of CACSD is the fact that the users' knowledge and their level of experience varies considerably. Thus "user-friendliness" has different meanings for different users. In contemporary human-computer systems the user interface is designed mainly for end-users, i.e. for persons having no experience in programming nor any extensive familiarity with computers.

The following main ergonomic requirements for a user-friendly interface are mentioned in [2]:
- adaptive and flexible dialogue;
- clear and determined behaviour of the system;
- simplicity of use;
- simplicity of learning;
- reliability, error-safety.

In the case of using CACSD system for a certain control system design, users of the system are design engineers, who are mainly interested in the flexibility of dialogue and in maximum freedom for formalizing their problems. In using the same system for teaching, the main interface requirements are: simplicity of use and learning, reliability and error-safety.

Systems used for teaching purposes are usually based on the safest types of interface: menu-driven and question-and-answer dialogues, which are unfortunately too rigid for design engineers and for other more experienced users. In such dialogues the computer provides a question or a list of alternative possibilities for problem solving, and the user gives an answer or makes a choice. It may seem that, in general, there are no interface problems in the case of such a fixed dialogue, with excellent possibilities for organizing fault protection. A dialogue can be designed according to the structure of the problem, the necessary data flow and the number of various solution methods. This should ensure an adequate dialogue for the required tasks. Actually, in the case of menu-driven dialogue some psychological aspects have to be taken into account. This means joint contributions of both computer science and psychology to the construction of human-computer interfaces.

3. HUMAN ABILITIES IN INFORMATION PROCESSING

A brief survey of basic questions and methods of cognitive psychology is given by [3]. Influenced by the modelling method of cybernetics (feedback mechanism), and by the method of modelling with the technique of a computer program, cognitive psychology is developing a general theory of human actions regulated by an internal information processing system. There exist different models of human's 'brain machine' characterizing human abilities in information processing. (Most computer-like models are given in [4] and [5].) The main shortcomings of such a system (mentioned in [5]) are a very limited capacity of operative (short-term) memory: 7 ± 2 units (chunks), and slow information transfer processes (speed about 30 bit/sec.). Therefore, a person is neither able to perform labour-consuming computations nor make rigorous decisions in the case of too many alternative possibilities.

With a menu-driven dialogue we usually have a choice of given alternatives. CACSD systems, as a rule, offer quite a large number of alternatives at every design step:
– several methods of object description,
– several object analysis methods,
– several regulator algorithm types,
– several mathematical methods for solving problems of regulator synthesis, etc.
If users have insufficient knowledge or too little information to make a choice between the given alternatives, they usually choose only what they know, or the first alternative in the menu. Therefore, if it exists, it would be reasonable to put the most suitable alternative highest in the menu. Usually it cannot be done, for usually the appropriate choice depends on the specific task. The user should then be given some help.

There are two ways of making the choice easier:
1. give corresponding comments for each alternative. This means including some fixed text to explain the differences between the alternatives. Such a comment is like an additional criterion for making the right decision. There are also several problems in this case. Firstly, the comments are physically limited (for example by display screen area). Secondly, if the user has to read all the comments to make the decision, the interaction will become considerably slower.
2. add a corresponding help procedure to give dynamic advice on the best choice in the particular conditions. This is a more complicated addition to the dialogue than the previous one. The concept of the state of the dialogue offered in [2] is useful for designing help procedures.

4. THE STATE OF THE DIALOGUE

For the study and modification of menu-driven dialogue it is very useful to utilize the state of dialogue SD, which is a triple

SD = (H, P, R)

where   H is the history vector of the dialogue,
         P is the state of the problem,
         R is the type of the dialogue.

The *history of the dialogue* begins with starting the CACSD system and ends with the exit from the system. The history vector saves all dialogue steps including help procedures. The history can be of different lengths for different problems and different users. The history vector H is useful in several respects.

For instance, the H vector is used in *designing help procedures*. The first step is to determine where and when the user needs help. This problem can be solved by studying dialogue histories. We can fix the steps or states of the dialogue to which users return most frequently. If such steps exist, the reason for returning can be the indefinitely formulated text of the dialogue or insufficient information for making the right decision. If the semantics of the text is unequivocal, we have to add a special procedure to help the user to decide.

In the same way we can *determine unnecessary parts* of the whole system. If there are parts that are never used, we may leave them out of the actual dialogue, and give corresponding reference to them if somebody should ever need them.

Mistaken data input steps can be fixed in the same way. In such steps some other request types have to be used, for example, a request with prescribed answer format, or some other possibility to raise the error-safety.

In using dialogue histories some psychological phenomena can be studied, for example, the semantics of the different word, and at the same time, the motivation of different users. For example, if one solution method is described by the word "fast" and the other by "precise", then students mainly choose the first and system engineers the second.

In actual work with the CACSD system the *state of the problem*, the second component of the state of the dialogue is determined by the history vector.

The state of the problem is the characteristic with quite a different meaning than the history vector. The state of the problem P characterizes the state of the input/output data of the problem. For the computer a problem is a network which begins with the initial data input and ends with the output of results. Such a network represents the structure used for designing the dialogue as well. In the actual work process, at every interaction step, the state of the problem is determined according to the history vector and system structure. The initial state can be defined differently, but the final state is reached when all the input data have been used and all results have been computed.

The state of the problem determines *the help procedures*: help procedures give advice for the next step according to the state of data as well as the previous steps. By using the state of the problem it is also possible to organize a *dynamical menu-driven dialogue* – only appropriate alternatives for the actual state of data will be offered in the menu. In fact such a dynamical menu represents expert aiding – determining all possible alternatives in the actual data conditions. Such an action can also be taken as an intelligent help procedure, which has lately become very popular in the CACSD area. (Examples can be found in [6 – 8].)

The third component of the state of the dialogue characterizes the actual *type of dialogue* if different dialogue types are available. The type of dialogue R is an additional parameter which determines the formation of the history vector and computing the state of the problem. Different dialogue types also entail different ways of computing.

Including the vector of the state of the dialogue in the interface requires additional efforts but results in quite a user-friendly and even somewhat intelligent interface, and makes it possible to study several interesting aspects of the dialogue.

5. PRACTICAL EXPERIENCE

The user interface of a CACSD system called COMICS is studied by using the concept of the state of the dialogue. COMICS is a CAD system for the linear multivariable computer control system. This was designed and implemented at the Institute of Cybernetics of the Estonian Academy of Sciences in the late seventies and has been in practical use since 1981. (More detailed information about COMICS can be found in [9].) Besides using it for control system design purposes, COMICS is also used in a practical course on control system design and in supporting a theoretical course on control theory at the Faculty of Automation of Tallinn Technical University.

The aim of such interface studies was to get information for radical reorganization of a full system with a view to transferring it to PC computers (it still works on PDP mainframes). From the state of the dialogue mainly the first component (the history of the dialogue), is in use. According to the simple tree-like structure of COMICS, the history of the dialogue is implemented as a simple counter of dialogue steps. The third component (the type of dialogue) has not been used to date because only menu-driven dialogue is used in the old system. The state of the problem is used for the design of help procedures.

The menu-driven dialogue is unsuitable for design engineers, and some other interaction types have to be added for more experienced users. But the menu-driven dialogue is appropriate in the teaching context in virtue of its simplicity for use and learning. A menu is a suitable aid for teaching, especially where there are sufficient comments and corresponding help procedures.

The problems to be solved with CACSD systems all have a similar structure, therefore the user interface requires quite a limited vocabulary. The corresponding help procedures are sufficient aids to learning both the vocabulary and its semantics. Some demo systems can additionally be used for that reason.

The need for organizing fault-safe input procedures can also be noted as essential in our experience. Interaction is the most time-consuming part of the

CACSD system, so it is more useful to add extra procedures to improve error-safety and provide a logical check on input data than to return to data input because of incorrect data. Interestingly, faults are made mainly in these dialogue steps where the semantics of the answer differs from the semantics of natural language.

While checking the unnecessary parts of the system, it first appeared that there was no need for quite a number of parts. However, changing the positions of the alternatives in menus the result became different and even the opposite. This means that with insufficient information users choose the first available alternative. After adding corresponding comments, there were very few steps that were never used. The need for essential help procedures in CACSD systems can be mentioned as another experience in these studies. In principle this means adding expert aiding to the user interface. Such future trends are actually mentioned in CACSD systems.

6. CONCLUSIONS

In this paper several user interface features of CACSD systems have been discussed. In spite of its rigidity, menu-driven dialogue can be employed in CACSD systems which are in use as teaching aids. Ergonomical aspects have to be considered in designing the menus and all the information forms. A dynamical menu with corresponding intelligent help procedures is most suitable in this case. The best interface type for all CACSD system users is a combined interface described in [1] and [7]. Such a combined interface offers various possibilities for a more experienced user, for example, a command language, which can be learned using corresponding menu-driven dialogue. In future, menu-driven dialogue can serve as one possible way of interacting with CACSD systems, especially in learning to work with the system. The vocabulary of the dialogue can be learned by using help procedures, which are simple to organize because of the fixed structure of the menu-driven dialogue. Thus it is simple to observe the state of problem solving. Such advanced menu-driven dialogues can be developed using modern windowing environments, as described in [7].

7. REFERENCES

1 Taylor J.H., Frederick D.K., Rimvall C.M., Sutherland H.A. Computer-aided Control Engineering Environments: Architecture, User Interface, Database Management, and expert aiding. In Preprints of the 11th IFAC World Congress, Tallinn, 1990.
2 Dehning W., Essig H., Maas S. The Adaptation of Virtual Man-Computer Interfaces to User Requirements in Dialog. Springer-Verlag, Berlin, 1981.
3 Tauber M.J. Top-down Design of Human-Computer Systems from the Demands of Human Cognition to the Virtual Machine – an Interdisciplinary Approach to Model Interfaces in Human Computer Interactions. In Proceedings of the IEEE

Workshop on Languages for Automation: Cognitive Aspects in Information Processing, Palma de Mallorca, 1985.

4 Card S.K., Moran T.P., Newell A. The Psychology of Human-Computer Interaction, Lawrence Erlbaum Associates, Hillsdale, NJ, 1983.

5 MacFarlene A.G.J., Gruebel G., Ackermann J. Filter Design Environments for Control Engineering. Preprints of the 10th IFAC World Congress, Munich, 1987.

6 Jordan D. Specification of a Man-Machine Interface for Control Systems Computer Aided Enginering Software Packages. UMIST, Control Systems Centre Report No. 630, Manchester, 1985.

7 Barker H.A., Chen M., Grant P.W., Harvey I.T., Jobling C.P., Townsend P. The Impact of Recent Developments in user-interface specification, Design and Management on the Computer Aided Design of Control Systems. In Preprints of the 11th IFAC World Congress, Tallinn, 1990.

8 Rimvall M., Künding M. Intelligent help for CACE applications. In Preprints of the 11th IFAC World Congress, Tallinn, 1990.

9 Oit M., Jaaksoo Ü. Dialogue-based CAD for multivariable controllers. CAD of Control Systems, Nauka, Moscow, 1982 (in Russian).

HUMAN JOBS AND COMPUTER INTERFACES
M.I. Nurminen and G.R.S. Weir
Elsevier Science Publishers B.V. (North-Holland)
© 1991 IFIP. All rights reserved.

Interfaces in a flexible manufacturing system - a case study

M. Vartiainen[a], H. Tiitinen[b] and V. Teikari[c]

[ac]Laboratory of Industrial Psychology, Helsinki University of Technology, Otakaari 4 A, SF-02150 Espoo

[b]Department of Psychology, University of Helsinki, Ritarikatu 5, SF-00170 Helsinki

Abstract
A flexible manufacturing system, its interfaces, and the job content of a work group operating the system were studied. The goal was to identify the hindrances in the work which prevent the operators from achieving optimum work, i.e. maintaining well-being and productivity.

The manufacturing system and its components, including the dialogue structure and the interfaces, were described. The operators controlled the system with the help of five visual display units. These VDU's all had different dialogue layouts and structures. A questionnaire completed by the operators showed that the operator group consisted of two sub-groups; the 'experts' and the 'novices'. This was in contrast to the intended organizational structure planned during the implementation. It seems that the inconsistent interfaces 'conserve' easily the Tayloristic type of traditional work division. If the objective is a flexible sociotechnical work system with its multi-skilled employees, it is not only necessary to organize tasks as group work and to train employees but also to develop technology, especially, integrated and consistent interfaces.

1. INTRODUCTION

1.1. Computer-aided work as an activity system
Discussion concentrating only on man-machine interface design, or the design of industrial or office automation should be given up, and a discussion on the design of computer aided work or computer aided factory work or computer aided office work should be started. The latter approach emphasizes the criteria of 'good work' and the complete task structure as the aims of the man-computer system design. Therefore, in designing man-machine systems and the man-computer interaction, or more generally, sociotechnical systems, the starting point should be the holistic

analysis of work activities, in which machines with or without programs are used as tools (Figure 1).

Vygotsky (12, 2) remarked that humans use tools and signs to mediate their activities. Concrete tools, e.g. computer, software, are aimed to master, control and influence the external object of activity. As a result, changes occur in objects. Signs belong to the broader category of 'psychological tools'. Examples of psychological tools are: language, various systems of counting, mnemonic techniques, algebraic symbol systems, works of art, schemes, diagrams, maps, etc. Psychological tools have - in addition to their control of behavioural processes - the important characteristics of 'reverse action', i.e. they operate on the individual and his/her consciousness. Thus, the two types of tools are in parallel and hierarchical relation to each other. If computer-aided work is studied as an activity system, it is evident that to concentrate only on the interface problems does not result in the best possible solution for the development of both well-being and productive work.

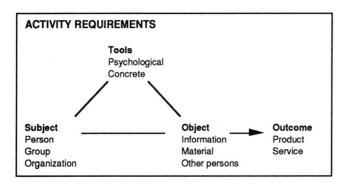

Figure 1. An applied Vygotskian (12) approach: work as a tool-mediated activity.

The above is not a new idea. Jordan (6) criticised the Fitts' list (5) as the basis for design of man-machine function allocation. In Fitts' list the functions for which man is superior to machine, and vice versa, were compared. A conclusion from the Fitts' list was that people are flexible but cannot be depended upon to perform in a consistent way, whereas machines are consistent but they have no flexibility. The *comparability* of man and machine was questioned by Jordan. He noted that "men and machines are not comparable, they are *complementary*". The term "allocation of task to men and machine/programs" is meaningless. Rather we should speak about a task that is done by man and machine/program in a certain organizational and physical environment.

The main difference between man-computer systems and traditional man-machine systems has been characterized as the greater ability of the computer to perform information processing, i.e., interpreting, analyzing data, etc. The development of man-machine systems into man-computer systems has been easy to see on the shop floor when following the development of machine tools into flexible manufacturing systems (FMS), and towards wider systems of computer integrated manufacturing (CIM).

1.2. The aim of the sociotechnical design and its barriers

The man-computer interface design is, of course, an interesting object of research. However, it is impossible to meet real shop-floor problems of industrial and office automation from this narrow perspective. Before turning to the wider approach, let us look at the challenges and their barriers in working life on the shopfloor.

The key word in the sociotechnical design of work is *flexibility*. For years many enterprises have applied the Just-In-Time philosophy of production and implemented small production units to achieve the flexibility necessary to meet the needs of their customers. In manufacturing, this means individual products, and in administration, diverse services. Enterprises and organizations are competing among themselves in both domestic and foreign markets to supply goods on the basis of quality, product range and delivery time. There are, however, some barriers which prevent organizations from achieving the above-mentioned aim.

The organizational barrier is primarily a consequence of the *Tayloristic division of labor*. The goals of flexibility cannot be achieved by increasing the division of labor, i.e. by separating organizationally the planning of the work from its execution. This kind of division of labor causes several problems in jobs. The most important of these is the absence of thinking demands. Therefore, when designing man-machine/computer systems the division of work and job content must be studied and evaluated in order to reach a human-centered solution. Various trials have been conducted over an extended period of time with the objective of rebuilding the hierarchy. Most private enterprises and organs of state administration, however, still have hierarchical organizations with an excessive number of levels. On the organizational side the necessary prerequisite for the flexibility of production is *multi-skilled* and *motivated personnel possessing the ability to think and solve problems* independently.

The psychological barrier is a result of the organizational barrier. The residual allocation of tasks between persons result in partialized task structure (10). This means, in the case of an individual, impossibility to realize basic psychological mechanisms, which are the cyclic structure of actions (preparation, execution, control) and their hierarchical mental regulation (intellectual, conceptual-perceptual and sensorimotor levels). The theory of mental regulation of work activities (3, 10) regards the concepts of complete and incomplete, i.e. partialized actions (10), as crucial. The partialized task structure shrinks the developmental possibilities of the intellectual level of regulation. To summarize: partialized work is neither sequentially nor hierarchically complete (4). The sequentially complete work structure includes preparation (goal-setting, planning, action programs, autonomous decision-making), executing, checking and organizing. In addition, the work should be hierarchically complete. There should be demands on various levels of regulation, i.e. real information processing including non-algorithmic intellectual demands.

Norman (8) also presented a model of the cyclic interaction between a person and a computer system. The interaction involves four stages of activities: forming the intention, selecting the action, executing the action, and evaluating the outcome. Generally speaking. Norman's model reminds one of the TOTE-model (7) and the VVR-model (3). Norman stressed that the system should support the different stages with tools. For example, supporting for sub-intention formation by providing information on the current status of things and what is possible, or supporting for selecting the action by providing well-designed menus. Roe (1) later presented the so-called 'action facilitation approach' which was derived from Hacker's theory of the mental regulation of work actions (3). Action facilitation aims at improving or maintaining a user's performance, simultaneously decreasing his/her mental and/or physical load. The software tools should support the user's actions in such a way that action facilitation results. The problem is to find the concrete means to include such tools and aids in software and work environment.

The technological barrier, which prevents organizations from achieving the above-mentioned flexibility, is the traditional allocation of functions between man and machine/program when *designing tools* (programs, machines, technological systems and their interfaces). The allocation is still often based on the idea of comparability of man and machine. On the technological side, flexibility requires *new* types of *computerized tools*, e.g. flexible manufacturing systems, integrated office systems. The approach which regards these complicated industrial and office systems as tools to achieve certain goals has emphasized the meaning of man-computer interfaces in regulating the work process. The demands of usability and user-friendliness are well-known. In designing man-computer interaction we should, first of all, aim at complete work activities. Tools should extend man's sensory and motor abilities, i.e. they should increase his/her possibilities to regulate work activities.

In summary, to achieve high productivity, flexible production and well-being of personnel, enterprises should have good work environments, highly qualified and internally motivated personnel. The concept of 'work environment' includes not only physical and chemical but also sociotechnical factors, e.g. man-computer interface and job content.

2. THE PROBLEMS AND METHODS OF THE STUDY

In this study, a flexible manufacturing system, its interfaces, and the job content of a work group operating the system were studied. The main idea was to find the hindrances in the tools, their interfaces and activity requirements which prevent FMS-operators (N=12, two shifts) from optimum work, i.e. that which maintains well-being (job satisfaction, proper mental load) and productivity.

The problems were:
(1) What are the components and software of the system?
(2) How do the users control the system?
(3) What kind of interfaces are there to operate the system, and how they are evaluated by the employees?
(4) How is the work organized to operate the system?

The system and its operators were studied six months after the start-up. As the starting point, a description of the system components and interfaces was formulated. Then system specialists and system operators (members of the work group) were interviewed. The formal dialogue structure of each operating system was analyzed and described as a tree-structure (9), graphically fixing the connections between individual elements (menus, information and data entry masks). Finally, a questionnaire concerning the work environment, machines and their interfaces was answered by the FMS operators. Ten operators returned the completed questionnaire. In this study, questions concerning (a) time used in different activities by employees when operating the machinery, (b) error feedback and help given by software, and (c) general satisfaction of users with usability, flexibility, etc., of the system software, are reported. Five step scales were used (1 = very bad....3 = moderate.....5 = very good).

3. RESULTS

3.1. Description of the FMS and its environment

The factory studied produces pneumatic actuators which operate as turning devices for ball and butterfly valves. A 10-pallet Okuma machining center was purchased at the end of 1985, because of the increased demand for actuators. The purchase of a machining center laid the foundation for the FMS strategy. The adaptation of FMS technology was prepared by rationalizing production. For example, unmanned production was learned over three years so that in 1989 ten machines were running unmanned from 3 to 8 hours during the night-shift. Some machines were running for over 6000 net hours per year. The demand for products was still increasing.

The decision to build a new plant which would be totally based on FMS technology was made in spring 1988. That year was the beginning of the research project too. A lot of attention was paid to the training of the employees, and the personnel as a whole made visits to other FMS-based organizations, participated in lectures, played a simulation game several times, and were practically trained to use flexible manufacturing systems in a separate training center. Up to seven percent of the working time in 1989 was used for training. The new FMS-factory was opened in the beginning of 1990.

The manufacturing system consists of three machining centers, two flexible turning cells, one FMS washing machine, three separate CNC-machines, three manual machines, one manual washing machine and automated warehouse. The components manufactured in machining centers are prismatic, and those in turning cells rotational.

The software is produced by Valmet with the programs running on a Digital PDP 11/53 minicomputer, a Siemens PLC and an IBM PC. There are *three levels* in the control system (Figure 2). At the bottom, there is a machine tool control level which also controls the automated warehouse. Above this, is a process control system (PCS) which manages the flow of components to be manufactured and communicates with machine tool control. At the top level, there is an operative control system (OCS). All tool management is run on the IBM PC. The operative control system is connected to a production planning system from which a half week production schedule is transferred straight to the FMS control system. The operative control system takes care of DNC operations. All tool data, e.g. life, offsets, spare tools, can be stored in databases.

In future, the tool management system will be connected to a CAD system, and allow data transmission between the CAD system and the tool management system. CAD/CAM will be realized in a few years' time. At present, not the CAD system has been fully implemented. In the future, actuator plant operations will be integrated as far as possible, from costumer order to delivery of the goods. For this purpose, an extensive information network is being built between subsidaries and the head office so that orders from abroad will be transferred electronically.

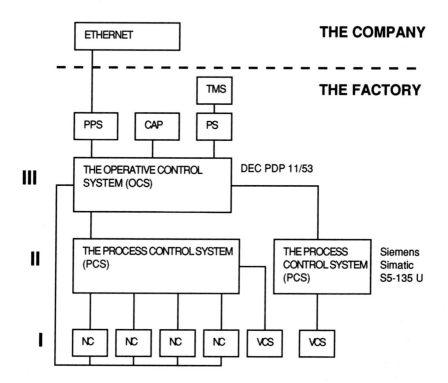

Figure 2. The three levels of the FMS control system (PPS = Production Planning System, CAP = Computer Aided Planning, PS = Production Control, TMS = Tool Maintenance System).

3.2. How the users control the system

The users control the operative control system (OCS) with the help of five visual display units:
- the first terminal is used for starting the whole system
- the second terminal is used to manage tool-setting
- the third terminal (located in the NC-programming room) is used for transferring NC-programs
- the fourth terminal is used to manage the automated warehouse information and the turning cells
- the fifth terminal (located in the room of production management) is used for production simulation.

In addition to the terminals, there are two printers for reporting and a separate magnetic tape unit for making back-up programs. The process control system (PCS) is used via the above-mentioned five terminals. In addition, there are two black-and-white terminals and two process control keyboards to operate the PCS. Each machine and piece of equipment also has its own local control and can be operated individually without the OCS.

3.3. The interfaces and their evaluation

The operating programs and interfaces may be divided into five groups each with different dialogue structures:
- programs used in OCS-terminals
- programs used in PCS-terminals
- machining centers (numerically controlled, NC) having their own operating system
- tool maintenance system (TMS) and
- quality control equipment.

The displays for data input and receiving information on the operative status of both the OCS and the PCS are based on menus. Examples of displays are shown in Figure 3. Function and alphanumeric keys are used for data input except for the tool maintenance system, which can also be operated using a mouse. In general, the user starts from the top level of a menu by selecting an operation (letter/number). Then the program moves to the lower level, etc. In the OCS, there are five main menu displays. An example of a display is given in Figure 3a. The dialogue of three NC-machines consists of a screen, menu keys and the operating panel with various keys, pushbuttons, switches and indicator lamps. The display is shown in Figure 3b. The tool maintenance system takes care of tool pre-setting. The pre-setting values are transferred from a microcomputer to the machining centers via the PCS. The dialogue is programmed in the MS-Window environment based on menu displays. The quality control equipment is used for quality control of products. The user fixes the product and starts the measuring program. The dialogue (Figure 3c) consists of a screen, standard keyboard, various other keys and indicator lamps. In addition, there is a separate control unit for moving parts of the quality control system.

In general, one might conclude that the five operating systems seem to have a number of different characteristics, e.g., general layout, the structure of the programs. The previously discussed theoretical accounts would suggest a number of potential problems, especially in the flexibility and ease of use of different systems for the FMS-operators.

The formal analysis of information exchange between man and computer showed immense differences in the levels and complexity of dialogue structures, and in the difficulty to use and learn to use them. The hypothesis is that the more levels and branches there are in the program, the more difficult is operation for the user. As examples, the dialogue structures behind *one* of the main menus of the OCS and the *whole* dialogue structure of the tool maintenance system are shown in Figure 4.

Closer inspection of the questionnaire completed by FMS-operators (N=10) showed some unexpected results, the main result being the fact that the group consisted of 'experts' and 'novices' holding different opinions about the five interfaces. The classification into experts and novices is somewhat artificial. Each respondent was classified either as an expert or as a novice (a) by means of their daily and weekly interface operating-time and (b) by the number of times they used a certain type of interface daily/weekly.

The FMS-operators were asked to judge the interfaces they used on a number of dimensions, e.g. consistency and complexity. There were a number of questions concerning each dimension. On average, the respondents used different interfaces

42

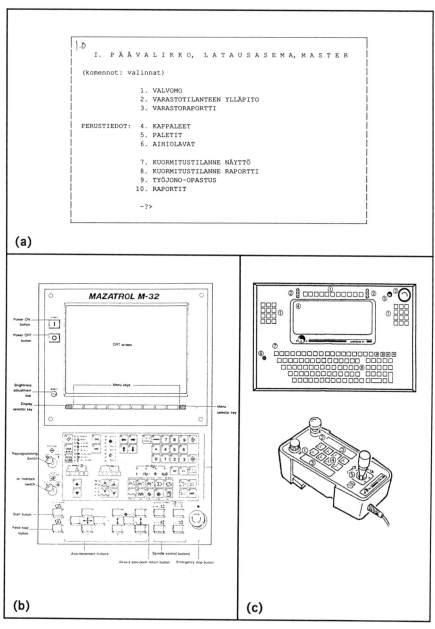

```
).D
      I. PÄÄVALIKKO, LATAUSASEMA, MASTER

   (komennot: valinnat)

              1. VALVOMO
              2. VARASTOTILANTEEN YLLÄPITO
              3. VARASTORAPORTTI

   PERUSTIEDOT:  4. KAPPALEET
              5. PALETIT
              6. AIHIOLAVAT

              7. KUORMITUSTILANNE NÄYTTÖ
              8. KUORMITUSTILANNE RAPORTTI
              9. TYÖJONO-OPASTUS
             10. RAPORTIT

              -?>
```

(a)

(b)   (c)

Figure 3. Examples of displays used by the FMS-group. (a) The OCS, (b) machining centers, and (c) the quality control equipment.

43

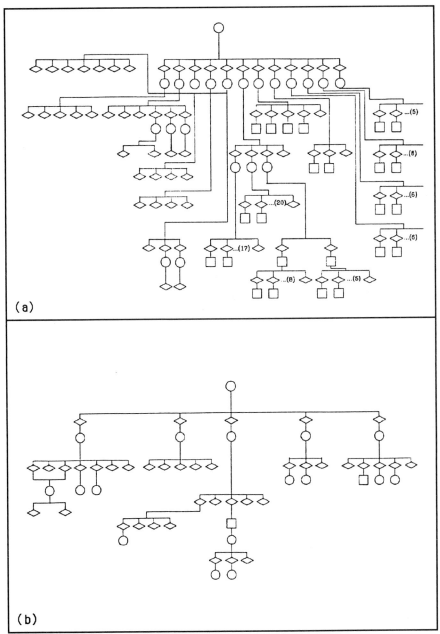

(a)

(b)

Figure 4. The dialogue structure of a menu (a) in the OCS and (b) in the tool maintenance system. O = information, □ = data entry, ◇ = menu.

17 times per day, the average operation time being about ten minutes. During an average eight-hour working day the operators used the interfaces for approximately 1 h. 40 mins. In general, they agreed that the five interfaces were quite useful in accomplishing the tasks being done. They were also quite satisfied with most of the interfaces in general, perhaps excepting the quality control equipment, in which there were some still unsolved programming problems.

With regard to, for instance, disturbance time, there were differences amongst novices and experts. While novices said they had trouble with the interfaces practically every day, most of the experts had an occasional problem, once a week or so. Similar polarization between the novices and experts was found among a large number of questionnaire-items ranging from "the clarity of error messages", "easiness of data-input and acceptance" as well as "the meaningfulness of the codes and abbreviations, etc.

In general, whereas the experts found the interface quite reliable, easy to use and not-so-error-prone, the novices claimed just the opposite. On average, the experts found the different interfaces studied more satisfactory than did the novices.

3.4. The organization of work

The existence of 'experts' and 'novice' was a surprise because it contrasted with the organizational aim during the system implementation. The aim was to organize jobs as group work. There were going to be four separate groups and a group of clerical employees. Three general alternatives for organizing group work in the new plant were made by the specialists:
1. The 'radical' alternative: complete job rotation in all tasks among all groups.
2. The 'compromise' alternative: complete job rotation within each group.
3. The 'traditional' alternative: each person is doing his/her own specialized tasks.

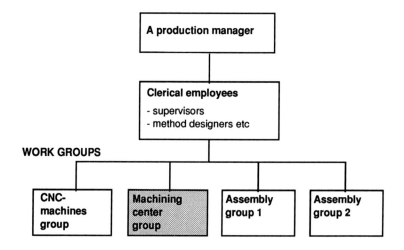

Figure 5. The organization of work in the factory. The FMS-group studied is shown as a gray box.

The 'compromise' solution was selected by the personnel themselves. There were two groups operating machining tools (Figure 5). The FMS was operated in two shifts. The aim was an even job rotation among the groups. The questionnaire, however, showed that there were groups of 'experts' and 'novices' with regard to their ability to use the five studied system components. This division seems to be clearly related to the observed differences in the complexity level of the dialogue structure (see, e.g., figure 4). Practically all the FMS-operators had had the same amount of training, so it seems reasonable to conclude that even though the basic training was very intensive, the inherent properties and structure of different interfaces were too problematic for some of the operators. This resulted in the emergence of the two 'sub-groups'.

5. DISCUSSION

Our study showed that the interfaces in a flexible manufacturing system are very inconsistent both in their *physical layout* (see Figure 3) and in the *dialogue structure* of their *programs* (see Figure 4).

Although the aim of the organization had been an even job rotation among the tool machining groups, the study showed a clear-cut difference in the aforementioned groups. This difference (statistically significant $p<.005$) could be described as the emergence of 'experts' and 'novices' within both the groups.

Those operators who had worked in more demanding jobs, e.g. programming NC-machines in the old factory, could manage the different dialogue structures of all systems ('the experts'). It also seems evident that for this reason they had learned to appreciate the different systems and regarded the interfaces as satisfactory.

Despite extensive pre- and post-FMS training, some members in the machining groups had obviously found the different layouts and dialogue structures too complicated ('the novices'). This was evident both from the amount of time spent on the more complicated programs and the reported amount of run-time failures during operation: the novices did not use the programs as much as the experts, and while using them, they ran into problems more often. This, in turn, was reflected in their level of satisfaction with the interfaces. In most cases, the novices ranked the interfaces as 'poorer' than the experts.

The results of the study showed both objective and subjective differences; in the physical structure of the equipment and in the opinions of the FMS-operators, respectively. Taking into consideration the theoretical points concerning the structure and planning of sociotechnical systems, one might conclude that not only design of the systems but also their implementation must be done in a wider context, taking into account organizational, training and software matters. Computer-aided-manufacturing is *only* a tool. Inconsistent and complicated interfaces may, however, be the result of old, Tayloristic approaches to work division. More importantly, the inconsistent interfaces may conserve the traditional organizational structure; they may be hindrances to achieving more flexible structures. In building complicated, computer-aided work environments, such as FMS and CIM, straight-forward and relatively simplistic accounts about 'man-machine interface design' are not sufficient bases for building efficient, 'powerful', easy-to-operate systems. What is needed instead is a theory driven framework for outlining the task structures involved, thereby setting certain criteria (1), which can then be used in a more quantitative manner, along the guidelines set by, for instance, activity theory.

ACKNOWLEDGEMENTS: This study was made in the project 'The tools and methods of the learning organization' financed by the Academy of Finland.

REFERENCES

1. Arnold, A.G. & Roe, R.A. Action facilitation: a theoretical concept and its use in user interface design. In Work with computers: organizational, management, stress and health aspects. M.J. Smith and G. Salvendy, Eds. Elsevier, The Netherlands, 1989, pp. 191-199.
2. Engeström, Y. Learning by expanding. Orienta-Konsultit Oy, Helsinki,1988.
3. Hacker, W. Allgemeine Arbeits- und Ingenieurpsychologie. VEB Deutscher Verlag der Wissenschaften, Berlin, 1973.
4. Hacker, W. Arbeitspsychologie psychische Regulation von Arbeitstätigkeiten. VEB Deutscher Verlag der Wissenschaften, Berlin, 1986.
5. Fitts, P.M., Ed. Human engineering for an effective air navigation and traffic control system. National Research Council, 1951.
6. Jordan, N. Allocation of functions between man and machines in automated systems. J. Appl. Psychol. 47 (1963), 161-165.
7. Miller, G.A., Galanter, E. and Pribram, K.M. Plans and the structure of behavior. Holt, Rinehart & Winston, New York, 1960.
8. Norman, D.A. Stages and levels in human-machine interaction. Int. J. Man-Machine Studies 21, (1984), 365-375.
9. Spinas, P. Arbeitspsychologische Aspekte der Benutzerfreundlichkeit von Bildschirmsystemen. ADAG Administration & Druck AG, Zürich, 1987. Thesis for Ph.D.
10. Volpert, W. Handlungsstrukturanalyse als Beitrag zur Qualifikationsforschung. PahlRugenstein, Köln, 1974.
11. Volpert, W. Psychische Regulation von Arbeitstätigkeiten. In Arbeitspsychologie. U. Kleinbeck und J. Rutenfranz, Eds. Hogrefe, Göttingen, 1987, pp. 1-42.
12. Vygotski, L.S. Mind in society: the development of higher psychological processes. Harvard University Press, Cambridge, Mass., 1978.

HUMAN JOBS AND COMPUTER INTERFACES
M.I. Nurminen and G.R.S. Weir
Elsevier Science Publishers B.V. (North-Holland)
© 1991 IFIP. All rights reserved.

Industrial Interface Design: Discussant's Note

Risto Suitiala

VTT/TIK, Technical Research Centre of Finland, Laboratory for Information Processing, Lehtisaarentie 2 A, 00340 Helsinki, Finland (email: rhs@tik.vtt.fi)

1. INTRODUCTION

An abstract discussion about human jobs and computer interfaces requires more concrete material for illustration. These two presentations on industrial interface design satisfy this kind of requirement. However, the possible applications range from the designers using CAD-systems to operators using computers to control the factory at the floor level. In reality, there is no unified industrial interface, there are only particular examples from a great variety of systems.

2. COMMENTS ON "MONIKA OIT: HUMAN-COMPUTER INTERFACE IN COMPUTER-AIDED CONTROL SYSTEM DESIGN"

The interface that Monika Oit depicts supports the computer-aided control systems designer, e.g. a person that designs the operator's interface and implements the algorithms that are used in the automatic control. In reality, the automatic control is not merely a simple mathematical model but a situation where there are many unknown parameters and the operator must have the final decision. The designer is faced with a complex environment and he/she must, on one hand, determine the regularities in the environment, and on the other hand leave the operator the possibility to react to the many expected and unexpected events.

Oit mentions three areas that have progressed recently: advanced user interfaces, data-base management, and expert aiding. Windowing and new forms of interaction, some call it direct manipulation, have greatly influenced the design of user interfaces (Smith et al. 1982). It is to be expected that the quality of user interfaces will be higher with these enhanced design principles. However, the essence of the user interface is something other than simply the surface of the computer. However similar they look at the interface, the systems can have e.g. discrepancies as compared with the old ways of working (Grudin 1989). The second area of progress, data-base management, integrates the systems inside an industrial plant and is useful in coordinating work and sometimes also in centralizing work. The third area of progress, expert systems, is more questionable in my opinion. There has been no real progress and even the philosophical basis has been hotly disputed (e.g. Göranzon & Josefson 1988).

Another problem is to use these systems for teaching as Oit is doing. In this case, there are rather a lot of people involved. The teacher wants to transfer his/her knowledge to the students. Students are using the system and trying to simulate the behaviour of the design engineers. Through the design engineers there is a link to the operators of the system. It will be challenging to be a designer for a system for use by teachers to teach students to be design engineers that design the operator's work.

Oit uses cognitive psychology as the foundation for user interface design. A wider perspective would encompass human jobs. Critics of the "function allocation" model can be found e.g. in the subsequent paper by Vartiainen et al. in this issue. The separation of humans and computers leads us to think about the computer as an object in itself. The computer is then something that exists without humans. The contemporary human job requires co-operation with other humans. So it is more relevant to see the relations between humans than between the computer and the human.

When Oit suggests the use of helps to give dynamic advice, she somehow makes the situations permanent. The state concept is needed as a prerequisite for these dynamic help texts. The designer of the help texts will convey his/her best knowledge through texts. However, because they are static the student always gets the same advice in any specific situation. As I see it, the help texts are generally aimed at two purposes: patching and hiding a bad user interface and shifting the responsibility to others. I have not enough information to decide which is the case here. I would prefer personal communication in the teaching. Only some very carefully designed parts of teaching could be computerized. Also, students would like to experiment with the results of their design. The rather permanent help system could be replaced by components that make such experiments possible. It is hard to give any details in this specific case. However, one example is simulation that could offer more possibilities for experiments.

I think that a good user interface "grows" with the user. There are two dimensions in the growing. The first dimension is the operation of the interface. When the user is faced with the interface for the first time, he/she concentrates on getting the work done with the computer. In this situation, he/she should be able to browse through the possible operations. Gradually, he/she learns how to operate the interface. The requirement to make routine operations as easy as possible arises. The second dimension is knowledge from the subject field. A student has (perhaps) little knowledge when he/she starts using the system. A design engineer has the required knowledge already. The problem is mainly how his/her knowledge "co-operates" with the knowledge inside the computer program. It is very challenging to make a computer interface that would serve the users in both of these dimensions.

3. COMMENTS TO "M. VARTIAINEN, H. TIITINEN AND V. TEIKARI: INTERFACES IN A FLEXIBLE MANUFACTURING SYSTEM - A CASE STUDY"

It is very interesting to propose a theoretical framework and then apply it to a special case. Activity theory (Engeström 1988) is relevant in studying work and especially the changes in work. A one-dimensional view would study only the computer interface between man and computer. As Vartiainen et al. note, there is more involved in this situation than simply man and computer. The activity theory could offer a way to new dimensions and new conceptual structures.

The problem in this kind of study is to find the connection between the theory and the case study, so that they support each other. Let us take the problems one at a time.

"(1) What are the components and software of the system". The theory would study the ideas behind the software. Which conceptual tools (models) are used in the software? What are the presuppositions in the software?

"(2) How do the users control the system?". Perhaps the software is a vehicle for controlling the system? What/who is the system? Are the people controlling themselves?

"(3) What kind of interfaces are there to operate the system, and how are they evaluated by the employees?". The interface is only the tip of the iceberg. Why concentrate on it? What is the internal model behind the interface? Evaluation without actual practice is very hard. You should try the work yourself. You should observe the work instead of collecting questionnaires. Questionnaires are a way of throwing the problem onto others. The system view as a hierarchical menu is rather syntax-oriented. What about semantics? What about pragmatics?

"(4) How is the work organized to operate the system?". Reorganization was done by the personnel. However, they were given a menu of three alternatives. How about other alternatives?

In the paper there are concepts like "optimum work" and "sociotechnical work system". Although it is not explicitly mentioned, it resembles a known participative, sociotechnical approach, originating from e. g. Enid Mumford (Mumford 1987) (humanized activity in terms of Engeström). There is a further level of development, a collective activity. It is described in more detail by Engeström. It means that we develop ourselves new forms of activity. It is not a choice in a menu offered by management but it is a new kind of activity found by resolving conflicts in work.

Although some references are made to Engeström, no real application of these theories is made. In the background, there seem to be the sociotechnical ideas.

4. REFERENCES

Yrjö Engeström: Learning by expanding, Orienta-Konsultit, Helsinki 1988

Jonathan Grudin: The case against user interface consistency, Comm. ACM, 32 (1989) 10, 1164-1173

Bo Göranzon, Ingela Josefson (eds.): Knowledge, Skill and Artificial Intelligence, London: Springer 1988

Enid Mumford: Sociotechnical systems design, Evolving theory and practice, in Computers and Democracy, A Scandinavian Challenge, Gro Bjerknes, Pelle Ehn & Morten Kyng (eds.), Avebury 1987, 59-76

D.C. Smith, E. Harselem, C. Irby, R. Kimball, and W. Verplank: Designing the Star user interface, Byte 7 (1982) 4, 242-282

Section 3

Interfaces and Special Needs

HUMAN JOBS AND COMPUTER INTERFACES
M.I. Nurminen and G.R.S. Weir
Elsevier Science Publishers B.V. (North-Holland)
© 1991 IFIP. All rights reserved.

A Computer Interface for Lawyers

Eve Wilson

Computing Laboratory, University of Kent at Canterbury, CT2 7NF, United Kingdom

Abstract

This paper examines the criteria for interface design for lawyers. Lawyers epitomize discretionary users; they are highly motivated professionals with well-established working practices. They will use only computer systems that improve performance without affecting their work pattern, in which the user interface can be easily mastered and remembered. The paper looks at existing databases and systems, then discusses the advantages of a hypertext interface to integrate different tasks in a lawyer's workbench. It ends by considering hybrid systems, consisting of a hypertext front-end to a traditional search engine. These can give a simple, consistent interface across a variety of different retrieval systems, and the techniques used in their implementation may be extended to afford user preference in interface specification.

1. DISCRETIONARY USERS

During their early development, computer interfaces had no need to be user-friendly. Interacting with the computer could be restricted to a few staff who had been chosen for their compatibility with the computer; that is, they could adapt to obscure machine languages and intricate control sequences and even revel in their complexity. However, intricacies of computer communication that might intrigue computer professionals frequently irritated the growing community of users who regarded their computer as merely a tool in their real work. Such users expected the computer to act reliably and predictably, and did not want the problem of instructing it to be a demanding intellectual discipline in its own right. The number of task-oriented users continues to grow; in many industries to-day there is a computer on the desk of almost every employee. Designers of computer interfaces can no longer afford to remain insensitive to the preferences of ordinary human beings who have neither the time nor the inclination to lavish intensive intellectual effort on mastering a new technology to which they may be antipathetic by nature or previous training. Computer interfaces have to be designed to appeal to people; they must be easy to use and have the appearance of technological simplicity; in other words, they must be user-friendly. To-day, it is chiefly this quality that determines whether a computer system will be a success.

One force in promoting this revolution has been the industrial market, where manufacturers and software houses have vied fiercely with one another to produce more user-friendly application packages. But many of these packages have been designed independently of the user – they may no longer be computer-centric but many are still designer-centric rather than user-centric. In designer-centric systems the full resources of the windowing and operating systems are exploited in a dazzling exhibition which flatters the designer's technical virtuosity, often at the expense of clarity of presentation and simplicity of use. It is fortunate for sales that many people can still be constrained to use a computer, either because their employer decrees they shall, or because there is no other way, although the task may be confined to their leisure pursuits, for example, accessing the on-line catalogue in their local branch library.

The other force in the interface revolution has been discretionary users: users who cannot be constrained to use a computer. Most obviously, they are people who buy computers for use at home. They may feel a computer would be a useful administrative assistant around the house, but unless they feel that using the computer will be easy to learn and to remember they will not buy one. Few industries or professional groups are in the same independent position. Law is one of them. Except for forays into the field of word-processors – where not lawyers but their secretaries confront technology – most lawyers in Britain have not been beguiled by computer technology. This is not for want of many fertile application areas, but because the lawyer is the epitome of the discretionary user. An interface to suit a lawyer must surely possess attributes of general merit in interface design.

This is not to imply that lawyers are a uniform group. There is probably no professional group whose interests and activities vary more widely: solicitors in quiet country practices, dealing predominantly with will drafting and contracts for sale and lease; barristers in the courts, interested in law reports of previous hearings relevant to their current client's affairs; draftsmen composing new Statutes to meet the wishes of Parliament and civil servants seeking to administer statutory provisions, whose chief interest is Acts of Parliament, and how new acts impinge on old; university researchers who are concerned with the underlying principles, the history and development, the social implications — lawyers for whom even a statute repealed 200 years ago may be relevant; lawyers who use their legal expertise in other professions: teachers, business managers, trade unionists, members of Parliament. It is because the group is so diverse that it is so challenging. However diverse their objectives, lawyers' source materials are identical: statutes and statutory instruments; law reports; precedents of legal documents such as contracts and wills; commentaries and textbooks to improve understanding; dictionaries to define legal terms.

The chief interest in this paper is the need for a coherent interface for tasks that require the retrieval of information, the integration of information from diverse sources, the incorporation of information in its original or amended form in new documents and the production of a final version to the required high quality printing standard. Obviously, there is much work done by lawyers that is merely peripheral to the actual legal work, e.g. time-recording, accounting and billing. Tasks such as these are largely self-contained, and common to many professions besides law; they are marginal to our concerns here where we concentrate on the principles that should illuminate interface design in the access and use of legal information and the production of legal instruments.

2. INTERFACE REQUIREMENTS OF A LAWYER

The interface requirements of lawyers and other discretionary users are largely the requirements of ordinary users. Discretionary users are more likely to have their requirements met because they are under no more compulsion to accommodate the designer-centric systems of today than they were to accept the computer-centric systems of yesterday.

The system must be oriented towards the user and the user's objectives. It must perceive the world – or at least the information structures that represent the world – as the user perceives them; and it must work in a way that seems natural to the user.

The essential attributes of a well-designed interactive interface are a frequently discussed topic: (1 – 8). I am going to rehearse the features that seem particularly important for lawyers and try to justify them as they relate to lawyers' work and lifestyle.

To avoid an unstructured list I have divided interface characteristics into three main groups:

i.   characteristics appertaining to appearance
ii.   operational characteristics
iii. functional characteristics.

Some features have relevance or implications for more than one group.

2.1. Characteristics appertaining to appearance

• *Uncluttered*

The user interface should look clean and uncluttered. Just as an untidy desk may inhibit work, clutter and complexity in the display make learning and use more difficult for the non-technical user, who may see only chaos where the system designer saw elegant exploitation of all available technology. In many ways the designer's desire to use available resources to the full is entirely admirable, but the exercise is too frequently undertaken without regard for the preferences and orientation of the user. The technology of windowing, multiple overlays, and a rainbow of colours is part of the designer's chosen discipline; it is entirely alien to the lawyer. His natural medium is paper with printing – usually white paper with black ink.

• *Familiar to look at*

Lawyers are used to documents on paper. Law leans heavily on linguistic abilities and the interpretation of natural language, and lawyers have a substantial investment in the skills of literacy. They understand the use of indices, tables of contents, and cross-references. They can interpret text structure, format, and typographic conventions. The form of legal documents has evolved over centuries, and law reports were some of the first documents to find their way into print. Lawyers may more easily be enticed to use computers if the computer gives better access to the traditional tools of the trade. Certainly, it must never present them with computer jargon, system mnemonics, or any information not directly relevant to the legal task.

• *Integrated*

A disadvantage of books is that they are static and self-contained. The most committed researcher of paper documents will admit that working from a dozen different books with several paper markers in each imposes a great strain on the short term memory. Currently available computer packages suffer from the same disadvantages. Information from one package often has to be transported to another package before it can be used; sometimes, it even has to be re-typed. A document drafted using an expert system has to be formatted on a wordprocessor before it can be printed. Unless all the tasks can be integrated under a single interface, the systems will always be difficult and confusing to use. The interface of a hypertext system can give the user an impression of a seamless information universe.

2.2. Operational characteristics

• *Easy to learn*

Lawyers are busy people whose time is valuable; if the system is frustrating to learn they are likely to give up quickly. Nor do they have time to attend special training courses. They want to learn by experience while solving a real problem.

• *Easy to remember*

Lawyers' work often takes them out of the office – sometimes for days or even weeks at a time: for example, a major case in court. Computer usage is bound to be intermittent, therefore retention of what has been learned is important.

• *Transparent*

Law as a discipline is problem oriented. Lawyers want to concentrate all intellectual resources on their legal problems. They do not want to dissipate intellectual energy on computer interface problems. They would prefer to be unaware of the existence of an interface: the interface must be simple.

• *Fast response*

Response to queries that the lawyer regards as simple must be fast. The patience threshold of the profession as a whole seems low! In any case immediate feedback helps to establish user confidence in the system and helps to maintain concentration on the task in hand. Some observable response should be received to every action; if a wait is anticipated, a message or icon to that effect should be shown.

• *Little manual dexterity*

Many lawyers have resisted learning to type. The interface should allow them to achieve many of their objectives without any special manual skills.

2.3. Functional characteristics

• *Consistent*

Much of the confusion in existing computer systems stems from their isolation from one another and from the different dialogue types used by each. That dialogue modes are different is not surprising; a tenet of interface design has been that each task should be realised optimally. Wordprocessors rely on sophisticated typing skills and the use of function keys; information retrieval relies on boolean algebra and some knowledge of how the computer system works; expert systems use a variety of techniques from simple question/answer to menu driven.

This may be good design theory: different types of dialogue are appropriate for different jobs. To a lawyer who sees only one job where the system designer has seen three, the constant switching of method can be disconcerting; it increases what they must learn and remember about the computer system. Learners tend to give up if they become too frustrated or feel that there are no limits on what needs to be learned and remembered. The user view of what is a logical job must prevail and consistency of response to a user action is crucial to user satisfaction.

• *User controlled*

Lawyers are independently minded: they know how they want to achieve their objectives. An interface that constrains them to work unnaturally will not succeed.

• *Flexible*

Within wide parameters, lawyers must be able to choose the order in which they do things. They should be able to undo any action at will, and the system should not rely on their remembering where they are or what they have done. Contextual information should be immediately available on request. They should be able to save a task that is incomplete and return to it at a later date.

• *Annotation and editing*

Many lawyers make marginal notes in their own copies of books or documents: this facility should be provided by the computer system. Lawyers are also used to working from precedents. A precedent is simply a past instance of a document that may serve as an example for a future document. All lawyers keep office precedents, many of which have come from precedent books or have been inherited from predecessors. Editing an old document to fit new circumstances must also be an integrated part of the system.

• *Different methods of access*

Different methods of access should be available; a minimum subset should include: browsing, direct access to a specified document, access via an index, and boolean query. Browsing, direct access, and access via an index are techniques learned with printed books and involve no typing skills. Boolean query requires only minimal typing skills but greatly increases the power and flexibility of the system, particularly if implemented through a hypertext interface or menus.

3. DATABASES AND SYSTEMS CURRENTLY AVAILABLE TO LAWYERS

3.1. Databases

In all countries the legal database is voluminous and dynamic. *The Directory of European Databases and Databanks* [9] published by the Commission of the European Communities lists 114 law databases for Community countries alone. Below are examples from the *Directory*, with supporting information from *Law Databases* [10]. (For a discussion of similar issues in Nordic countries, see Seipel[11]; for a discussion of the legal issues in international databanks, see Saxby[12].)

• *Belgium*

BJUS   Credoc-Bjus Doctrine Juridique and Jurisprudent Belges.
         About 140,000 citations and abstracts of juridical articles and periodicals, and selected jurisprudence directly transmitted to Credoc by Belgian courts and tribunals.

BLEX   Législation Belge.
         23,000 citations to items in *Moniteur Belge* on law, legislation and regulation, administration, in Belgium.

Host   BELINDIS

• *France*

CONSTIT	Conseil Constitutionnel
	All decisions made by the French constitutional council since 1958.
DIF	Fiscal legislation in France.
FISC	Législation et Réglementation Fiscale
	French tax legislation, regulations and administrative principles.
LEGI	French legislation relating to commercial tax law, social legislation.
SOC	Industrial law and social legislation.
TAX	Tax law in France.
Host	L'Européenne de données

• *Germany*

JURIS	Juristiches Informationssystem für die Bundsrepublik Deutschland.
	Jurisdiction of the federal constitutional court and highest law courts; court jurisdiction and juridical literature and administrative regulations.
JURIS-L	Rechtsliteratur – Abstracts from 180 legal journals and 400 other sources.
JURIS-N	Normen – Laws and statutory orders.
JURIS-R	Rechtssprechungs Databank
	Summaries of court decisions, bibliographic information and details on content of judgments.
JURIS-V	Verwaltungsvorschriften
	Administration regulations for social legislation and tax law.
Host	JURIS
DBUN	Deutsches Bundesrecht
	Full text of German federal law
Host	EDICLINE

• *Italy*

CONSTA	Giurisprudenza del Consiglio di Stato.
	Administrative case law with the official provisions taken from the rulings of the council of state.
CORTEC	Giurisprudenza della Corte dei Conti
	Digest of the court of auditors
COSTIT	Giurisprudenza Costituzionale
	Decisions of the Constitutional Court since 1956.
PENALE	Giurisprudenza Penale
	Digest decisions of the supreme court in criminal cases.
Host	CED

• *United Kingdom*

LEXIS   A full text database that covers many countries in addition to the UK: Australia, New Zealand, European Community, France, USA. For England and Wales, it has forty-two series of law reports (800–1200 cases a year) since 1945; tax cases since 1875; All public General Acts and statutory instruments; 2500-3000 transcripts of 'unreported' cases.

Host   Mead Data Central

• *European Community*

CELEX   Texts of treaties and amendments, secondary legislation, complementary community legal acts, preparatory acts for the European Parliaments and judgments by the European Court.

Host   CED, CERVED, CONTEXT LIMITED, EDICLINE, EUROBASES, ICEX, JURIS, L'Européenne de données, PROFILE INFORMATION, TBD TIME SHARING.

There are two main problems:

i.   Even within a single country, related information can be held on disparate databases. While it might seem reasonable to divide such quantities of information into subsets for ease of handling, it is not practical except for teaching or experimental systems. Kyle Bosworth of Butterworths has an anecdote from the introduction of Lexis in the United Kingdom when the only material in the database was on finance and company law, but, within that domain, the database was, the purveyors hoped, complete and exhaustive. The system was given to certain specialist lawyers for field trials. "Do you use the system frequently?", one was asked. "Well, no", he replied apologetically, "You see, it only contains what I already know". Lawyers are experts and proud of their specialist knowledge, but law encompasses every aspect of human activity and all areas tend to overlap. It is when their area impinges upon another that the lawyer is most in need of help. No system that does not treat legal information as a seamless universe is going to meet with unqualified approval from the legal profession.

ii.   Different data bases have different hosts: only European Community legislation is available on several hosts. Lawyers increasingly need information about an unfamiliar legal system, information which is available only in a foreign language. These are problems enough, yet users of more than one database host must grapple with different access procedures and different query languages for information retrieval.

3.2. Information retrieval

Even working in their native language within their own legal system, lawyers have taken to computerised information retrieval reluctantly. The reasons for this are not clear: expense could be a factor, but, for lawyers living and working outside big cities, physical access to a law library has long been expensive and time-consuming. Informal research suggests that the interface has been the real stumbling block.

Information retrieval techniques for full text have not changed in principle for over twenty years: for a fuller account of the development of information retrieval in law, see Bing [13] and Campbell[14].

60

A retrieval system usually comprises:

i. a text file with tagging to delimit components in a largely linear structure.

ii. a sorted inverted index file of all but the most frequently occurring words, giving the locations of the words in the text file.

iii. a Boolean search and retrieval package.

Lawyers need training in the use of a retrieval system based on a concordance and search strategy that do nothing to resolve the natural language problems of synonyms, homonyms and lexical hierarchy. Not surprisingly the system is more popular in larger firms where a law librarian or paralegal can be trained to provide a service for all members of the firm.

An example in using JURIS, taken from Fanning [15] will illustrate the problem:

......the user wants to find a recent article on 'Hacking and Computer Misuse in the Federal Republic of Germany'...... The user commands (in bold type), always followed by carriage return (CR), and the consequent system response, are as follows:

*s_hack&&+computer (CR)
SUCHWORTLISTE IN DATEI L
1 HACK&&   (59)
2 COMPUTER(1783)
AUSGABEENDE
   *

......To find those documents with both 'hack&&' and 'computer' in them, terms 1 and 2 must be linked together with the Boolean Operator AND (*UND*, abbr, 'u')......thus:

*1_1u2   (CR)

However, it would also be useful to have the result of (1_1u2) as a search term.
...... Hence:

*1_1u2!msl (CR)
SUCHWORTLISTE IN DATEI L
1 HACK&&   (59)
2 COMPUTER(1783)
3 &&1u2   (8)
LOGISCHE VERKNUEPFUNG
003
ANZAHL DR DOKUMENTE: 8
AUSGABEENDE
   *

......The instruction 'sort data' (*sortiere nach Datum abstiegnend*, abbr. 'soda') sorts the references into chronological order, the most recent first. 'Soda' entered with the text display command, 'text_n' ('Text', abbr. 't') where n is the serial number, produces the required article:

*soda!t_1 (CR)
DOKUMENT 1, DOKNR 297801,
SEITE-NR 1
Typ:Aufsatz
Verfasser: Gravenreuth, von,
Rechtsanwalt
Haupttitel: COMPUTER VIREN,
HACKER, Datenspione, Crasher
und Cracker
Titelzusatz: Ueberblick und
rechtliche Einordnung
Fundstelle
NStZ 1989, 201-207

Kurzreferat

(F)

Der Verfasser eroertert unbefugte Datenmanipulationen durch ...

The *Fundstelle* is the source of the article. In order to find out what the abbreviation 'NStz' stands for, the user need only type:

    *abkjp_nstz (CR)

Quite!

3.3. Wordprocessors

Wordprocessors are ubiquitous in lawyers' offices. It has been a revolution from below because the wordprocessor is still the tool of the secretary. Its advent has been welcomed by lawyers, who recognise the increased efficiency of secretarial staff since its introduction. But it is not seen as conferring any great benefits on lawyers themselves. They see it as a glorified typewriter with a particularly abstruse interface. It has not encouraged them to learn to type, or to acquaint themselves with the properties of the function keys essential for editing existing texts. The most common method of working is still manual amendment of an existing document. This is then retrieved from disc and edited by the secretary, where previously it would have been retyped from scratch.

Wordprocessing systems in use in legal offices are many and varied. Documents are still exchanged in hard-copy format only. If a solicitor wishes to amend a contract sent for inspection it must be retyped. A new printed version is then sent back to the solicitor who drew up the original version. The two versions are compared by eye to find and check all alterations. These are inserted, with perhaps further changes that the client now wants, and the document is returned. The process is recursive and, as currently realised, inefficient.

3.4. Expert systems

This is not the place to indulge in a discussion of the principles underlying expert systems or their long-term viability: for a fuller discussion of those aspects see Gardiner [16]. Expert systems in law are in their infancy. Implementors frequently have more technical than legal expertise, and experimental systems have been written using every tool in the expert system workbench: conventional multi-purpose programming languages like *Cobol*, du Feu [17]; specially designed languages such as *Prolog*, Sergot [18]; standard expert system shells like *Apes*, Hammond [19] and *Crystal II*, Capper[20]; and specially developed shells such as *LES*, Mowbray [21], to mention but a few. There is a plethora of languages and dialogue techniques. Work is unlikely to flourish unless practising lawyers can be persuaded to use the systems and provide feedback for the technical implementors. Yet lawyers might feel justified in believing that what current expert systems best simulate is the Tower of Babel.

4. A WORKBENCH FOR LAWYERS

Thus, lawyers have to contend with interface inconsistency from two causes:

i.   variation of interface between different hosts for the same task
ii.   variation of interface with the legal task.

Inconsistency from the first cause is unnecessary; variation from the second cause is greater than it need be. Lawyers are right to resist it; they are members of a well-established and confident profession. Legal information structures and methods of accessing them have evolved over centuries. Lawyers are not going to change their way of working because a systems designer thinks that it will be easier to implement or will lead to a fuller exploitation of computing resources. A system for lawyers has to convince lawyers that they can continue to work in their natural way but more efficiently and effectively than they could with only printed material. Because of the scale of the information problem an electronic database and a printed data base are going to operate in parallel for some time. The transition will be less traumatic if the lawyer feels he is simply doing what he has always done in the way he has always done it – indeed, unless he is secure in that belief, it may not happen at all.

Hence, when we began to design a workbench for lawyers the main objective was to convert automatically disparate legal source materials into a hypertext database that the user would see as a seamless information universe. The original structure of each individual document would be preserved but the user would be able to switch between documents without being aware of a change of environment. This was successful; a suite of programs, collectively known as *Justus*, converted primary legal sources such as statutes and law reports, and secondary sources such as a textbook and a dictionary into an integrated electronic book for the *Guide* hypertext system. (Guide was originally devised and developed by Prof P J Brown at the University of Kent [22]; a version of Guide has also been developed by Office Workstations Ltd.) The interface seemed perfectly suited to the requirements of the task and the orientation of lawyers. Local lawyers with no computer experience were invited to try the system and happily used the basic browsing facility by themselves after about ten minutes demonstration.

A detailed description of the Justus system can be found in Wilson [23, 24, 25]. The interface characteristics that are particularly valuable in Justus are summarised below.

4.1. Contextual clarity

Guide has a variable node size and a scrolling mechanism. This means that all documents can be represented naturally. A long paragraph from a judge's opinion does not have to be split up into card sized chunks; it appears as a single unit. It can be scrolled forward and backward to show context as fully and as naturally as would a printed book. This is important. In any text a change in structure may alter meaning; lack of context impedes understanding, and may even convey a false meaning. Physical or implementational constraints of a hypertext system should not be allowed, however subtly, to come between the authorised text and the reader. Hence, I feel that card-based hypertext systems are unsuitable for law, and a scrolling mechanism is essential.

4.2. Textual clarity

Buttons (or node icons) in Guide have an expansion level control. This was originally devised as a means of organising different paths through a document for readers with different levels of background knowledge and, consequently, different information requirements. In Justus, expansion control ensures that users are never confronted by button-names that convey no information. For example, so that a search could be carried out for words in the same sentence or in the same paragraph a judge's opinion is divided into sentence level nodes, the sentence level nodes are accumulated into paragraph nodes and, finally, the paragraphs into an opinion. But, unless readers search specifically for a sentence or a paragraph, they are unaware of the text divisions at this level. At normal reading level, they see the judge's opinion as a single node, expanded by selecting a single button: paragraph and sentence nodes are expanded automatically as soon as the opinion node which contains them is selected. Similarly, in statutes, subsection nodes have only numbers, not headings. The nodes are needed so that subsections can be cross-referenced; but, unless a subsection is a target of a cross-reference, the user sees only section nodes with informative headings. Immediate expansion avoids meaningless lists of subsection buttons.

4.3. Textual cohesion

Another facility indispensable when presenting a simple, clear, interface to the user is *aliasing*. Aliasing allows many different versions of a name to be mapped onto the hypertext system name for that node. This means that the natural wording of a text need never be changed to incorporate a link or target in the hypertext system. In the appropriate circumstances, all the following might map on to the same system node:

paragraph (c) of subsection (2) of section 10 of the Industrial Relations Act, 1971

Industrial Relations Act 1971 10(2)(c)

section 10(2)(c) of this Act

section 10(2)(c) of that Act

subsection (2)(c) of this section

subsection (2)(c) of that section

paragraph (c) of this subsection.

paragraph (c) of that subsection.

This means that the text always reads naturally, and cohesion arising from the flow and rhythm of natural language is not lost.

The use of system names rather than user comprehensible names as actual hypertext node names is likely to increase as hypertext systems grow and name uniqueness becomes a more formidable problem than it is currently. Ambiguity in names has existed in law for a long time; different series of law reports are frequently referred to by the same abbreviation:

A.L.R. Adelaide Law Review

A.L.R. Aden Law Reports

A.L.R. Argus Law Reports, Victoria

Osborn's Law Dictionary [26]

Such ambiguities can only be resolved by manual intervention, but aliasing provides one means of ensuring the correct target without altering the original. At some point the legal community may need an international standards body to agree naming conventions for legal documents, perhaps an equivalent for law of the International Standard Book Number (isbn) used by publishers for printed books.

4.4. Structural simplicity

Justus was designed for naive computer users. In simple browsing mode, it opens with one large screen. The reader uses a mouse to select a document, which can be expanded rapidly to show structure (e.g. chapters, sections, subsections) and, finally, to give text. The screen is automatically reformatted to accommodate node expansion within the text. In a monochrome display, nodes that will give expansion within the text are shown in boldface; usually they are nodes corresponding with a structural component of the document, where in-text expansion is entirely natural.

Cross-references are highlighted by underlining; when the reader selects a cross-reference the main window is split; text corresponding with the reference is displayed in the secondary window so formed. This means that readers never lose their place in the main document; they can always see exactly where they are by positioning the cursor in the scroll bar and holding down the mouse button: a pop-up window gives their trail. They can discard text by positioning the cursor on it and pressing the *undo* button on the mouse. Hence, it is difficult to become completely disoriented, and new users can soon achieve results: confidence in moving the mouse is the most advanced skill required for basic tasks.

Nevertheless, the glossary subscreen can become extremely confused, and more work is needed into browsing techniques. One solution may be to create a new main window for every new document, so that only intra-document references, i.e. references to disparate parts of the same document, footnotes, and references to an integral glossary appear in the subwindow. This would reduce confusion in the subwindow by increasing the number of windows in the display. There is no easy solution. However, the simple two window display seems popular with inexperienced computer users, so it remains standard in Justus; users may, of course, create a new view for themselves whenever they so choose. Ideally, users should be able to define the interface they want when they start a session. Ways in which this might be achieved are discussed in the following section.

4.5. Interface consistency over diverse tasks

Not all books are simply passive depositories from which information is extracted for use elsewhere. Precedent books contain examples of private instruments such as wills and contracts. The wording of clauses in precedents has often evolved over many years and may have been tested in the courts. Preferred clauses depend on a client's circumstances and precedent books contain advice to help lawyers to choose clauses that fit the circumstances. The advice must be read and understood before the lawyer can choose appropriate clauses, although it is often stored in the printed text as footnotes to the precedents. These footnotes are frequently couched as directives:

> 'This agreement is unconditional: contrast Form 4 post (agreement determinable on death, bankruptcy etc of tenant or guarantor); Form 6 post (existing tenant to remedy dilapidations before completion of new lease); Form 7 post (agreement conditional on exclusion order); Form 8 post (agreement conditional on tenant acquiring existing underlease and on superior landlord's consent to new underlease); and Form 9 post (agreement conditional on tenant obtaining planning permission). Where the premises are to be built, refurbished etc before completion see also Forms 11-14 post.'
>
> Encyclopaedia of Forms and Precedents [27]

To treat such directives as passive text would be to ignore the computer's potential to make them much more. In Guide they can be implemented as *enquiry buttons*. Enquiries are a way of realising menus in hypertext. The lawyer is offered a list of mutually exclusive conditions, and selects the appropriate condition with the mouse in the usual way. However, condition buttons need not always be merely links to replacement texts: they may initiate programs to select clauses or set parameters that will ensure that the wording of selected clauses fit the circumstances specified by the lawyer. For example, the enquiry which asks whether a party to a contract is male or female uses the information to ensure that all pronominal references agree. The interface is what a reader who has used Justus to retrieve information intuitively expects: the applicable condition is selected with a mouse.

Used like this the hypertext system is acting as an expert system shell. All the information linking facilities of the hypertext are still available: references to other clauses are turned into buttons which allow those clauses to be retrieved and considered; references to external documents such as statutes are recognised automatically and turned into links which the user can select. The user may not be fully aware that the prime function of Justus has changed from information retrieval to document drafting: the interface is the same.

The interface also handles form-filling. While input is kept to a minimum, sometimes users must provide information:

- when they want direct access to a specific part of a document without going through the document index;
- when they want to enter a search term;
- when they want to add their own notes to retrieved text;
- if the document they are drafting needs specific information such as the term of contract, the amount of rent, the name and address of a client.

Entering information in draft documents is probably the most significant of these tasks. The chief mechanism is form-filling implemented by local buttons without replacement texts; these buttons act as field names. The interface remains consistent: the user selects the field to be filled, the field name vanishes and is replaced by a marker flag. When the information has been typed in, the user moves on to the next field. There are no function keys to remember, not even an enter key to press when input is complete.

The system is flexible: a session can be saved at any point – either to be resumed later by the lawyer or, for a draft document, to have tedious detail like names and addresses completed by an assistant.

5. THE WAY FORWARD

5.1. Evaluation

Work on the Justus system has shown that hypertext's real advantages are its ability to handle interconnected documents and the simplicity of the interface. The same interface is suitable for a variety of functions: document browsing, expert system shells, form-filling. It is simple and uncluttered. No more than two windows are in use at any time. The information is exactly that of the printed book and a monochrome display screen is adequate for presentation. Familiar typographic conventions like boldface and underlining are used to highlight where a section of text may be expanded or the text of a cross-reference requested. All the facilities and the text are integrated under a single interface – the Guide interface – in an apparently seamless database.

In limited trials, the system has proved easy to learn and to remember. The user needs neither knowledge of function keys nor any awareness of underlying data structure. Minimal typing skills (or a secretary) are needed to input information unique to a client or to add personal notes or memoranda. Response time for most tasks in the current system is good; more trials are needed to see how a large database affects performance.

However, the hypertext system also had shortcomings:

- The text editing facilities in hypertext are basic compared with the best word processors. In the Justus project this had not, initially, been a consideration because the project had its roots in information retrieval, not document production.

- While high quality document production was not originally part of the Justus project the hypertext documents were produced automatically from the tapes used by the publishers to produce the printed documents. Consequently, there was no doubt that the information to produce top quality output was available, although the original type-setting codes had been lost in the hypertext version. Because Guide formatting conventions are comparable with those used by the *troff* text formatter, Guide formatted texts could be mapped automatically into troff. While not rivaling book quality this gives copy adequate for texts retrieved by lawyers and annotated for their own purposes. For documents with a complex format it would not recapture all the information contained in the original printers' tapes; exact replication of the printed text as published would require a return to the source tapes.

- Because it might still be required for hard copy, the original version must be preserved. This means that at least two different versions of the database have to be maintained.

- However, the same data is probably already part of a traditional information retrieval system in yet another form. This form, too, would have to be preserved – at least until the hypertext version of the database was as comprehensive as the traditional information retrieval database, and search and retrieval in the hypertext system as efficient. For large quantities of data, associative retrieval and boolean query under hypertext systems remains unproven: traditional systems have been honed to efficiency through years of experience.

5.2. Standardised mark-up, hybrid systems, and prototyping

Information retrieval, printing, and hypertext, all work on forms of tagging: tagging of named fields for information retrieval; printers' mark up to show typographical changes that emphasise individual components of the document, and lay-out that makes structure more apparent; finally, hypertext formatting conventions to ensure that the information is presented with a clear information structure and that all implicit and explicit links are highlighted. It is true that tagging for different purposes differs in detail, but, in principle, there is much in common. Economically and aesthetically it would be preferable to have a single database, marked-up so that information retrieval, printing, and hypertext browsing could be achieved using the same information. Standard General Mark-up Language (SGML) exists to help us do this.

SGML is a declarative mark-up language in which structural and non-structural components of a text can be tagged so that they may be used for a variety of purposes. Many texts are already tagged to SGML standards: that is, they conform to a document type which has a formal specification or, in SGML, a Document Type Definition (DTD). Law publishers should be encouraged to adopt this practice for law documents. It would not be difficult: many law documents already have a well-defined structure. With standard tagging in the public domain, it is easier to provide coherent, integrated systems with consistent interfaces. Hybrid systems are also possible. For example, hypertext can be used merely as an interface to a conventional information retrieval engine. People read slowly and, by electronic standards, need short textual extracts for long periods. Hypertext buttons for cross-references can be used to trigger programs that will

i. initiate a search by a traditional search tool in a tagged database of well-defined structure;

ii. convert the retrieved tagged text to hypertext format;

iii. present the retrieved text to the user, who should be unaware that the system is not pure hypertext.

Since the hypertext interface will be based on the formal specification (DTD) and the conversion of the document performed on-the-fly only when the user accesses the text, a procedure could be organised which would allow users to add to the DTD parameters to specify how they wanted the document to be displayed, e.g.

- a new window for each document;

- a glossary window for intra document references;

- pop-up windows for footnotes;

> and so on.

Such a procedure is a feasible mechanism for interface prototyping. (For a more detailed account of a system using this technique, see Wilson [28]). This gives the best of all worlds:

i. All documents are instances of a document type with a formal specification, not just copies of documents with no explicitly recognised structure;

ii. The formal specification can be used to produce documents in a lawyer's office and transfer them electronically to another lawyer's office, perhaps with a different system, using Office Document Architecture principles;

iii. Efficient information retrieval can continue through existing search engines, in which there has been considerable investment of resources, and where multiple users have effective support;

iv. Good browsing facilities with a user-specified display could be provided through a standard hypertext interface, which could be common to all information retrieval systems whatever their host or country of origin. Differences in the syntax of queries between different systems would be the concern only of the provider of the hypertext interface to the information retrieval system.

v. High quality printout, equal to that of the original printed document, would be available on demand through a formatting program working on SGML tags.

ACKNOWLEDGMENTS

I should like to thank Dr Jorma Kuopus and two anonymous referees for suggestions which have improved the paper. I am also grateful to Mr. R. C. Saunders, University of Kent at Canterbury, for advice and comments on draft versions of the paper, and to the editors, especially George Weir for meticulously reading the final version.

REFERENCES

1. Huckle, B.A. *The Man-Machine Interface: Guidelines for the design of the end-user/system conversation*, Savant Institute Studies, 1981.

2. Apperley, M.D. and Field, G.E. "A cooperative evaluation of menu-based interactive human-computer dialogue techniques" *Proceedings of the IFIP Conference on Human-Computer Interaction* INTERACT 1984, North-Holland.

3. Rubinstein, R. and Hersh, H.M. *The Human Factor: designing computer systems for people*, Digital Press Burlington MA, 1984.

4. Lee, A. and Lochovsky, F. "User Interface Design" in Tsichritzis D (ed) *Office Automation*, Springer Verlag, Berlin 1985, pp. 3-21.

5. Brown, C.M. *Human Computer Interface Design Guidelines*, Ablex, Norwood, NJ. 1986.

6. Shneiderman, B. *Designing the User Interface*, Addison-Wesley, Reading, Mass, 1987.

7. Whitefield, A. "Models in human-computer interaction: a classification with special reference to their uses in design" *Proceedings of the Second IFIP Conference on Human-Computer Interaction* INTERACT87, North-Holland 1987.

8. Rubin, T. *User Interface Design for Computer Systems*, Ellis Horwood Limited, Chichester, 1988.

9. *Directory of European Databases and Databanks*, Commission of the European Communities, 1989.

10. Raper, D. *Law Databases 1988*, Aslib, London, 1988.

11. Seipel, P. "Coordination between the legal data-banks of various countries: reflections on Nordic experiences" in *Fourth International Congress on Law and Computers*, Rome, 1988.

12. Saxby, S. "Information and the challenge of the new technologies" in *Fourth International Congress on Law and Computers*, Rome, 1988.

13. Bing, J. & Selmer, K.S. *A Decade of Computers and Law*, Universitetsforlaget, Oslo, 1980.

14. Campbell, C.(ed) *Data processing and the law*, Sweet & Maxwell, London 1984.

15. Fanning, M. "Juris: the German Legal Information System", *Computers and Law*, April, 1990.

16. Gardner, A. "An Artificial Intelligence Approach to Legal Reasoning", MIT Press, Cambridge, Massachusetts, 1987.

17. du Feu, D. "Selecting welfare benefits by computer" in *Computer science and law*, Niblett B. (ed), Cambridge University Press, 1980.

18. Sergot, M.J. et al "The British Nationality Act as a Logic Program" 29(5) *Comm ACM*, 1986.

19. Hammond, P. *Representation of DHSS Regulations as a Logic Program*, Computing Department, Imperial College, London, Report number 82/86.

20. Capper, P & Susskind, R. E. *Latent Damage Law – The Expert System*, Butterworths, London, 1988.

21. Mowbray, A. *LES: Legal Expert System Generation User Manual*, DATALEX Project, University of New South Wales, 1985.

22. Brown, P.J. "Interactive Documentation" *Software Practice and Experience, 16(3)*, 1986, pp. 291-299.

23. Wilson, E. "Integrated Information Retrieval for Law in a Hypertext Environment" *Proceedings of the SIGIR/ACM 11th. International Conference on Research and Development in Information Retrieval*, Grenoble, 1988, pp.633-677.

24. Wilson, E. "Electronic Books: the automatic production of hypertext from existing printed sources" *Proceedings of the Fourth Annual Conference of the UW Centre for the New Oxford English Dictionary, Information in Text*, Waterloo, 1988, pp29-45.

25. Wilson, E. "Reference and Reference Inversion in Statutes and Cases; a hypertext solution" *Informatics 10*, York, 1989.

26. 'Osborn's Concise Law Dictionary.' Sweet and Maxwell, London, 1976.

27. *Encyclopaedia of Forms and Precedents*, Fifth Edition, edited by Sir Raymond Walton, Butterworths, London, 1986.

28. Wilson, E. *A hybrid system: using hypertext as an interface to an external search tool* Laboratory Report 1990, available from the Computing Laboratory, University of Kent at Canterbury.

HUMAN JOBS AND COMPUTER INTERFACES
M.I. Nurminen and G.R.S. Weir
Elsevier Science Publishers B.V. (North-Holland)
© 1991 IFIP. All rights reserved.

Design Considerations for Microcomputer Based Applications for the Blind

Karl P. Dürre and Karl W. Glander

Computer Science Department, Colorado State University,
Ft. Collins, CO 80523, U.S.A.

Abstract

For blind individuals, access to microcomputers can help overcome an essential part of their handicapping condition and help them work competitively in many jobs previously not open to them. The limiting factor for these individuals is not the speech synthesis and volatile braille display peripherals but rather the application software interfaces that are primarily designed by the sighted for the sighted. This paper describes the objectives and provides recommendations for the design of application software for the blind.

Keywords

Nonvisual human-computer interaction; computer-assisted integration of blind individuals; real time blind-sighted communication.

Introduction

Two approaches, shown in figure 1, are commonly taken in designing application software for the blind. In the first approach, a dedicated application system is designed in which a non-visual interface is structured exclusively for a blind user. In the second approach, a general application system is designed with a standard visual interface and then a non-visual interface is designed that overlays the visual interface to allow blind users access to the application. Both of these systems have desirable and undesirable qualities.

A dedicated system is desirable in that the system enables blind users to access, through a tactile braille display or speech synthesis, previously inaccessible information; however, a dedicated system is undesirable for two primary reasons. First and foremost, a dedicated system does not aid the integration of blind users into the work place since their sighted peers will of necessity be using a different application system. Secondly, since the marketability of such systems is low, the incentive for software companies to develop and maintain dedicated systems is absent. Therefore, the diversity and availability of

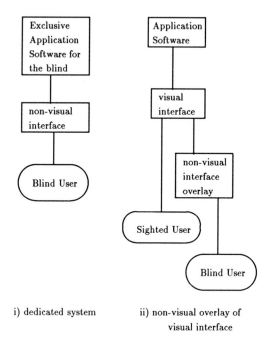

i) dedicated system   ii) non-visual overlay of
visual interface

Figure 1: Two common methods for non-visual computer applications.

dedicated systems is not comparable to the amount of software for sighted computer users.

Overlaying a non-visual interface over a visual interface is desirable in that it addresses the undesirable features of a dedicated system. Sighted and non-sighted users may be integrated since both can use the same application software, and depending on the availability of specialized hardware for the blind users, both may arbitrarily use any available computer. Secondly, the application software, by having a visual interface, can be marketed to anyone regardless of their visual abilities. Overlaying a non-visual interface over a visual interface, however, does not solve all problems. For example, most currently available application systems make extensive use of the visual senses by displaying information on the computer screen in a two-dimensional pattern that relies heavily on the ability of visual senses to quickly assimilate the displayed information. Such displays do not easily conform to any method of sequential tactual screening and are thus problematic for non-visual interfaces. A blind individual forced to use such a system would consistently be required to make guesses as to the current status of the cursor, the current location in the application software, etc. The blind user is thus at an unnecessary disadvantage as compared to a sighted user when dealing with computers.

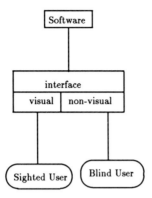

Figure 2: Interactive system for blind and/or sighted user.

A new approach is needed that addresses the undesirable qualities of both methods above while maintaining the desirable qualities. The ideal system, shown in figure 2, incorporates a non-visual interface into, as opposed to over, the visual interface. This paper addresses the design considerations of implementing this ideal system. The first section establishes objectives of this system while the second section presents recommendations for implementing the system.

System Objectives

The primary system objective is to offer both the blind and sighted user interactive editing techniques. By interactive editing techniques we mean the immediate presentation of a manipulated object in a form that allows quick recognition, and in a manner similar to the interactive techniques offered to the sighted user by the visual interface component. A user should be able to stop at any point in the text and correct old or enter new information. The information changed by such direct manipulation [7, 8] should be immediately available in its new form. An application system which does not offer such actual interactive editing techniques is undesirable since it would not allow full computer access to either the blind or the sighted user.

The system, in addition to providing the above interactive editing techniques, should provide an efficient communication bridge between the sighted and non-sighted [3]. A large part of the apprehension on the part of sighted individuals who find themselves having to work with non-sighted individuals is due to the inability to communicate fully. Unless the sighted individual is proficient in braille, the only form of communication with the non-sighted individual is through speech. A system that allows communication between sighted and non-sighted without requiring the sighted user to know braille is highly desirable.

Finally, the system should be capable of working with not only foreign language text, but also with scientific and mathematical texts. Each of these types of texts require special consideration. Many current systems for the blind do not process these texts, thus unjustifiably excluding blind individuals from many occupations while those systems that do handle these types of texts do so in an awkward manner that puts the blind at a severe disadvantage.

System Recommendations

For a computer system to support blind users, it may provide output by either a tactual braille screen or by a speech synthesizer. A tactual braille screen is an output device that typically contains 20 or 40 braille cells, though it may contain any number between 1 and 80 braille cells. Each braille cell has six or eight pins—one pin for each dot in the braille code. (With a six pin braille cell, when dots 7 and 8 are required by the braille representation, they are represented by vibrating up and down the pins in the cell a varying speed, dependent on whether dot 7, dot 8 or both dots 7 and 8 are included in the braille code.) A speech synthesizer, on the other hand, effectively 'reads' text to the user with software options that allow the verbal spelling of a specified word, and the repeat of a specified, letter, word, sentence, or paragraph. Experience has indicated that the advantages of using a tactual braille screen overshadow those of speech output.

There are several reasons for preferring tactual output over speech output. Most importantly with a tactual display, information distributed over a two-dimensional surface may be explored in a fashion identical to the way in which the visual senses scan print characters. The recognition of information patterns such as paragraphs and tables is greatly facilitated, in fact, in conjunction with a moving exploration of distributed information, referred to as 'haptics' [9], the tactual sense is suited, much like the visual sense, to perceive spatially distributed information. With a tactual display, the blind user is free to scan tabular information by column rather than by row and is thus able to perceive the implicit relations that a table provides to a sighted individual.

A preference for a tactual display is further supported when foreign language, scientific, and mathematical texts are to be handled by the system. The advantages of a textual representation in a universal braille code over speech are overwhelming since each 8-bit ASCII character can be uniquely represented by an 8-dot braille cell [5]. If the text can be displayed on a computer screen, it can be displayed with a simple character mapping on a tactual display. There is thus no need to include alternate pronunciation tables when foreign language texts are being processed, pronunciation tables do not have to be expanded to include the technical words that are particular to each scientific field, and mathematical formulas, equations, etc. are represented tactually in the same way they are represented visually. (With a speech based system, mathematical formulas, etc. are 'spelled' out, thus making the comprehension of these formulas more difficult to obtain.)

Additionally, with a tactual display, a blind reader is free when confronted with a complicated text to linger and review a sentence (or paragraph) in order to better understand an ambiguous passage or formula. Such scanning modes are natural and easy when reading print visually and braille tactually [6]. Sound and speech cannot be scanned in such modes [10]; therefore reading complicated texts by listening becomes cumbersome and time-consuming, even if convenient functions for repeating and spelling out are offered.

Finally, tactual output is superior to speech output when the user is interactively editing a text. Typically, when editing in this manner, the interaction modes frequently switch from input to output and back as the user locates the desired point to change, makes the change, and then checks the change for correctness. A complete comparison of tactual and acoustical (speech-based) interfaces can be found in [4].

Conceptually, a full page braille screen may appear to be desirable; however, either a 20 or 40 cell braille screen is recommended. A full page braille screen will have an advantage over a limited length screen if the computer is used solely for reading and not as a tool to manipulate texts through reading and editing. Using a full page screen with interactive editing, however, will cause greater hardships for the blind user by being too large to be used effectively in an interactive setting. Consider a word processing application where text is to be inserted into the middle of a file at the current cursor location. For sighted users, visually scanning the computer monitor to find the location of the cursor is quickly accomplished. For a blind user using a full page braille screen, finding the cursor in the screen takes substantially longer since (s)he must sequentially check each character to see if it is the cursor. A small braille screen, while not containing as much information as a large braille screen, is advantageous because the blind user can quickly locate the cursor and perform interactive operations on the file [3].

Toward the system objectives of providing a communication bridge between sighted and non-sighted computer users, the representation of a tactual braille screen in software as a limited-length window which is primarily, though not necessarily, bound to the system cursor is recommended. By binding the window to the system cursor, the window is restricted to tactually displaying information that is visible on the computer monitor. Then, by highlighting or otherwise setting the contents of the window apart from the rest of the information on the monitor, the sighted user is given access to the location and content of the braille screen without requiring him/her to know braille. Since both sighted and non-sighted users can identify, and even change the location of the braille window within the text, they are able to talk about and manipulate the text in a straightforward and equal manner. The sighted user can see immediately on the screen anything that the blind user has entered, while the blind user can simultaneously see tactually anything entered by the sighted user.

Pop-up menus are convenient for the purpose of implementing interactive editing techniques since their main menus and submenus are hierarchically arranged in a simple tree structure that is frequently easy to remember and use. Selections are made in these menus by choosing a desired option from a menu by either moving the cursor onto the desired option or by entering the first character of the selected option. This method is highly versatile in that it implements an implicit command language. Novice users can rely on the menus to guide their function activation by positioning a selection bar over the option they want and then activating the function simply by entering a carriage return. The more experienced users, on the other hand, can quickly activate the desired function by entering a command string consisting of the first characters of the desired options.

The design of an application's pop-up menus should not be arbitrary. The menus

Figure 3: Example menu showing combination of short and long form menus.

should be designed so the time and effort spent reading and selecting a function is kept small. Each menu should consist of a short form and a long form. The short form menu has a dual purpose. It not only uniquely identifies the particular menu (by a title), but it also gives the first character of all of the options available in the menu. The long form of the menu is an explicit list of the available options intended for novice and infrequent users of the system. The short form of the menu is provided so that the blind users can quickly identify the menu and options available. An example pop-up menu is given in figure 3. When a pop-up menu is first displayed, the short menu is highlighted by the visual component of the braille display window and thus by the tactual screen. This allows the blind system user to, if needed, quickly scan the menu title and remind himself/herself of the number of options the menu offers. If they are unfamiliar with what the specific options are, the braille window, being tied to the cursor, may be moved to each specific option.

Finally, we again recommend that speech play a minor role within the interface since it does have some benefits. For example, after extensive editing, the blind user may find it convenient to have the option of listening to the complete file. At any point in the recital, however, the user should be able to interrupt the speech and proceed tactually from the point in the text at which the speech was interrupted. Speech output is additionally convenient when the text being read is organized in a well-known form or when the text structure, given by lines, indentations and paragraphs, is not important for the full comprehension of the text content.

Conclusion

Three simple objectives concerning interactive editing, user communication, and special text handling are established that should be considered when combining a non-visual interface with a visual interface. These objectives are followed by several recommendations for designing and implementing a microcomputer-based application for the blind. Most of these recommendations have been implemented and tested in both educational and professional environments [1, 2]. The underlying philosophy in the design presented here is the need for a system that serves blind and sighted persons alike, either independently or simultaneously.

References

[1] Dürre, K. and I. Dürre. *Electronic Paper for Blind Children.* **Education & Computing** 2, 1986, 101-106.

[2] Dürre, K. *A Blind Student in a Regular Classroom Using a Computerized Pen-and-Paper Substitute.* **Proceedings of the 10th Annual Conference on Rehabilitation Technology, RESNA, San José, CA.**, 1987.

[3] Dürre, K. *BrailleButler: A New Approach to Non-Visual Computer Applications.* **Third Anual IEEE Symposium on Computer-Based Medical Systems**, 1990, 97-104.

[4] Dürre, K. and K. Glander (unpublished). *Importance of Tactual Interfaces to Blind Users of Full Text Systems.*

[5] Dürre, K., D. Tuttle and I. Dürre (unpublished). *A Universal Braille Code for Literary and Scientific Texts.*

[6] Foulke, E. *Reading braille.* In W. Schiff & E. Foulke, **Tactual perception: A sourcebook.** Cambridge, MA, Cambridge University Press, 1982, 168-208.

[7] Shneiderman, B. **Designing the User Interface: Strategies for Effective Human-Computer Interaction.** Reading, MA, Addison-Wesley Publishing Company, 1978.

[8] Shneiderman, B. *Direct manipulation: A step beyond programming languages.* **IEEE Computer** 16, 1983, 57-69.

[9] Warren, D.H. *Development of haptic perception.* In Schiff & Foulke, **Tactual perception: A sourcebook.** Cambridge, MA, Cambridge University Press, 1982, 82-129.

[10] Waterworth, J. *Speech Communication: How to Use it.* In A. Monk, **Fundamentals of Human-Computer Interaction.** London, England, Academic Press, 1984, 221-236.

Section 4

Office Applications

HUMAN JOBS AND COMPUTER INTERFACES
M.I. Nurminen and G.R.S. Weir
Elsevier Science Publishers B.V. (North-Holland)   81
© 1991 IFIP. All rights reserved.

Human factors issues in the electronic newsroom:
A briefing guide for media managers

Donald L. Day

School of Information Studies, 4-290 Center for Science & Technology, Syracuse University, Syracuse, New York 13244, U.S.A.

Abstract
     The print media have encountered the electronic age. Computer-
ized phototypesetting equipment that had replaced Linotypes in
the back shop have been joined in the newsroom by editing
terminals and in the morgue by microcomputer database systems.
     As a result, today's media managers are faced with issues that
reach beyond the traditional tasks of text generation, publication design and production.
     This paper examines those issues, including productivity,
quality assurance, employee health, regulation and humanitarian
concerns, and recommends a training-intensive approach for
dealing with human factors in media management today.

1. INTRODUCTION

     During the mid-1970s, print media encountered the electronic
age. Computerized phototypesetting equipment that had replaced
Linotypes in the back shop was joined in the newsroom by editing
terminals and in the morgue [1] by microcomputer database
systems. Hot metal linecasters had been 10,000 strong in 1970.
By the dawn of the Eighties, there were four times as many video
display terminals (VDTs), and the ranks of Linotypes had shrunk
to fewer than 200 (Lindley, 1988). Today's carpeted newsroom is
largely a quiet one, minus clacking typewriters and booming
mechanical teletypes.
     In the production arena, computer-controlled offset presses
now use laser-etched dry dot plates and backshop preparation
includes colour electronic prepress systems. Sophisticated and
expensive workstations allow art directors, advertising designers and even copy editors to assemble spreads with great
speed and flexibility.
     "There hadn't been such a drastic change in production since
the 1890s, when a belated industrial revolution which had swept
through the mills and along the railroads finally got to the
newspapers (Lindley, 1986). In fact, the introduction of
electronic editing has restored the newsroom environment to that
of a century ago, when the editor -- unencumbered by Linotype
crews -- had responsibility for final content and appearance
(Randall, 1979).

Some critics claim that the cost of change has been a dehuman-
ized journalism in which throughput outweighs depth of presentation. Others perceive a threat to interpersonal contact and editorial respect, the elimination of legions of proofreaders, and
an increase in sloppy editing.
So it is that today's media managers are faced with issues
that reach beyond the traditional tasks of text generation, publication design and production. Human factors have begun to
impact product quality and to threaten widespread disruption in
the workplace.

2. PRODUCTIVITY ISSUES

2.1 Time and Money
Elimination of the need to re-type markups for typesetting is
touted as a major cost-and-time benefit of having workstations
in the newsroom. Most organizations that automate editorial
operations experience a 20 percent improvement in writer productivity, a one-quarter drop in basic typesetting costs, and
nearly total elimination of author's alterations charges --
which otherwise account for 20 to 30 percent of all composition
costs. [2]

2.2 Proofreading
A proofreading analysis conducted by Wright and Lickorish
(1983) studied the speed and accuracy of proofreading text on a
CRT versus proofing the same material manually. Both speed and
accuracy were impaired when the document was presented on
screen. Reading speed on screen is about 30 percent slower than
on paper.

2.3 Training
In order to realize potential gains, however, today's newsroom, production and accounting personnel must be hired for or
retrained in operation of computerized text generation, prepress
and billing systems. [3] Although the knowledge and skills required to use these systems may be drawn from an existing pool
of capabilities (Long et al, 1983), staff still must possess an
aptitude for (and commitment to) retraining. [4]
The call to instill new skills in old staff stretches well
beyond the domain of distribution, advertising and billing
clerks. For example, copy editing duties have been expanded to
include proofreading and other production tasks. Slot editors
now provide the 'editorial backstop' formerly provided by com-
positors.
An early Eighties study of electronic editing found that 69
percent of personnel newly trained on computer equipment had
been taught directly by another staff member. Nearly 40 percent
had learned from a manufacturer's representative, and 30 percent
were self-taught. Seven in 10 of these people felt comfortable
in their new roles within two weeks; another quarter required as
much as four weeks (Shipley and Gentry, 1981).

2.4 Specialist Knowledge

A sensitive relationship exists between the domain of the tool (the computer) and the domain of the application (the work to be done). Each is accompanied by an associated set of specialist knowledge, presuppositions and biases (Long et al, 1983).

A primary cause of new user problems in operating computers is the lack of this specialist knowledge (i.e., an ignorance of presumptions incorporated in the system). Although many irritated workers complain about the cryptic command languages required to operate some systems, it is actually their lack of computer literacy that is the problem. "Even when unnecessary jargon [is] eliminated, it [is] still a requirement for users to learn a whole new terminology before systems [can] be grasped (Long et al, 1983).

2.5 User Acceptance

Even to the otherwise sophisticated, computer literate individual, the introduction of computerized editing and production equipment can invoke reactions ranging from enthrallment to distrust. "Some users [have] no clear conception of the limitations of a computer and so [misperceive] its capability (Long et al, 1983). Others "...remember the hot type era as some enthusiasts remember the days of the steam locomotive (Lindley, 1988).

Workstations used in media applications have received mixed reviews. Editors have responded favorably to spell checking programs, but report that they can read leads in hardcopy much faster than on a VDT. They also decry a tendency to let the technology control process.

Also, any new system, electronic or manual, can be a threat to status. "Skills learned over time are declared obsolete, and the respect that comes from knowing a hundred ways through or around a problem is reconsidered (Lindley, 1986).

2.6 Interface Design

Reactions to the way in which computers have begun to dominate work reflect in part the inadequacies in the design of human-computer interfaces. [5]

Computer users perform two types of tasks: Those which involve direct interaction with a program and those that help the user to make his way to or through the program. Some poorly designed interfaces produce more frustration than text, as users search for meanings and try to back out of blind alleys. Poor or missing feedback, inactive prompts, misinformation, and unprompted or duplicate functions abound.

Other poor systems presume a user's reading speed or predict how long the user will take to absorb a message. Confusing, outdated prompts may linger on the screen when the monitor is redrawn (to reflect a mode change) without deleting information from the previous display. Interfaces that use numerous modes -- subsystems in which keystrokes may trigger different results at various times -- are especially confusing.

2.7 Machine Reliability

Workers cannot be productive if machines do not meet their needs or are simply inoperative. Machine reliability issues that may affect productivity in the newsroom include interconnectivity, workstation portability, and the ability of keyboards and disks to survive in newsrooms where carbonated beverages, coffee and smoke are an ever present danger.

3. QUALITY ASSURANCE ISSUES

3.1 Standards Integrity

At the dawn of the electronic age in journalism, publishers were forced by deadlines and profitability concerns to adopt electronic editing, but their editors had serious misgivings. Many predicted a drastic degradation in editing and appearance standards (Randall, 1979). It would be an era, some said, of relying upon software to make quality assurance checks previously performed by skilled craftsmen and of wholesale re-use of file material without the close scrutiny inherent in re-typing. As Lindley (1986) noted

> Coding accurately is essential to clear the copy. Editing carefully...is not that necessary. In a time bind, which gets priority? In a choice of job candidates, which rates higher?

The way some computers accustom users to quick responses and uncomplicated, unambiguous procedures also may affect the style, accuracy, texture and nuances of media content. Reinforcement of short attention spans and of impulsive, impatient approaches to problem solving may become characteristic of computer users who have not had experience with manual techniques.

3.2 Publication Design and Illustration

High resolution electronic integration of illustrations and type is possible, but detailed graphics necessary for high fidelity artwork is expensive. Quality approximations of traditional publication design and illustration can be performed on Lightspeed and Scitex computer systems, but these are not the grade of equipment available to everyday production facilities. Thus far, Macintosh-based publication design does not meet professional standards, despite impressive advances in PostScript laser printers and page makeup software (e.g., Quark Xpress and PageMaker). The ability to integrate type with art in full-page makeup is critical to modern newspaper and magazine production.

In one study of page layout for technical manuals, researchers were able to automate decisions regarding how much text to place on each page, how text and graphics should be laid out, and how pages should be split (Sylla, 1988). Software developed for the study automatically resolved page overflow situations, and applied a 30 percent white space standard. Unfortunately, the system required that a rigid format style be defined in advance. Although such 'canned' templates are commissioned routinely by smaller publications that do not employ their own art directors, templates do not provide the flexibility necessary for creative, non-formula design.

3.3 Production Errors

Three studies have attempted to assess the quality assurance aspects of newsroom automation. The hypothesis of a 1979 effort by S. Randall was that

Newspapers using electronic editing systems have shorter sentences and fewer errors in spelling, punctuation, sentence construction, hyphenation and typography than newspapers not using electronic editing systems.

Findings supported this hypothesis, although data were insufficient to prove that electronically composed sentences were shorter than manual ones. [6]

Two years later, Shipley and Gentry (1981) surveyed 137 copy editors from 42 newspapers in nine states to evaluate the speed and accuracy of VDT editing versus that with pencil and paper. Few of the observed differences were statistically significant, but trends indicated that editing probably is slower but more accurate when VDTs are used. Shipley and Gentry found that the brand of VDT used, a person's copy editing experience, his years spent in a newsroom, and his experience on VDTs were all irrelevant to error rate.

Although one might expect negative feelings toward automation to result in slower production and more errors, this did not appear to be the case in the Shipley and Gentry study. No significant differences were observed in mean elapsed time or errors, regardless of whether individuals liked, disliked or were indifferent to editing with VDTs.

Prior studies reviewed by Shipley and Gentry indicated that

1. Students edit redundancy and punctuation errors skillfully with VDTs, but take considerably longer than with paper and pencil.
2. Students using VDTs detect fewer errors; manual editing results in slightly shorter stories.
3. Fewer typographical and grammatical errors occur with electronic editing.
4. Electronic editing affects editing procedures during the first few weeks after installation, but there is no permanent change in editing patterns.
5. Editing on a terminal can take as much as 32 percent longer than doing it by hand.
6. Daily papers with video display systems report gains of an hour or more in routine deadline flexibility, even though the process actually takes longer.

4. HEALTH ISSUES

Concerns about health problems related to VDT use were voiced

first in Europe during the 1970s. In the U.S., the National Institute of Occupational Safety and Health (NIOSH) first studied
VDT health issues in 1975.

4.1 Direct and Indirect Effects

Health problems associated with VDTs could stem from direct
effects (e.g., hazardous radiation from terminals) or indirect
effects (e.g., job insecurity, deteriorating vision, or poor
posture). Evidence suggests that there are relatively few direct
health effects. However, there is a wealth of evidence implicat-
ing indirect effects (Sauter et al, 1983).

In a study of direct effects, Hedge (1987) noted that DC elec-
trical fields and ion concentrations near terminals were typical
of levels in the natural environment. Despite widespread suspi-
cions to the contrary, VDT radiation has not been shown to constitute a risk of pregnancy complications. A March 1991 article
published in the New England Journal of Medicine reported a
study by NIOSH's Alan Wilcox that discounted any link between
VDT use and miscarriages among a sample of 2,500 women ("All
Things Considered", 1991).

Epidemiological and experimental evidence also fails to
support claims that VDT use may result in cataracts or other
organic damage. Hedge (1987) reported, however, that there had
been some association of facial dermatitis with VDT use, perhaps
as a result of a combination of electrostatic charges and low
humidity. Another potential ailment is hypervitaminosis A
(vitamin A intoxication), which may result from long term
exposure to low levels of ultraviolet radiation.

A study of indirect effects by Smith et al (1981) found that
clerical VDT operators exhibit much higher levels of vision,
musculoskeletal and emotional complaints than control subjects
and professionals (see Table 1).

Sauter et al (1983) evaluated nearly five dozen specific medical signs and symptoms covering all major categories of indirect
health disturbances. At least 75 percent of respondents reported
occasional problems, including statistically significant changes
in colour perception (p < .01). Chapnik and Gross (1987) identified a dozen ergonomic factors which may affect worker health:

1. Height of work area.
2. Angle of work area to the individual.
3. General physical relationship of worker and equipment.
4. Musculoskeletal stress.
5. Glare.
6. Reflectivity.
7. Noise.
8. Humidity.
9. A detached keyboard.
10. A tiltable screen.
11. An adjustable chair.
12. A variable height terminal stand.

4.2 Visual Dysfunction

Some operators complain of headaches that apparently are due to the flicker seen on most screens each time the display scrolls. This effect may be compounded by fluorescent lighting which flickers at the same rate, but out of phase. The result can be nauseating. However, fears of some that screen flicker might trigger photosensitive epileptic seizure also appears to be baseless (Hedge, 1987).

Table 1
Variables assessed for each study group that
were considered relevant to VDT problems among workers

Life Stress and Personal Problems

Job	Finances	Health	Unknown
Career	Other People	Time Pressure	Family

Job-Related Stress

Involvement	Peer Cohesion	Lack of Self-esteem
Innovation	Physical Comfort	Workload Dissatisfaction
Boredom	Role Ambiguity	Quantitative Workload
Work Pressure	Role Conflict	Supervisory Control
Staff Support	Task Orientation	Workload Variance
Clarity	Autonomy	Job Future Ambiguity

Mood

Anxiety	Depression	Anger	Vigor
Fatigue	Confusion		

From Smith et al, 1981

In a study by Gunnarson (1984), the organization and duration of work were found to be crucial factors affecting visual strain. Also, a Swiss study reportedly found that eye strain carries over from one day to the next (Smith, 1984).

The reflectivity of source documents versus that of VDT screens has been associated with eye problems. Operators such as editors who glance frequently from source documentation to their displays and back again need VDTs offering glare control and good screen characteristics (well-formed characters and good character-to-background contrast). Although Sauter et al (1983) reported that corrective eyewear and ambient lighting are predictors of visuo-ocular disturbances, other studies have failed to validate VDT-related visual dysfunction. Hedge (1987) found that optometric measurements did not correlate consistently with subjective complaints. He also reported that large individual differences have been found in the need for screen and workplace lighting.

4.3 Musculoskeletal Problems

Evidence suggests that the physical environment (in particular, the musculoskeletal demands of work) causes many

VDT-related health problems. Studies have shown that chair and workstation configuration are particularly important predictors of musculoskeletal disturbances (Sauter et al, 1983). There appears to be an association between (1) constrained postures and (2) hand, arm, shoulder and neck problems (Hedge, 1987).

In particular, Carpal Tunnel Syndrome occurs in workers because of damage to the median nerve and flexor tendons that extend from the forearm into the hand through a 'tunnel' formed by the wrist bones and transverse carpal ligament. The repetitive twisting of the wrist to reach some keys causes the flexor tendons to rub against the sides of the tunnel, irritating the tendons and causing them to swell (Sheehan, 1991). The result can be progressive numbness, tingling and pain as the cross-section of nerves bundled in the wrist is reduced by as much as 35 percent (Pinkham, 1988).

Also known in other forms as repetitive strain injury and cumulative trauma disorder, 115,000 such injuries were reported to the U.S. government in 1988 (versus only 23,000 in 1981). Repetitive strain injuries account for nearly half of all workplace illnesses. OSHA's Robert Stephens predicts that by the Year 2000, fifty cents of every dollar spent in the U.S. on workers' compensation will go toward such disorders ("A Growing Danger...", 1990).

Previously, 50,000 to 100,000 workers annually chose surgery (to sever the transverse ligament) as a cure. However, new techniques using fiberoptics and video cameras to guide slight incisions allow victims to return to work in an average of 25 days, versus 46.5 days when the older techniques are used (Koenig, 1990). Also, a special keyboard has been designed to lessen the strain by changing the traditional geometry of the keyboard, but industry has been slow to adopt the new layout. To reduce editors' risk of wrist strain, Smith (1984) recommended including a rest on their workstations.

4.4 Disparate Impact

Health effects associated with workplace automation impact some classes of employees more than others. Smith's 1981 study examined four newspapers or related operations in San Francisco. Tasks studied included data entry and retrieval, word processing, writing, editing and telephone sales, as performed by clerical versus professional workers.

For all significant factors, clerical workers reported the highest levels of stress, professionals the least. Clerical workers reported a higher workload, more boredom, greater workload dissatisfaction, greater job future ambiguity and lower self-esteem. Clerical operators also expressed more health complaints than did professionals.

Professionals reported the highest levels of job involvement, autonomy, peer cohesion and staff support. They had the lowest levels of work pressure, and role ambiguity. However, a newspaper industry study of terminal users in New Zealand found that editors experienced the most work pressure, followed by workers performing tasks manually, then clerical workers, suggesting cultural differences regarding these issues.

The San Francisco survey found that VDT use tends to magnify the pressure of stressful tasks, but has little effect on less stressful activities. Smith and his colleagues reported that the VDT was not the primary cause of reported stress and health problems. They noted that other factors such as job content and the work system are major contributors. [7]

4.5 Emotional Problems
The disparate levels of stress experienced by clerical workers may stem as much from emotional factors as from work pressure, although Hedge (1987) found that complaints appeared to be independent of job pressure and hostile attitudes toward the electronic office.
Emotional disturbances reported in the California newspaper study fell into two general categories: mood disturbances and psychosomatic symptoms. It was noted that

The mood disturbances typically are of a neurotic nature including anger, frustration, irritability, anxiety, and depression. The psychosomatic disorders reflect a typical distress syndrome, including gastrointestinal disturbances, muscle and psychic tension, heart palpitations, and frequent sweating (Smith, 1984).

This study found that clerical VDT operators and professionals using VDTs reported higher levels of anxiety, depression, tension, and mental fatigue than nonoperators. Smith concluded that "This emotional effect could be related to the job demands that required tight deadlines and resulted in pressure to produce."
Emotional problems were experienced in part because work procedures had become controlled by computers rather than by human beings. The selection of information presented on the screen, the order in which images appear, and the sequence of functions can direct work in a regimented, insistent manner (Gunnarsson, 1984), leading to mood and other psychological effects.

5. REGULATION

Computer-related health problems have attracted sufficient attention from organized labor, government and industry to be of serious concern to media managers.

5.1 Organized Labor
In hearings before the U.S. Congress during 1984, Charles Perlik (President of the Newspaper Guild, AFL-CIO) presented a model state act to provide occupational safeguards for operators of video display terminals. The act would have required employers to comply with minimum standards, but would have been implemented by state departments of labor. All employers would have been required to comply, regardless of staff size.
The model statute would have regulated minimum compliance levels for

1. Illumination and glare.
2. Furniture arrangement.
3. Which furniture is required (included: wrist and foot rests).
4. Terminals (detachable keyboards mandated).
5. Radiation protection (metal cabinets for VDTs).
6. Semiannual terminal inspections.
7. Eye examinations.
8. Rest breaks.

Civil penalties suggested for violations of the statute were as high as $10,000 per incident or $1,000 per day (Hearings, 1985).
Some labor unions have distributed brochures to VDT users. Others have sought protective provisions in collective bargaining agreements. The 1985-88 contract between New York State and its Civil Service Employees Association mandated development of guidelines for state agencies to use in planning and operating video display equipment. [8] At the University of New Haven, the local union negotiated eye exams and work transfers for pregnant women who use VDTs in their work, and required adjustable furniture for all terminals (Chapnik and Gross, 1987).

5.2 Governments

Legislatures in 14 U.S. states considered VDT legislation during 1983 and 1984, while several congressional subcommittees studied the issues. In 1986, the U.S. Occupational Safety and Health Administration (OSHA) began to instruct compliance officers to review musculoskeletal and visual stress as part of their inspections of workplace safety. OSHA explained that computer-based technology had increased the number of chronic repetitive motion and constrained posture injuries on the job (Chapnik and Gross, 1987).

Legislation was passed in Suffolk County, New York, in 1988 and in San Francisco in 1990 to mandate that businesses apply ergonomic standards in selection of equipment for employees (Lewis, 1991). The San Francisco law requires the use of adjustable chairs and tables, lighting, angle-adjustable screens and keyboards, work time away from the computer, training of workers and supervisors and the use of printer covers to reduce office noise.

There also has been government action in Sweden, Germany, Austria, Canada and Norway. A directive published in 1979 by the Swedish National Board of Occupational Safety and Health provided that

If eye fatigue or visual discomfort tends to develop, the work must be organized in such a way that the employee can intermittently be given periods of rest or work involving more conventional visual requirements. (Gunnarsson, 1984).

In 1980, the Swedish Board recommended that

Work should be designed so as to provide the employee

with an opportunity of influencing and varying the pace
of work and the working methods used, and of surveying
and verifying the results of his or her labors. A shift
from rigid and monotonous working procedures towards
greater independence and greater vocational responsibility is essential as means of achieving greater involvement in measures of occupational safety and health
(Gunnarsson, 1984).

The Swedish Federation of Civil Servants has demanded that
intensive VDT work be limited to a maximum of two hours per day.
The Civil Servants also have joined the Swedish Union of Insurance Employees to draft extensive and detailed guidelines
related to VDT work.

5.3 Industry
Thom Foote-Lennox of the Pelican Group in Minneapolis has
submitted human-computer interface guidelines for adoption as an
IEEE standard (Foote-Lennox, 1986). The suggested guidelines
specify that workstations

1. Provide prompts for all requested inputs.
2. Rapidly acknowledge all completed inputs, and ensure that
each response indicates success or failure.
3. Allow the user to select from several choices, but never
more than seven things at a time.
4. Avoid offering the user menu choices whose selection would
not be acceptable at their time of presentation.
5. Use real world analogies to represent complex software
concepts.
6. Make use of audio signals and visual symbols.
7. Provide a means for the user to correct any operational
error.
8. Integrate error message subsystems with user correction
subsystems.
9. Ensure that the help system includes examples, and relates
directly to the functions currently being executed by the user.
10. Allow the user to browse through help information.
11. Apply the interface consistently throughout the system.
12. Provide a means for experienced users to circumvent labori-
ous command schemes meant to guide the inexperienced through the
system.
13. Recognize the need for multilingual capabilities.
(Hwang, 1988).

6. HUMANITARIAN AND OTHER ISSUES

6.1 Isolation
The use of computerized devices can reduce interpersonal contact in the workplace. Lindley (1986) found that editors tend to
send messages to staff via electronic mail rather than dealing
with them face-to-face. He also found that copy editors do not
confer with subordinates as much when VDTs are used.

Employee-supervisor interaction problems are compounded by the use of a specialized vocabulary to refer to computers and their activities. Command language interfaces are difficult because of their complexity and perceived inconsistencies. Determining the status and appropriateness of information in the computer is a difficulty which has been found to contribute to emotional problems (Long et al, 1983). Inadequate training, a lack of worker participation in system implementation, job security, and monitoring of employee performance only add to the level of distress (Smith, 1984).

Systems that fail to recognize the nature, needs and expectations of users force workers to place a premium on the availability of friends who know how to use the machine (at a time when use of the system actually is discouraging interaction with colleagues). A realignment of the otherwise natural patterns of interpersonal contact results.

> If a piece of work is conceived in terms of the relationships between individuals necessary for its successful completion, the introduction and extension of computerization profoundly affects those relationships (Long et al (1983).

Users often establish new friendships with people who perform specialist functions vis-a-vis the computer, at the expense of relationships with individuals concerned with product content. This can threaten long term product quality and disrupt established lines of authority in the newsroom.

6.2 Monitoring

The disparate impact of computerization is exacerbated among clerical personnel by production monitoring. Clericals report significantly less peer cohesion, involvement, staff support, and job autonomy than professionals -- problems that are heightened by 'over the shoulder' supervision.

NIOSH estimates that about two-thirds of American VDT operators are monitored electronically to determine work speed, accuracy and efficiency (Chapnik and Gross, 1987). Smith et al (1981) found that clericals were monitored closely by their computers, which issued up-to-the-minute reports of production rates and errors to supervisors. As a result, clericals had a feeling of being watched constantly.

Smith (1984) noted that employee monitoring creates a dehumanizing work environment in which the worker feels controlled by the machine. The result is a high stress response that fuels an adversarial relationship between supervisor and employee. The VDT in effect becomes an overbearing boss to whom the clerical worker is chained. Every keystroke is a betrayal.

6.3 Job Security

Job security typically is a concern during automation, regardless of the work setting. When conversion to electronic production became widespread, labor unions negotiatied lifetime job guarantees for printers and photoengravers, resulting in a surplus of labor at many newspapers. [9]

After wholesale layoffs, transfers and job buyouts during the Seventies, manpower reductions in newspaper composing rooms and pressrooms because of new technology have slowed to a trickle. Job guarantees and buyouts are slowly disappearing from the labor scene. Employment levels of newspaper production workers peaked at 184,900 in 1972 (172,500 in 1987). Meanwhile, newsroom staffs had grown to 55,300 in 1988 versus 43,000 in 1978 (Goltz, 1988).

Although unions remain concerned about job security in the electronic newsroom, automation does not necessarily trigger labor strife. One paper was able to pace the introduction of technological innovations to coincide with the natural attrition of composing room workers. In a two-year transition at another newspaper, severance pay and job transfers averted a potential strike or slowdown by the International Typographical Union. No new editorial employees were added to the workforce, even though page makeup had shifted to the newsroom.

6.4 Restrictions On Creativity

Workstations are fast becoming the premier tool of media professionals. However, it is likely that printing and production requirements or interface standards would restrict the ways in which users could apply their electronic tools. Future AI-based systems might allay this concern to some degree, since their interfaces would be educable to the needs and preferences of each user. AI also might facilitate greater interface flexibility in response to standards requirements. [10] Standards could be an agenda setting element that would limit how and what an entire class of media specialists could do in their profession.

Widespread acceptance of computing tools in journalism and commercial art depends upon an ability to temper the conflict between creativity and instrumentality. Computers are not anti-human; they are non-human. In fact, some professionals use their machines to promote interpersonal communication.

6.5 Data Security

The electronic storage of confidential information on local networks and shared hard disks complicates questions of source anonymity that long have been sensitive in the news business. The ease and speed with which workstation background notes can be obliterated (almost without a trace) has exacerbated the ongoing dispute between courts seeking evidence and journalists anxious to protect their sources.

7. APPROACHES TO HUMAN FACTORS PROBLEMS

The consideration of approaches that media management might take in dealing with these and other human factors issues requires evaluation of priorities, timing, and potential solutions.

7.1 Priorities

Although the problems of human factors in automation are new, the background of publishing priorities against which they must be considered has changed little since invention of the Linotype. Editors still must generate and distribute a product of standard quality in a timely manner. The introduction of computers to newsroom and pressroom can make this task easier. However, if automation is managed ineptly, human factors problems that accompany computerization can neutralize many of the potential benefits.

Three issues should be addressed by the media manager faced with human factors problems during (and after) automation: training, task assignment, and supervision.

7.1.1 Training

Human resources development has seldom had high priority in the industrial sector (publishing included). However, in the electronic age training can no longer be considered a perk to be given as time permits to those deserving of reward. Media managers should recognize that training is an investment of time, money and resources to develop a valuable raw asset (the worker) in order to better leverage that asset in the generation and distribution of product.

Although training is an obligation of management, it also is a responsibility of the employee. The worker is expected to contribute as much as possible to further the goals of his organization; management is obligated in turn to provide the support necessary to help the employee make the most of his potential.

Computer literacy is the most important skill that workers in an electronic environment can acquire. This does not mean that individuals necessarily know how to operate the brand of personal computer or terminal installed in their newsrooms or business offices. It also does not mean that these employees can use WordPerfect, Lotus 1-2-3, dBASE or Ventura. What it does mean is that people have a basic understanding of how computerized data processing systems operate; in particular, how data are entered, modified, stored and transmitted from one device to another. The conceptual framework provided by reasonable computer literacy is vital to a worker's ability to adapt to the repeated changes in technology which are and will be part of the job environment.

Employees (and managers) also must be trained regarding the potential health problems associated with extensive work with computer workstations. In a narrow sense, it is in management's best interest to ensure that workers adopt good posture and other appropriate work habits. Totally aside from health plan expenses, preventable ailments suffered by the ill-trained employee reduce production, cause deadlines to be missed, and impair quality.

Computer training and the personalized attention it entails also support employee morale and promote the sense of self-worth essential if workers are to be productive. Management sends an implicit but clear message when workers are asked to deal with new technology but are not trained thoroughly in its use. Everyone infers that the work performed by such employees is not of high value to the organization.

7.1.2 Task Management

The special problems inherent in VDT use place unusual demands upon the ability of media management to structure, assign and evaluate tasks for clerical workers. Studies have shown that computers in the workplace are concentrators and multipliers of stress already in the environment. Conscious effort is necessary to defuse potentially debilitating aspects of that environment and to address problems before they occur. The organization and duration of work assigned to clerical workers, the employee's understanding of the importance of tasks and their relationship to activities valued highly, and the regular scheduling of breaks and non-computer tasks are especially important.

7.1.3 Supervision

Although informed supervision is essential to an office in the throes of automation, the need to cultivate understanding and mutual respect between supervisor and employee continues long after vendors leave and systems begin generating copy and page layouts. The unique strains of the electronic workplace require the manager to be a facilitator more than a taskmaster.

Special consideration should be given to clerical workers in order to avoid adversarial relationships which feed common psychological and emotional problems. The practice of monitoring production and error rates is not in the best interest of either management or employees unless (1) only aggregate trend data are analyzed (i.e., individuals are not identified) or (2) performance data are clearly divorced from employee appraisals, advancement and compensation. Only under these circumstances can such data collection and analysis be a legitimate part of product quality assurance.

7.2 Timing

Everything in media management has a deadline. Unfortunately, the deadline for considering and implementing solutions to human factors problems was yesterday. Personal computers, terminals, database machines, integrated production networks and prepress systems already are in place throughout the industry.

The effective management of human resources is an urgent concern that requires management attention now. The need for immediate action is especially strong at those sites where organized labor has taken up the banner of health effects allegedly stemming from VDT use.

The impact of emotional factors upon morale and productivity make workers' feelings of persecution or dehumanization (and their sense of shared purpose) central to the long-term success of automation in the newsroom. As a result, it is management policy and technique rather than employee adaptation to technology that is key.

8. POTENTIAL SOLUTIONS

Many approaches are possible; only some are feasible. Generally, media managers can wait for the flow of current events to impose solutions piecemeal (the 'default approach') -- a strategy that would be wasteful of human and financial resources. In another approach, management would take the initiative to understand unique demands of an electronic environment and implement informed policies and programs to satisfy those demands (the 'proactive approach').

8.1 The Default Approach

The market is merciless. The media manager who chooses to address automation problems as they occur will experience high staff turnover, higher than necessary health care costs, poorer product quality and internecine rivalry pitting professionals against clericals (and both against management).

Traditional media such as newspapers find it especially difficult to take the initiative in dealing with new problems. Unless the high ground is seized early, however, management will find itself forced to adopt the very policies in the long term that could have been implemented earlier at much less cost.

8.2 The Proactive Approach

The savvy media manager who is able to see beyond today's deadlines might implement a multifaceted approach in order to (1) apply human factors in the newsroom, (2) study the work environment impact of technological changes, (3) involve employees in system design and hardware selection, and (4) use flexible task scheduling to minimize employee boredom and fatigue.

8.3 The Training Imperative

Although the proactive approach may appear to be the best of all worlds, the world which news and production managers inhabit is not that world. It is a world of irritable staff, computers that fail at critical moments, telecommunications links that garble important copy, and computer-controlled presses that run amok.

It is unrealistic to expect that media managers trained in gathering and distributing information about the outside world (with minimum concern for the subtleties of personnel management) would comprehend and implement new human factors techniques in tandem with their new computer systems. The field of human-computer interaction is relatively new, without guidelines that could ensure reasonable success for managers interested in cookbook solutions.

Enough is known, however, to highlight the crucial role played by comprehensive and continual training. Automation is unique, discernible from other changes that affect news gathering and dissemination, in that it guarantees waves of ever-faster change in the future. Even the media manager who may understand the issues highlighted in this review and who takes reasonable action to protect his operation today will be hapless tomorrow, unless he makes an attempt to keep current not only with computer applications, but also with human factors developments. If any one practical solution can be identified, it is training. But in order for training to be effective now and in the future, the first student must be the media manager. Human factors has joined copy editing, investigative journalism and production management as a key component of the world of media.

9. NOTES

[1] A 'morgue' is a comprehensive file of stories published previously by the newspaper, arranged by subject.

[2] Some gains are lost, however, because of the ease of "unlimited and unbridled revision" (Romano, 1988). But despite such increases in the volume of revisions, a monthly publication's production schedule can be shortened by at least two days due to the new technology.

[3] Some media have found it necessary to create a new position: systems editor.

A new expert has been added to the newspapers staff -- the systems editor or systems manager -- who provides technical advice. One project some of these people will be discussing is how to test prospective employees for ability to deal with computer systems (Lindley, 1988).

The creation of such a position carries with it complex implications for hiring and promotion. For example, how is a technician with few traditional editing skills to be advanced within an organization that values such skills highly?

[4] Computer literacy, at bottom a cumulative phenomenon (Sullivan, 1988), affects the degree to which individuals anticipate and understand the functioning of software and the conventions of screen design. The willingness to accept automation -- generally, to deal with the unfamiliar -- is a personality trait which will reward many who must deal with workstations, in media and out (Nickell, 1986).

[5] Experienced users actually are handicapped in dealing with innovative interfaces, which attempt to break away from previous mechanically based techniques. Their expectations relate to dramatically different systems, implemented at a time when software was limited seriously by hardware speed and storage capacity. People who are neither electronics hobbyists nor computer professionals are better able to adapt to human-engineered systems.

[6] Randall's 1979 study of the Charlotte Observer sampled a base period (manual systems only), an interim period (computerized typesetting) and a final period (full automation). Samples

were taken six years apart. Randall found that errors increased
from the base period to the interim period, then decreased as
full automation was implemented to a rate lower than that for
the manual base period (p < .001).

Randall's later (1986) study concluded that the key
factors in any editing technology are the ease with which the
process is completed, the number of steps and the amount of
error inherent in the process.

[7] In evaluating results of Smith's San Francisco study, one
must consider its findings in light of significant (if unavoidable) methodological flaws. Study sites and participants
were not selected at random. Union health complaints were known
to be high at the newspapers studied, and respondents were vol-
unteers. Also, difficult labor negotiations were underway during
data collection, which may have heightened respondents' sen-
sitivity to problems.

[8] In January 1987, New York State issued VDT ergonomic guidelines for its agencies. Rest breaks and alternative work were
recommended, as were proper lighting and glare shields.

[9] Absent such guarantees, the typical buyout was a year's pay
plus continuation of benefits until the worker could get another
job. One Seattle paper still buys out 20 printers a year at an
average payment of $25,000 each. However, the paper also offers
voluntary training programs to composing room employees who
prefer to continue working in other departments, with the right
to return to the composing room within nine months.

[10] See Day, D. (1990), "AI Applications in HCI Design for
Innovation-Resistant Users" (unpublished manuscript).

10. REFERENCES

1. "A growing danger on the job" (1990). Ladies' Home Journal,
   April 1990, 112-118.

2. "All Things Considered" (1991). National Public Radio
   (U.S.), 6:20 p.m. EST March 13, 1991.

3. Chapnik, E. and Gross, C. (1987). Evaluation, Office Im-
   provements Can Reduce VDT Operator Problems. Occupational
   Health & Safety, 56, 34-37.

4. Foote-Lennox (1986). Ergonomic Guidelines for Computerized
   User Interfaces. Proceedings, Computer Standards Conference
   1986, pp. 38-41. IEEE Computer Society Press, Washington.
5. Goltz, G. (1988). Man versus machine. Presstime, 10, November, 36-38.

6. Gunnarsson, E. (1984). The impact of organizational factors
   on visual strain in clerical VDT work. In B. Cohen (Ed.),

Human Aspects in Office Automation. (Amsterdam: Elsevier Science Publishers).

7. Hearings (1985). Hearings before the Subcommittee on Health and Safety of the Committee on Education and Labor, House of Representatives; 98th Cong., 2d session (1985). SUDOCS Nr. Y 4.Ed 8/1:Oc 1/12, pp. 8-11.

8. Hedge, A. (1987). Office health hazards: an annotated bibliography (1980-1986). Ergonomics, 30, 763-772.

9. Hwang (1988). An Experimental Study of Chinese Information Displays on VDTs. Human Factors, 30, pp. 461-471.

10. Koenig, R. New operation to repair wrist speeds recovery. Wall Street Journal, Sept. 27, 1990, B1 and B4.

11. Lewis, P. More computer safety laws may be coming. The Lowell (Massachusetts) Sun, Jan. 6, 1991, 37.

12. Lindley, W. (1986). How the computers shook up editing. Editor & Publisher, 119, May 24, 16E.

13. Lindley, W. (1988). From Hot Type to Video Screens: Editors Evaluate New Technology. Journalism Quarterly, 65, 485-489.

14. Long, J. et al (1983). Introducing the interactive computer at work. Behaviour and Information Technology, 2, 39-106.

15. Nickell (1986). The Computer Attitude Scale. Computers in Human Behavior, 2, pp. 301-306.

16. Pinkham, J. (1988). Carpal Tunnel Syndrome Sufferers Find Relief With Ergonomic Designs. Occupational Health & Safety, 57, 49-53.

17. Randall, S. (1979). Effect of electronic editing on error rate of newspaper. Journalism Quarterly, 56, 161-165.

18. Randall, S. (1986). How Editing and Typesetting Technology Affects Typographical Error Rate. Journalism Quarterly, 63, 763-770.

19. Romano, F. (1988). Focus on editorial systems, not automation. Folio, 17, 108-112.

20. Sauter, S. et al (1983). Job and health implications of VDT use: initial results of the Wisconsin-NIOSH study. Communications of the ACM, 26, 284-294.

21. Sheehan, M. (1991). Avoiding carpal tunnel syndrome: A guide for computer keyboard users. Syracuse University Office Technology, Spring 1991. Syracuse, New York.

22. Shipley, L. and Gentry, J. (1981). How electronic editing equipment affects editing performance. Journalism Quarterly, 58, 371-374.

23. Smith, M. (1984). Ergonomic aspects of health problems in VDT operators. In B. Cohen (Ed.), Human Aspects in Office Automation. (Amsterdam: Elsevier Science Publishers).

24. Smith, M., et al (1981). An investigation of health complaints and job stress in video display operations. Human Factors, 23, 387-400.

25. A.C. Sullivan (personal communication, December 17, 1988).

26. Sylla (1988). A Human Factors Design Investigation of a Computerized Layout System of Text-Graphic Technical Materials. Human Factors, 30, pp. 347-358.

27. Wright, P. and Lickorish, A. (1983). Proofreading texts on screen and paper. Behaviour & Information Technology, 2, 227-235.

HUMAN JOBS AND COMPUTER INTERFACES
M.I. Nurminen and G.R.S. Weir
Elsevier Science Publishers B.V. (North-Holland)
© 1991 IFIP. All rights reserved.

The formalization of activity requirements in an insurance office

V. Ruohomäki and M. Vartiainen

Laboratory of Industrial Psychology, Helsinki University of Technology, Otakaari 4 A, SF-02150 Espoo

Abstract
The activity requirements, possible action hindrances and the amount of computer use were analyzed and described in an insurance office. The analysis was made on organizational, job and action/task strategy levels. Special attention was paid to the interaction episodes and communication between a customer and an employee. Interaction in natural situations was videotaped and recorded. The customer-employee interaction in two simulated tasks was also studied. In the interaction, both the observable performance and verbal communication were analyzed. Several disturbing requirements were found, e.g., noisy working environment and continuous changes in products. In the interaction, the employee was the active participant. Computers were utilized as an aid, but there were also several other tools in use. The role of the computer was smaller than expected. The work in an insurance office is much more than mere acquiring, processing and transferring of information between a customer and an employee using a computer as a tool. The interaction episodes are "loaded" with social and emotional requirements.

1. INTRODUCTION

1.1. The aims
Any job, for example in an insurance office, may be described as an activity system taking place in an action field. The 'action field' is defined as an area of possible actions. The action field is all the possible actions for an actor in a certain moment. In the action field, there may be hindrances which prevent a subject from achieving a given or self-set goal. On the other hand, there may be multiple aids, e.g. a well-designed interface, to facilitate activities. The aims of the study are to analyze and describe activity requirements and possible action hindrances (1) in an insurance office, and to find out to what extent computers are, in fact, used as an aiding tool.

1.2. The conceptual framework

Lewin (5) stated that behaviour (B) is a function (F) of the person (P) and of his/her environment (E), B = F(P,E). The 'behaviour' may be replaced with the 'action' (A) and the 'person' with the 'subject', thus: A = F(S,E). Work activities are realized by a subject (i.e. person, group, organization) using both practical (i.e. hammer, computer, software) and psychological (e.g. mental models) tools (T). The tools are used to transform objects (O) (e.g. material, information) into different outcomes (i.e. products, services) in a certain environment (e.g. an office). Then, Lewin's formula may be transformed into: A = F(S,T,O,E).

The structure of any specific activity may be analyzed as a transformation of a general goal into a sequence of subgoals which are realized through actions and operations. This is presented, for example, in the model of the hierarchical-sequential organization of an action (8). In the hierarchical order it is supposed that first the goal is set and then the series of transformations is produced. The series of transformations is then performed in a given order. Each transformation can be considered a unit, which has a goal and single steps of its own, so that the main goal can be specified. A hierarchical structure emerges in which superior units are divided into subunits on several levels. The sequential order is concerned with arrangements in time; tasks and subtasks are performed one after the other.

To understand or to predict actions, the subject and the environment have to be considered as one constellation of interdependent factors. Lewin called the totality of these factors the "life space" or the "life field". In addition to the "life space", i.e., the person and the psychological environment as it exists for him/her, there are a multitude of processes in the physical and social world which do not affect the life space. Certain aspects of the physical and social world, however, do affect the state of the life space, i.e., a "boundary zone". Such aspects are, for example, perception and the execution of an action. In summary, there are: (a) the life space, (b) the independent physical and social world, and (c) the boundary zone.

Oesterreich (6) adapted Lewin's ideas in his 'action field' (Handlungsfeld) model. There are two differences between the models of Lewin and Oesterreich (9). First, in Oesterreich's model it is possible to make a clear distinction between a subjective and an objective action field of a subject: there is a 'real' action field, and its mental, subjective representation, they may be different from each other. Second, it is possible to describe the action field model formally which allows comparisons of various action fields.

The action field can be described by means of three elements: actions, effect probabilities, and consequences of actions. An action starts when one of several possible actions has been selected, and it stops when there are, once again, several action alternatives to be selected. At any moment an actor is in a situation where s/he has possible actions among which to make a choice. Depending on his/her decision, an actor reaches the next consequence. An actor once again has several alternative actions to choose from. It is supposed, in the model, that an action results only with a certain probability in the particular consequence. The probability of reaching a given consequence is called the effect probability and may vary from 0.0 to 1.0.

In the action field, there may be some hindrances which lower the effect probability and, consequently, an actor's opportunities to reach his/her goal and subgoals. Action hindrances may be biological, chemical, physical, emotional, social, cultural, etc. Using Lewin's terminology, hindrances should be sought both in the subjective life space and in the boundary zone. In addition, potential sources of hindrances should be sought in the processes of the physical and social world which do not directly affect the life space of a subject. In an office, this means studying both subjective feelings (e.g. fatigue), and perceptions (e.g. job characteristics), and physical work environment (e.g. an interface and tools), and social interaction between an employee and a client, which is a basic episode in client service.

1.3. The problems of the study

From the point of view of man-computer system design, it is necessary to study action fields as activity requirements and try to define the hindrances, 'bottlenecks' etc. which prevent employees working or make it hard for them to work. This is important when trying to find out how to support the work of employees. Because there may be subjective 'hindrances', it is also necessary to study subjective perceptions of employees about work. The formalization of both the objective and subjective sides of work is also needed to develop new methods of work analysis.
The problems of the study are:
1. What are the activity/action requirements in an insurance office?
2. What kinds of methods are there to analyze action requirements?
3. What is the role of computers and their interfaces in the job content of employees?

2. METHODS

Our methodological perspective was systemic: from broader entities towards more specific analysis including cognitive and social aspects of working processes. The levels studied were: organizational level, job level and individual level of action/task strategies. The methods used, aims and research objects are shown in Table 1.

2.1. Organizational level

The working environment in which the work activity was taking place was studied and described. The data were collected by observing and interviewing employees. Written documents were also used. The information was gathered about the organization of the company, its products and business idea, types of clients, work flow, the division of work, tasks and job content of employees, tools, etc. In this paper, only data concerning the organization of the office are shown.

2.2. Job level

Job characteristics, job satisfaction and job motivation were studied using the Job Diagnostic Survey (JDS) questionnaire (3).
The mental work load of a normal working day was estimated using the BMS-scale. The BMS-scale (Belastung-Monotoni-Sättigung) I A and I B (7) measured experienced mental fatigue, monotony and affective aversion. There are 31 statements in the scale, e.g., "I feel myself tired just now", and two alternatives to answer: "agree" and "disagree". Each statement has a weighted value. Version A is used at the beginning and version B at the end of the working day in order to determine changes in mental well-being during the working period.

2.3. Action/task strategy level

The individual working strategies or working procedures of customer service employees (N=3) were studied in two ways:

a) The interaction of employees with customers was videotaped and recorded (4) *in natural situations* during a normal working day for about an hour per person.

Table 1
The levels studied, the aims, methods and objects used to describe the work in an insurance office.

	AIMS	METHODS	OBJECTS
ORGANIZATIONAL LEVEL	- An overview: products, line of business, organization, etc.	- Documents, interviews with supervisors	- The whole organization/ company
	- An overview of an office: clients, tasks, division of work, work flows, etc	- documents, interviews with employees, observations	- A typical office of the company
JOB LEVEL	- To determine job characteristics, job satisfaction and motivation	- Job Diagnostic Survey (JDS)	- All employees in the office (N=14)
	- To measure mental load of employees	- Belastung, Monotoni, Sättigung (BMS)	- All employees in the office (N=14)
ACTION/TASK STRATEGY LEVEL	- To analyze activity in general, natural working processes, time used for each action, tools, etc.	- Videotaping and recording normal cases with clients, classifying performance	- Customer service employees (N=3)
	- To analyze observable interaction and verbal communication between employees and customers, and to determine hierarchical-sequential goal-structure of employees	- Videotaping and recording simulated cases (simple and complicated), analyzing verbal protocols	- Customer service employees (N=3)

b) *Two simulated experimental tasks* were created on the basis of natural situations. The tasks were chosen with help from the supervisors of the office. The aim was to find typical, representative cases from which it would be possible to make generalizations to the whole work. The purpose of using simulations was to activate employees' mental models or action programs. The simulated tasks required different amounts of skill and knowledge, and action regulation at different levels. One task was simple and quite easy, i.e., issuing motor and vehicle insurance. The other task was complicated and more difficult, i.e., to insure an owned house. In the simulated tasks, the 'customer', as typical and neutral as possible, was always the same person (instructed to behave similarly in each interaction).

The working strategies were studied by analyzing the observable interaction both in the natural and simulated tasks and by analyzing the verbal communication process between an employee and a customer in the simulated tasks.

The *observable interaction* was decomposed into categories. The active part, either an employee or a customer was the focus of the classification, i.e., the acts that promoted task fulfillment in each moment, were coded. The main categories were: A. an employee speaks, B. an employee acts, C. an employee speaks and acts simultaneously, D. a customer speaks, E. a customer acts, and F. a customer speaks and acts simultaneously. The observable action of an employee, i.e. the outer performance (categories B and C), was then subdivided into specified subcategories on the basis of the videotaped cases in a normal working day: 1. writing, 2. using telephone, 3. using computer, 4. handling papers, 5. calculating, 6. reading, 7. handling money, and 8. only waiting. Time used in each category and subcategory was calculated and summed. Time used was expressed as a percentage in order to see portions of different actions in the whole action process.

The *verbal communication* between an employee and a customer during interaction was analyzed separately. The hierarchical-sequential goal structure of an employee was formalized quantitatively and qualitatively on the basis of the contents of verbal protocols. Special attention was paid to transmitted questions and information packages: their amount, order, content and repetitions. A transmitted question was defined as a single, understandable question, one sentence or several sentences, asked by an employee or a customer. An information package was defined as a single, understandable information unit/entity, a meaningful thought told by an employee or a customer. To determine possible differences between simple and complicated tasks, t-tests were calculated. Employees were interviewed about their goals for the tasks.

3. RESULTS

3.1. The working environment

From the organizational level of analysis only data concerning the insurance office are shown here. The personnel (N=14) may be divided into four professional groups: supervisors (N=2), sales personnel (N=4), case handlers (N=4) and customer service (N=4). The activity requirements of customer service employees are of special interest in this study. These employees had long experience working at a desk interacting with clients, and advising customers by telephones. Each employee, sitting near another, has a similar working place: a desk, shelves, a computer terminal, a telephone, a typewriter, a calculator, various formulas, leaflets and manuals, etc. The room is restless and noisy; telephones ringing, machines humming and people rushing.

3.2. Job satisfaction, job content and mental load

General job satisfaction and internal motivation received medium scores, with the exception of sales personnel who received low scores on job satisfaction. Most of the employees were dissatisfied with their wages. There was also dissatisfaction with supervisors among customer service employees. Most of the employees gave a rather low evaluation of the feedback from supervisors and co-workers. Customer service employees also considered their task identity as low and degree of skill variety high, demanding extensive interaction with other people.

There were changes in the mental work load during a normal working day. At the end of the day, affective aversion estimated by the BMS-scale was at a level that requires work redesign for all of the employees except the case handlers. The customer service employees were fatigued at the end of the working day. When interviewed, customer service employees considered themselves stressed by complicated tasks, lack of information support and continuous changes (in products, computer programmes, etc.). All the employees cited time pressure as a factor in mental work load.

3.3. The individual working strategies.

a) *In natural situations* eight cases were studied. Each customer service employee served 2-3 customers during the studied hour. There were lots of them visiting the office, often forming a queue. Customers varied a great deal; in age, sex, their way of dealing with employees, their knowledge about insurance, expectations and attitudes creating a particular atmosphere for the situation. Customers usually required advice on several issues at a time.

The tasks to be carried out by employees varied a great deal, for example; to clarify customer's confused payments, to insure a motorbike, to change home insurance and insurance policy etc. The tasks concerned several kinds of products, for example, travel insurance, motor insurance, accident insurance. Most tasks were quite complicated and included several work phases, but others were simpler with only a few phases.

The time used in tasks varied a great deal, from 2 min 21 sec to 47 min ($\bar{x}$=21 min, S=15 min 30 s). The analyzed observable interaction processes showed that most of the time employees had a more active role than customers. The time that employees spent in different activities varied from case to case: speaking took 3-32% and acting 9-65% of the total time. There was quite a lot of simultaneous acting and speaking (mainly with handling papers and using computers) ($\bar{x}$=19%, S=6.6%), which may say something about the automated/routinized level of skill. Employees needed several tools, i.e., computer and programs, a calculator, a telephone, and all kinds of papers, documents, tables, forms, covers, etc., to handle and process information. Customer service employees used computers in every case studied. The portion of time employees spent operating a computer varied from 8%-65% ($\bar{x}$=26%, S=18%) of their total acting time in the working process.

b) *In the simulated experimental tasks* the total time used for the easy task was 5 min 58 sec on average, and for the difficult task 13 min 51 sec. The division of the *interaction* between employees and customers into observable categories is shown in Figure 1.

(a) AN EASY TASK

Main categories of interaction: T1 - T2 = 5 min 58 s

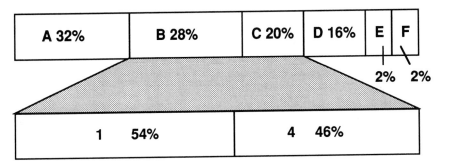

(b) A DIFFICULT TASK

Main categories of interaction: T1 - T2 = 13 min 51 s

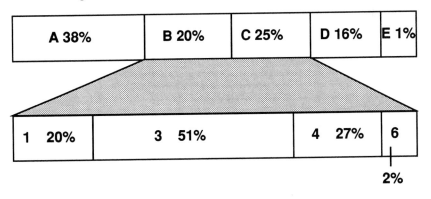

Figure 1. In the simulated situations, the division of observable interaction into categories on average: (a) an easy task, and (b) a difficult task. The main categories: A. an employee speaks, B. an employee acts, C. an employee speaks and acts simultaneously, D. a customer speaks, E. a customer acts, and F. a customer speaks and acts simultaneously. The subcategories: 1. writing, 2. using telephone, 3. using computer, 4. handling papers, 5. calculating, 6. reading, 7. handling money, and 8. only waiting.

An employee has the active role in the interaction both in the easy and difficult task, i.e., about 80 percent of the total time. Most of the active time in the easy task was used for speaking, then for acting (writing, handling papers), and, thirdly, for

108

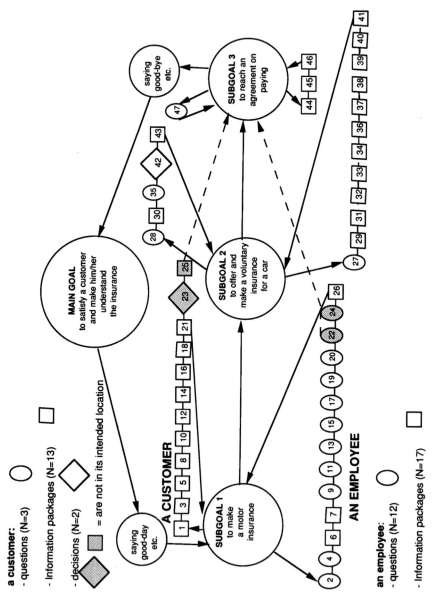

Figure 2. The formalization of the verbal communication in the easy task. The customer service employee number 1.

Table 2
The average number of subgoals, transmitted questions, information packages and
time used in the easy and difficult task.

TASK	SUBGOALS		TRANSFERRED QUESTIONS		INFORMATION PACKAGES		TOTAL TIME (sec)	
	N	s	N	s	N	s	$\bar{x}$	s
Easy	4.0	1.0	11	1.2	19	2.9	358	63
Difficult	5.7	0.6	24	2.3	49	3.7	831	287
t-test			p<.025		p<.025		p<.025	

simultaneous speaking and acting. In the difficult task, most of the time was used
for speaking, then simultaneous speaking and acting, and, thirdly, acting.

The content of acting in the easy task consists of writing and handling several
documents. Computers were not used at all. In the difficult task, the acting consists
mostly of computer use (51%), then handling documents and writing. There was
also a little reading. In the difficult task, one employee interrupted the use of a
computer program when making an insurance and continued writing by hand. She
was feeling uncertain and regarded the program as too complicated.

The verbal communication was an intensive flow of information between an
employee and a customer. In the simulated tasks, subgoals of employees were
identified on the basis of their questions and the information packages were
associated with the work phase in hand.

An example formal description of verbal communication in the easy simulated
task is shown in Figure 2.

The main goal of the employees could be divided into several subgoals.
Subgoals seemed to be quite clear entities. There were more subgoals in the
difficult task than in the easy one. Employees transmitted much information in the
communication process; they transmitted more information than they were asked
questions. In the difficult tasks there were more than twice the number of
information packages and questions compared with the easy task.

The number of subgoals, transmitted questions, information packages and the
total time used are shown in Table 2.

The communication process had a clear beginning, discussion, and end. The
employees' goal was to please and serve customers well. The communication and
subgoals served to fulfil the main goal. The process flowed sequentially from one
subgoal to another, from working phase to phase, by associated questions and
information packages. There were no repetitions. When giving information,
employees often used analogies to make their point clear. After fulfilment of one
subgoal the communication moved to the next.

The employees' working strategies varied more in the difficult than in the simple
task; there were more differences in the order and the content of communication
although the majority of subgoals were similar. The number of possible alternatives
to accomplish the task was larger for the complicated task than in the simple one.

4. DISCUSSION

The analysis of action requirements showed that the working environment of customer service employees was very restless and noisy. The feedback from supervisors and co-workers was rated as low. The employees considered themselves to be stressed by complicated tasks, lack of information support, continuous changes, for example, in products, and time pressure. The clients that employees must face in their work varied greatly. A great deal of information concerning insurance was processed in the verbal interaction between an employee and a customer, instead of processing it in the employee-computer interaction. There are not only cognitive but also high social and emotional requirements in the interaction between employees and customers. In the interaction, employees are more active than customers. Most of the time, employees do the speaking. When acting, the employees use several tools, of which a computer terminal is only one. The more complicated a task, the more employees use computers as their support. Since they also used other kinds of supporting tools, for instance, manuals and leaflets, it can be concluded that a lot of the support may, in the future, be transferred to software.

Our aim was to study and formalize the activity requirements on three levels, i.e., organizational, job and action/task strategy. All three levels were essential to understand the requirements of an individual employee. The most interesting data were derived from the analysis of observable and communicative interaction both in natural and simulated tasks. The role of the computer as a tool was smaller than expected. It was evident that not all of the potential information concerning various types of insurances could be received via the software. In addition, although the layout of displays and the dialogue structure were not analyzed, it could be concluded that employees could not find all the information that was in the computer. There were apparent deficiencies either in the usability of the software or in the skill level of employees.

The action facilitation approach (1, 10) provides an actor's point of view to remove action hindrances. Action facilitation is defined as improving or maintaining user's performance, simultaneously decreasing his/her mental and/or physical effort. Software tools should support the user's action in such a way that action facilitation results. For instance, the user should be able to prepare him/herself for a future action, the system error messages should be clear, etc. The action facilitation principle has been derived from Hacker's theory of the mental regulation of action (2). Hacker divides actions into three main phases: action preparation (goal setting, orientation, construction of sub-goals and action programs, decision among variants of execution), execution (e.g. motor, cognitive) and control of the execution. Further on, actions are guided at various levels of regulation (sensorimotor, perceptual-conceptual and intellectual). Based on the action facilitation approach, Roe and, later, Arnold (1) composed a list of software design recommendations. Software should support preparation, execution and control of user's actions. To be able to design and 'facilitate' man-computer interaction, job content of users, and the whole activity environment, it is helpful to analyze work as an activity system, and an action field as activity requirements.

ACKNOWLEDGEMENTS: This study was made in the project 'The tools and methods of the learning organization' financed by the Academy of Finland.

REFERENCES

1. Arnold, A.G. and Roe, R.A. Action facilitation: a theoretical concept and its use in user interface design. In Work with computers: organizational, management, stress and health aspects. M.J. Smith and G. Salvendy, Eds. Elsevier, The Netherlands, 1989, pp. 191-199.

2. Hacker, W. Allgemeine Arbeits- und Ingenieurpsychologie. VEB Deutscher Verlag der Wissenschaften, Berlin, 1973.

3. Hackman, J.R. and Oldham, G.R. Work redesign. Addison-Wesley, USA, 1980.

4. Laws, J.W. and Barber P.J. Video analysis in cognitive ergonomics: a methodologial perspective. Ergonomics 32 (1989), 1303-1318.

5. Lewin, K. Field theory in social science. Cartwright, D. Ed. Harper-Row, New York, 1951.

6. Oesterreich, R. Handlungsregulation und Kontrolle. Urban & Schwarzenberg, München, Wien, Baltimore, 1981.

7. Plath, H-E. and Richter, P. Der BMS (I) -Erfassungsbogen - Ein Verfahren zur skalierten Erfassung erlebter Beanspruchungsfolgen. Probleme und Ergebnisse der Psychologie, Heft 65 (1978), 45-65.

8. Volpert, W. The model of hierarchical-sequential organization of action. In Cognitive and motivational aspects of action. W. Hacker, W. Volpert, W. and M. von Cranach, Eds. North Holland, Amsterdam, New York, Oxford, 1982, pp. 35-51.

9. Resch, M. Die Handlungsregulation geistiger Arbeit. Hans Huber, Bern, Stuttgart, Toronto, 1988.

10. Roe, R.A. and Meijer, T. Action facilitation and mental information work. In Mental work and automation. P. Richter, and W. Hacker, W. Eds. Proceedings of 6th International Symposium on Work Psychology (Dresden, March 27-29). Stoba-Druck, Dresden, 1990, pp. 55-60.

HUMAN JOBS AND COMPUTER INTERFACES
M.I. Nurminen and G.R.S. Weir
Elsevier Science Publishers B.V. (North-Holland)
© 1991 IFIP. All rights reserved.

Computerization and the construction of new qualifications in the context of product and process innovation in the banking sector

Diane-Gabrielle Tremblay

Télé-université, Université du Québec, P. O. Box 5250, station C, Montréal, Québec, Canada H2X 3M4

In the present context of deregulation, increased competition, technological and product innovation in the banking and financial sector in general, a certain reorientation of banking activitites and professions is observed. Many jobs, such as those of teller, are being fundamentally restructured by computerization and new criteria for hiring are appearing. New tasks and professions such as executive banking counsellors, financial counsellors, financial planning specialists and others are taking more and more important places in the internal labour markets of firms.

On the basis of detailed research in a cooperative banking institution, and in traditional (capitalist) banks in Canada, as well as secondary material from a previous comparative research in France and Canada, we present some evidence on the evolution of work in the banking sector. The data concerns particularly the traditional job of teller and the newer job of credit agent or 'financial counsellor'[1], as well as the emergence of new qualifications for using the new computerized equipment installed in banking branches.

The research is based on in-depth interviews conducted with open questions at the head office of five different Canadian banks, including the cooperative one in which more detailed observation was conducted. In this last case, six branches of the institution were studied in more depth. In each of the six branches, we conducted observations of the whole process of decision-making concerning credit, from the moment a client presents a demand for credit to the final decision concerning his demand, in each of the six branches. We followed three or four demands in each branch, varying the types of credit decisions (personal, business, accepted and refused credit). At some point, we interviewed each of the persons who participated in the decision at some point to determine how the work was done. We also conducted similar observations with agents starting to work with an experimental expert system for credit decision-making. All of this led us to observe that new qualifications are required of credit agents and tellers, the two main job categories which we studied in detail. In fact, we concluded that it is a combination of computerization and product innovation, resulting in part from the deregulation of the financial sector, that brings about this change in the qualifications of personnel required at the level of local branches.

To a certain extent, particularly in commercial credit activities, 'professionalized knowledge' (more formal diplomas and financial experience) is taking over from 'local empirical knowledge' of the workers responsible for credit operations. The same evolution is observed in the credit commissions, that is an elected body of representatives of the 'local milieu', which characterizes cooperative banking institutions and is responsible for credit decisions, but we will concentrate here on the effects on the front office work force, particularly as concerns tellers and financial counsellors or agents.

Evidence indicates that computer and product innovation, as well as deregulation, clearly develop professionalization in the banking sector, as we observed in our research on the banking sector in Canada and in France, and this is particularly clear in the analysis of training activities. Training is less centered on empirical, 'on the job' observation and 'trial and error' activities. Formal training and theoretical learning, computer assisted training and work activities are becoming more and more important.

However, while Braverman (1976) and Marglin (1973) indicated computerization would result in a stronger division of labour and dequalification of all workers concerned, there is no unilinear trend in terms of dequalification or increased qualification of work in the banking sector. Evolutions are diverse and sometimes contradictory depending on the organisation concerned or specific branch studied. We explain this diversity of evolutions observed in a non-deterministic fashion.[2] We consider that human resources management strategies (and not just technology) largely determine the outcomes in terms not only of job content, but also in terms of the construction of qualifications needed in the use of specific equipment and the way in which these qualifications are obtained, i.e. through internal development of training or through the external labour market.

1. NEW FORMS OF INNOVATION, COMPUTERIZATION AND NEW QUALIFICATIONS

Innovation in the banking sector appears to take different forms as competition evolves. Over the last decades forms of innovation have been twofold. The recent strategic objectives of banking institutions (end of the 80s and beginning of 90s) are somewhat different from those of the 60s and 70s, although they are not totally unrelated, and this impacts on the type of qualifications needed. In the 60s and 70s, innovation in the banking sector mainly referred to technological change aimed at an increase in the processing capacity, and a reduction of the need for personnel.

The objective was mainly to replace human resources by machines as far as possible in order to meet the formidable increase in demand for processing services. In recent years, with the demographic decline in most industrialised countries and the saturation of traditional banking markets, banks are searching for new niches for profit. In this perspective, they are developing new products, new financial product innovations with *more value-added* than previous products/services. This is all the more so since the 'baby bust', which characterizes Canada as well as many other industrialised economies (but which is apparently much more sudden in Canada and also follows one of the strongest 'baby booms'), brings banks to seek new ways to attract the diminishing clientele. As the number of clients cannot be expected to increase over the next decades as much as in the post-war years, banks have adopted the strategy of 'mature' industries, which look to 'diversified quality production' for maintaining their profits.[3]

In the case of the banking sector, as in most service sectors, offering 'diversified quality products' actually means *diversified quality services*. While traditional banking services could rely on a rather unspecialized work force, often with only high school education, the new financial packages and counselling functions require a professional work force, not only capable of offering and delivering financial services but also competent to perform some financial analysis in a credit or investment perspective. Of course not all of the work force which is called upon for this professionalization, but as Automatic Teller Machines and other computerized services develop, all institutions clearly indicate that a larger part of their work force will be composed of professionals or semi-professionals of the financial field (financial analysts, credit and investment specialists, financial counsellors, etc.).

While the first generation of computerized technologies introduced in the banking sector aimed at mass production of calculations and processes, and did not require very highly qualified personnel, the recent period is centered on a more sophisticated treatment capacity which assists not only in calculations, but also in management, marketing, financial analysis, etc.[4] Associated with this different type of technologies, the new competitive strategy based on quality and diversity requires more qualified human resources.

It is therefore a search for product/service innovation which now leads the process of technological change and which illustrates the type of strategy necessary to renew competitiveness in 'mature industries' such as banking. This change in objectives, from assistance in the mass production of standardised goods (in this case, banking services) to the development of a diversified production of quality (strong value-added) services, has clear consequences in terms of the type of technologies and qualification of human resources required. In this paper, we concentrate on the evolution of the required qualifications.

2. TRANSFORMATIONS IN THE NATURE OF WORK

While the first phases of automation centred on the automation of basic non skilled tasks which had been organised along the lines of Taylorism (division between conception and execution), and therefore implied a disappearance of various manual tasks, more recent transformations imply new computerized functions which require an active participation of more qualified workers who must have a wider range of knowledge on the work process and content. Tasks that have been transformed by this more recent phase of computerization have become *more abstract and more diversified*. The teller's job is a good example of this increasing level of abstraction and diversity, not to say of *complexity*.[5] Credit agents' tasks have also become more abstract and more complex.

Although it is often considered 'easy work', as a lot of office work is often seen from the exterior, a teller's work should in fact be considered rather complex[6]. As is the case for credit agents, job complexity has increased over the years, particularly of late with the introduction of new products and services, and the increase in quality of service required by customers. Complexity is defined here on the basis of its diversity, of its level of abstraction, of interruptions of given tasks by other more urgent ones, and of the need to anticipate possible errors and malfunctioning of equipment[7], this last element being particularly important in the case of credit agents. An agent or teller's work is therefore considered complex because of the level of abstraction required for many of the tasks which involve work with computers, because of its increasing diversity (tasks, products and services), as well as because of the frequent interruptions of work in the case of the teller particularly. In the case of credit agents, the new expert system requires a sequential integration of information and therefore exerts more strain on memory. If the agent does not want to have to ask the client for information which he has just given voluntarily, in relation with another question, he or she must recall the information to be entered on the computer later on in the process. When things were done on paper, the agent just flipped the paper over and wrote down the information in the appropriate space.

In terms of abstraction, an important number of operations that used to be done manually are now done with computers and require the use of an increasing number of codes. A high level of mental work is needed to perform tasks such as planning of activities, analysis and filing of data, calculations, as well as various checks. All this requires a good dose of concentration and memorization.

As concerns the diversity of work, the organization of work in the banking sector as in many services, is usually not based on a precise division of labour. Personnel is called upon to do different tasks, to replace other workers, as 'work rules' are not as rigid as is the case in the manufacturing sector.[8] With the deregulation of the financial sector, new activities are now part of banking and this implies new tasks for the bank employees. Tasks related to investment planning, insurance, etc., are now introduced in banking agencies.[9] Financial agents and tellers often have to assume administrative functions, and these have not diminished with the arrival of computers. On the contrary, for tellers, controls and checks are part of the work, as are balancing cash, inter-bank compensation, putting cash in the Automated Teller Machines, etc. For credit agents, controls and checks of information given by the client with other financial institutions and with the credit bureau (reimbursement rates) are also an important part of the process.

Finally, interruptions refer to the fact that check-up phone calls with financial institutions and other activities often have to be taken up some time after having started another task, more urgent tasks sometimes temporarily interrupting the work. This implies a higher level of mental activity than is obvious at first sight, as has often been indicated by ergonomists.[10]

This complexity of tellers' and agents' work is often masked by the fact that management usually assumes that machines and computers will make the work easier, that tellers and agents will be able to do things more quickly and will therefore have more time to spend trying to sell new products and services to clients. This 'sales' function is a new task which has been introduced in the work in relation with the development of diversified quality services. Since tellers have contact with clients when they come to deposit checks or to get cash, they are asked to inform the clients of the new products and services which banks are eager to sell in the new context of financial sector deregulation: financial analysis and planning, executive banking services (including credit and investment), brokerage services, insurance, etc.

3. COMPUTERIZATION AND THE EVOLUTION OF JOB STRUCTURES

The increasing importance of product diversification brings about an increase in the number of employees in the counselling and professional categories, while the traditional job categories (tellers and clerks) become less important in the job structures. Tables 1, 2 and 3 illustrate the point clearly for the institution studied.

The percentage of employees in the financial counselling sector went from 3 % in 1975 to 4 % in 1980 and more than doubled to 11 % in 1986. Over the same period (1975-1986), junior clerks went from 12 % to 5 %, and tellers from 44 % to 40 %. Table 2 indicates clearly, for all sizes of branches, that the professionals and technicians are the only category which has known an increase, except for office workers in small branches; in this last case, it must be noted that very small branches are becoming less numerous, but also that they imply a greater flexibility of personnel, and sometimes a less extended range of financial products. Table 3 gives more detailed data, but again shows that the agents responsible for financial counselling of various types (credit, savings, etc.) benefit from the highest increase in numbers.

Table 1- Distribution by category, in percentage terms, 1975-1980-1986

	1975	1980	1986
Total	---	14,000	20,000
Junior clerk	12 %	4 %	5 %
Teller	44 %	44 %	40 %
Senior clerk	11 %	11 %	16 %
Secretary	5 %	3 %	3 %
Agent(counsel)	3 %	4 %	11 %
Accountant	8 %	6 %	1 %
Directors	10 %	10 %	6 %
Others	7 %	18 %	18 %

Source: Tremblay (1989)

Table 2- Variation in large categories of workers according to size of branch (1980-1985)

Size	Management	Technical/Professional	Office
0-9.99	-7,9 %	+4,7 %	+3,4 %
10-29.99	-3,6 %	+6,7 %	-2,7 %
30 and over	-0,8 %	+4,7 %	-3,3 %

Source: Tremblay (1989)

Table 3- Variation of detailed job categories by size of branch (in equivalent full time jobs),1980-1985

	0-9.99	10-29.99	30 et +	Total
Jr clerk	-1,2 %	+0,5 %	+3,2 %	+0,7 %
Teller	-0,1 %	-5,1 %	-2,7 %	-4,0 %
Sr clerk	+5,1 %	+4,9 %	+1,9 %	+4,8 %
Secretary	-1,0 %	-1,1 %	-0,2 %	-0,7 %
Office supervisor	-2,9 %	-1,2 %	-1,1 %	-1,9 %
Accountant	-5,9 %	-3,9 %	-1,7 %	-4,3 %
Agent-counsel	+1,1 %	+4,1 %	+1,0 %	+3,2 %
Agent current op.	+3,9 %	+2,6 %	+1,8 %	+2,7 %
Other tech. prof.	+0,6 %	+1,6 %	+2,8 %	+1,8 %
Ass. dir. counsel	---	-0,9 %	+0,1 %	-0,3 %
Ass. dir. curr. op.	+0,4 %	+1,4 %	+0,6 %	+1,1 %
Dir. 1st level	+1,0 %	---	---	-1,0 %
Dir. 2nd level	1,8 %	-2,0 %	-0,9 %	-2,5 %
Dir. 3rd level	---	+1,7 %	+0,5 %	+1,2 %

Source: Tremblay (1989)

4. COMPUTERIZATION AND THE CONSTRUCTION OF NEW QUALIFICATIONS

Although not affecting all of the work force, there is a trend towards a certain professionalization in the sense of 'closing' up a labour market and exclusion of workers who do not have the new qualifications required to work with the new equipement and to offer customized diversified financial services and products. At the present time, management of banking institutions is still undecided as to the strategy it will adopt in order to obtain these new qualifications, but it is nevertheless very busy in defining and constructing the new qualification required for tellers' work as well as for the more specialised work of financial counsellors. In this sense, in the deregulation context, the banking sector (as with many other financial activities) is clearly the object of a process of *construction of qualification* or a *closing* of labour markets.

As Doeringer and Piore (1971) indicate, the main factors which contribute to the development of internal labour markets are the *specificity of qualification and technology of a firm*, the desire to reinforce social cohesion of a group of workers, as well as to ensure loyalty of the workers. These elements are clearly present in the banking institutions' actual objectives. The goal of such a construction as internal or closed labour markets is to attach a group of workers to the firm by organizing mobility files and wages in such a way that workers possessing specific qualifications essential to the firm, and for which substitutes are not easy to find, will be inclined to remain with the firm. Those who do not possess the newly required qualifications will be pushed out of the firm by management practices which tend to make them more unstable through non-standard forms of employment, lack of wage progression and other similar practices[11].

The construction of a new professional category is not easy. The process of professionalization of new categories in the banking sector faces some difficulties. It is not easy to ensure loyalty of the whole group while transforming some elements of the mobility files, particularly as concerns access to the most interesting jobs and wages. It is no easier to counter individual defections and loss of loyalty from traditional occupational categories not called upon for entry into the newly formed 'closed' labour market related to specialized financial and credit activities, while differentiation and inequality in the employment system are increasing (expansion of the hierarchy).

5. FORMAL VERSUS INFORMAL 'ON THE JOB' KNOWLEDGE

In the coming years, banks will expect their personnel to be able to handle various dimensions of credit or investment analysis, with the help of computer support systems. Formal knowledge therefore becomes more important than it used to be. This shows up not only in the job descriptions, but also in training offered in the financial sector. Training is increasingly centred on theoretical learning, understanding of banking, credit and investment activities, not only on acquisition of more empirical knowledge, through 'on-the-job' observation and trial and error activities. However, for many of the new financial counselling jobs, qualifications required go far beyond the level of internal on-the-job training. Only for tellers and other low level office jobs is internal training considered sufficient.

This new strategy exerts some strain on the employment system and general organization of most banks. The employees who are most firmly embedded in local environments are often those who most cruelly lack the newly valued professional qualifications. Their informal knowledge is however important for customized service, which is more and more important in the present competitive context. On the other hand, future professional prospects who have the required qualifications and could do an excellent job on the professional side usually do not come from the local environment. Banks are trying to solve this dilemma, as they would like to obtain the new qualifications required by diversified quality services and more complex technologies without losing on its traditional grounds of local knowledge, as well as loyalty.

The present evolution of banking activities questions the relative importance of formal professional financial knowledge and more informal knowledge on people of the business and general community, the latter being sometimes as useful as the former in assuring sound credit decisions. Credit decisions are amongst the most crucial banking activities, if not the most crucial, and they therefore reveal what is at stake, the relative importance of informal and formal knowledge in credit and other banking activities.

A large part of our survey concerned human resources management practices, as they are in our view determinant in the adjustment process to new technologies and qualifications. This led us to define two main strategies or attitudes which can be used by banks in order to obtain the new qualifications required by process and product innovation.

6. CONSTRUCTION OF QUALIFICATION AND HUMAN RESOURCES MANAGEMENT

In the context of technological change and product innovation, firms are looking for new qualifications and can use different human resources management strategies in order to reach their goal of a requalification of their employment system. Criteria, rules and various characteristics of the employment and hiring systems are touched, some being destroyed and replaced by new rules or criteria, new ones appearing. Thus, the qualifications required for the new jobs tend to impose new criteria for hiring, for internal mobility, etc. All parameters of employment are not destroyed instantly, but many characteristics of the employment systems can be modified, the relative value of different skills or qualifications can be changed.

Our analysis of employers' strategies in the banking sector has led us to define two main categories of human resources management strategies use to adjust to change, particularly in the context of technological innovation. The first can be called a strategy of 'flexibilization'[12] of the employment system. It rests mainly on the use of the external labour market for access to jobs, but also on the development of non-standard forms of employment (short term contracts, occasional work, part time, etc.), as well as on wage adjustments, such as the reduction or elimination of cost-of-living adjustments (COLA clauses). The banks generally use the two first methods of flexibilization, wage adjustments in COLA clauses being more common in the manufacturing sectors.

The second strategy is one which aims at workers' stabilization in the internal labour market, their motivation and involvement in the 'firm's project'. This usually means more occupational training, development of a strong internal labour market, a more participatory work organization, etc.

A firm can very well rely simultaneously on both human resources management strategies identified earlier, either in different establishments or in one particular plant. It is even common, as we observed in the banking sector, to use different strategies for different occupational groups, and apparently even more so for different gender categories[13]. In the banking sector, and in offices in general, the duality of human resources management is particularly evident, since the internal labour market is generally closed to women, who are usually restricted to 'entry port jobs'[14].

These strategies are evidently very different in terms of methods, of job content and organization, of democratic or participatory dimensions[15] and of course, in terms of impact on the labour force. The first is a strategy of pure rationalization, of cost minimization through direct or indirect wage compressions, or through close adjustment of working hours to the volume of production (part time, occasional work, etc.) in order to ensure higher productivity of work. Workers pay the price of the firms' adjustment strategy in the sense that they are usually thrown out of their job and simply replaced by persons having the newly required qualifications.

The second is a more qualitative strategy which rests upon the internal development of qualification, the involvement of workers in the firm's project, their identification to the firm's 'culture' and their motivation to work being considered *determinant for productivity*. To a certain extent, it is a more 'modern' management strategy, resting on the belief that internal training, information and participation are the key elements to success not only in automation projects, but in any decision or strategy of the firm's.

It also appears to us that as concerns computer design, and therefore the possibilities for construction of qualification in a given computerized context, two possibilities are open and although firms rarely consider the two aspects simultaneously, computer design can in fact be related to the employment strategy. If the first strategy of flexibilization of the employment system is adopted, standardization of equipment and software may appear more efficient, as there is a strong turnover in personnel. However, if the second strategy of employment stabilization is chosen, it appears possible to develop local and user specific software. Therefore, there exists a relation between employment strategies and computer design strategies or possibilities, which in turn will determine possibilities open in terms of job qualification or job design.

At present banks still appear undecided between the two strategies; they actually use both, in different branches, for different gender categories, different age groups, etc. It must be added that as internal training is generally not very developed in Canadian and North-American firms, developing qualification and internal labour markets represents a certain change of organizational culture for a good number of banking institutions. Although it should be said that banks have always been amongst the Canadian firms that gave the most internal training to their employees, the training programs are generally very limited in scope as well as in length and formal recognition.[16]

It is important to note however that there exists a relation between employment strategies and computer design strategies or possibilities, which in turn will determine possibilities open in terms of qualification and job design. A strategy based on employment stabilization makes it possible to develop local and user specific software, while a strategy resting on flexibilization encourages high turnover and tends towards standardization of equipment and polarization of qualifications in job design. While the future still appears undetermined, it seems very few institutions and computer specialists think simultaneously in terms of job design, qualification of workers, and computer or software design.

REFERENCES

BERNIER, C. and TEIGER, C. (1987). Informatique et qualifications: les compétences masquées. In TREMBLAY, D.-G. (ed.). *Diffusion des nouvelles technologies: stratégies d'entreprises et évaluation sociale.* Special issue of the journal *Interventions économiques.* Montréal: Ed. Saint-Martin.

BRAVERMAN, H. (1976). *Travail et capitalisme monopoliste. La dégradation du travail au XXe siècle.* Paris: Maspéro. 359 p.

CORIAT, B. (1987). L'atelier flexible. *Les Cahiers français.* no 231. nai-juin. 30-35.

DOERINGER, P. and PIORE , M.J. (1971). *Internal labour markets and manpower analysis.* Lexington: D.C. Heath and Co. 211 p.

ECONOMIC COUNCIL OF CANADA (1987). L'encadrement du système financier. Ottawa: Economic Council of Canada.146 p.

FONDATION RESSOURCES-JEUNESSE (1989). *La formation et les jeunes en entreprises.* Rapport de recherche. octobre. 74 p.

KIRCHNER, E. J. (1983). *Conséquences sociales de l'introduction de nouvelles technologies dans le secteur bancaire.* Bruxelles: CEE. 145 p.

MARUANI, M. and NICOLE, C.(1988). Le clavier enchaîné; la construction de la différence. *Interventions économiques.* no 20-21. Montréal: Ed. Saint-Martin. Fall 1988. 123-134.

MERCHIERS, J. and TROUSSIER, J. F. (1988). L'analyse du travail: pratiques, concepts, enjeux. In *Formation Emploi.* no 23. July-Sept.

MICHON, F. (1988). Flexibilité et segmentation. *Interventions économiques.* no 19. Montréal: Ed. Saint-Martin. 45-71.

MARGLIN, S. (1973). Origines et fonctions de la parcellisation des tâches. *Critique de la division du travail.* Paris: Ed. du Seuil. 40-89.

MAURICE, M. (1980). Le déterminisme technologique dans la sociologie du travail (1955-1980). Un changement de paradigme? *Sociologie du travail.* Paris: Ed. du SEuil. no 1. 22-37.

MAYHEW, B.W. (1987). Relationship banking and the life cycle concept. *Canadian Banker.* mai-juin. 24-29.

MAYRAND, A. (1987). *Concentration et concurrence dans le secteur financier.* Ottawa: Document no 335, Conseil économique du Canada.65 p.

MOREAU, F. (1987a). La nouvelle réglementation du secteur financier. *Interventions Economiques.* No 18. Montréal: Ed. St-Martin.

PEITCHINIS, S.G. (1977). *Technological change in banking and their effects on employment.* Ottawa: Programme des études sur les innovations techniques, ministère de l'Industrie et du Commerce. Rapport de recherche. 16 p.

PINARD, R. et ROUSSEAU, T. (1985). L'informatisation dans les assurances et les banques au Québec. *Informatisation et bureautique.* Cahiers de recherche sociologique. Montréal: Université du Québec à Montréal. vol 3, no 2, 25-55.

POUPA-ROUAULT, M-M. (1986). *Méthodes d'analyse des processus d'appropriation de nouvelles technologies* (Etude de cas dans la banque). Doctoral disssertation for 3rd cycle thesis. Université de Paris I. 234 p.

ROSE, P.S. (1987). The changing bank customer: who,what, where, and how? *Canadian Banker.* mai-juin. 34-42.

SAINT-PIERRE, C. (1987). Le tertiaire en mouvement: bureautique et organisation du travail. Itinéraire d'une recherche. in TREMBLAY, D.-G. dir. (1987). *Diffusion des nouvelles technologies: stratégies d'entreprises et évaluation sociale.* Montréal: Ed. Saint-Martin. 304 p. 185-198.

122

SORGE, A. and STREEK, W. (1987). *Industrial Relations and Technical Change: The Case for an Extended Perspective.* Discussion paper no IIM/LMP 87-1. Berlin: WZB. 37 p.

STONEMAN, P. (1983). *The economic analysis of technological change.* New-York: Oxford University Press. 265 p.

TREMBLAY, D. G. (1990). *Economie du travail: les réalités et les approches théoriques.* Montréal: Editions Saint-Martin et Télé-Université. 544 p.

TREMBLAY, D.-G. (1990a). Technological innovation, work and participation: An institutionalist approach based on an analysis of employment systems. Forthcoming in Szell, G. (ed.) *Concise Encyclopedia of Participation and Management.* Berlin: Walter de Gruyter.

TREMBLAY, D.-G. (1990b). *L'emploi en devenir.* Québec: Institut québécois de recherche sur la culture. 120p.

TREMBLAY, D.-G. (1990c). *Technological innovation, employment systems and work organization: an analysis based on the Canadian banking sector.* Paper delivered to session no 3 of RC 30 of the International Sociological Association, Madrid, July 1990. Available through SA Abstracts.

TREMBLAY, D.-G. (1989). *La dynamique économique du processus d'innovation; une analyse de l'innovation et du mode de gestion des ressources humaines dans le secteur bancaire canadien.* Doctoral thesis delivered to the Université de Paris I, Panthéon-Sorbonne. Paris: Université de Paris I. 2 volumes. 711 pages.

TREMBLAY, D.-G. (1988). Technological change, internal labour markets and women's jobs. The case of the banking sector. *Women, Work and Computerization.* Amsterdam: Elsevier Science Publishers-North Holland Press. 263-272.

ZARIFIAN, P. (1987). Du taylorisme au systémisme: une nouvelle approche de la qualification dans l'industrie. *Cahier de recherche no 8.* Paris: GIP Mutations industrielles. 27 p.

FOOTNOTES

[1] Different titles are given to this job which has appeared recently: executive banking counsellor, financial counsellor and credit counsellor are the most common in English Canada, and "agent-conseil, conseiller, conseiller au crédit, conseiller financier" are the most common in French-speaking Québec.

[2] On the question of technological determinism see Maurice (1980), Saint-Pierre (1987) and Tremblay (1989).

[3] See Sorge and Streek (1987) or Tremblay (1990c) on this concept.

[4] As for most of the information collected in the case study, this information comes from analysis of internal documents and open interviews with different representatives of the institutions considered, as well as documentary evidence collected in banking journals and other specialized publications. For more information on the methodology, see chapter 1 of Tremblay (1989).

[5] On the definition of complexity, see Merchiers and Troussier (1988).

[6] As was shown by Poupa-Rouault, M.-M. (1986).

[7] The definition is that of Merchiers and Troussier (1988).

[8] See Osterman (1987) and Tremblay (1989; 1990c) on the differences between industrial and salaried (services) employment systems.

[9] See Economic Council of Canada (1987).

[10] See Bernier and Teiger (1987).

[11] See Tremblay (1990, 1990a) on the details of these management practices.

[12] See Michon (1988) or Tremblay (1990b).

[13] See Maruani (1988).

[14] See Tremblay (1988, 1988a).

[15] See Tremblay (1990c).

[16] On this question, we did a survey with the Chamber of commerce of Montreal, survey which indicated that one firm out of two had no personnel department, no training policy and no training budget. See Fondation Ressources-Jeunesse (1989).

HUMAN JOBS AND COMPUTER INTERFACES
M.I. Nurminen and G.R.S. Weir
Elsevier Science Publishers B.V. (North-Holland)
© 1991 IFIP. All rights reserved.

Office Applications Panel: Chairman's summary

Sture Hägglund, *University of Linköping, Sweden*

Panelists:

Donald L. Day, *Syracuse University, U.S.A*
Virpi Ruohomäki, *Helsinki University of Technology, Finland*
William S. Solomon, *Rutgers University, U.S.A*
Diane Gabrielle Tremblay, *University of Quebec, Canada*

The impact of automation and computerization on the job environment for office applications was the topic for a panel discussion with four contributors. This short paper will attempt to summarize a number of issues and problems of relevance for human jobs and computer interfaces in the office environment, as approached by the panel. These issues will be related to the essential findings reported in the contributed papers and to the ideas brought forward in the panel discussion.

The panel set out to address primarily the following themes:

• Job satisfaction, content, security, etc. Empirical findings.

• Evolution of jobs and effects on required qualifications and skills.

• Productivity issues vs. job and product quality.

• Deficiences in user interfaces: are there persisting problems?

• Relationsship between types of tasks and health problems?

• Solutions to problems: training, technology improvement, job design.

The contributed papers dealt with issues of introducing computer support for certain professions. Two of the papers focused on the effects of mechanizing individual work with computer support, namely Solomon's and Day's. The other two, by Ruohomäki and Vartiainen and by Tremblay, dealt with situations where the communication with a client is an important aspect for the design and analysis of a computerized support system. In the following we will discuss this and some other pertinent aspects of human jobs and computer interfaces in office applications.

Implications of client contacts

An interesting issue is thus whether there are any fundamental differences in situations where computer support is introduced for the individual office professional in isolation or in contact with a client respectively. Obviously the presence of a client in the human-computer cummunication process introduces significant complications. Ruohomäki's as well as Tremblay's studies indicate that in many cases the computer system plays a less important role than might be expected in the communication with the customer. Verbal interaction and non-computerized information retrieval also influence the work process to a very high degree. In Ruohomäki's studies and corresponding analyses of activities in an insurance office, the importance of social and emotional requirements in the process of communication with customers was pointed out. In general much remains to be studied regarding the effects of introducing computer support upon the user-client-computer contact as well as regarding how to design such systems in an effective way.

On the other hand we have the experience of introducing computer support for individual professionals, as reported by for instance Solomon. He presented and reflected upon the effects of computerization of newspaper copy editors work, in particular their attitudes towards the use of computer terminals, as studied both before 1985 and in a current investigation. A significant change of attitudes in favour of computer support was documented. In the first study, users referred to a lot of technical problems concerning reliability and robustness in the computerized work, while the later study mentions problems related to the copy editing work rather than with the computer system per se. Solomon's studies indicate that once a general familiarity with computer-based work was attained by the copy editors, no major problems persisted. An important issue that remains to be researched is however the impact of different workplace structures, e.g. cooperative instead of hierarchical, and changes in skills and tasks, in connection with the introduction of new technology.

Impact on flexibility in job design

A special issue of interest is whether the introduction of computer support will promote automation of office work or allow more flexible job design. In the short perspective, it appears that computerization of tasks tends to result in a stronger division of labour and dequalification of workers concerned. Solomon reported from copy editing work that the computerized systems confined editors both physically and technically, at least with first generation technology. However, this is not a unilinear trend. Tremblay argues that, for instance in the banking sector, it is basically the human resources management strategies (and not just the technology push) that determines effects on job content and qualifications needed.

Formalization of office work

An issue of much concern is whether the introduction of computer support leads to more or to less formalized ways of solving office tasks. The are certainly reasons to believe that in order to achieve the full potential of mechanization and automation, it is necessary to formalize and standardize the ways information is recorded and tasks are solved. On the other hand, as has been pointed out by the Swedish pioneer in theoretical analysis of information systems, Börje Langefors, there is curiously enough a small-scale economy for information. That is, the cost of producing, maintaining and exchanging information in a standardized format might be higher than the profits gained. At the same time, modern software technology promotes decentralized development of information systems and office applications with increasing efficiency, resulting in systems based on local control of information with a minimized need to communicate data.

This leads to the conclusion, that although studies such as Solomon's indicate that computer-based tools restrict and confine the ways in which tasks can be carried out, as compared with previous manual routines, we should be prepared to explore the possibilities of using the computer to support also processing of less formal information. Tremblay's and Ruohomäki's studies of client contacts in banking and insurance show that but a limited part of the information exchange follows the formalized structure of the computerized routines. Current development in the area of expert systems or knowledge-based system also emphasize the support for knowledge management and communication and support for making decisions based on incomplete and fuzzy information, rather than being systems for automating office tasks and problem solving.

Standardization or customized interfaces

Another problematic issue is to weigh the advantages of standardization and customization respectively against each other. And also; can we create systems adapted to local needs and user preferences or should we accept that standardized technical solutions set limits for how tasks are carried out? Thus we might have a situation where economical or technical facts force us to use a uniform interface to a system, rather than allowing the end user to participate in the development process and influence the final design.

But this issue is even more problematic than that. There are strong arguments in favour of both having standardized interfaces which look the same across a wide range of applications and for different users doing similar things, as well as allwoing customization depending on the task environment and individual preferences. It is well known and documented from many studies that the successful introduction of computerized services presumes that systems closely mimic previous manual routines. This may be in conflict with the desire to build systems that conform with the environment of computer-based services and standardized information representation rather than with the manual application. Present trends in designing system interfaces building on metaphors from office tasks significantly contribute to diminishing these problems, but there will always be a trade-off left between the virtues of standardization and customization respectively.

Strategies for the future

To wind up the discussion in the previous sections of this short paper, we will try to indicate some of the directions for future development identified by the panelists. For instance, Solomon emphasized the need to study how different workplace structures, e.g. cooperative as opposed to hierachical, affect and interact with systems solutions. Ruohomäki describe how activity studies on different levels can be used to improve our understanding and form the basis for better job design and system solutions.

In his paper on human factors in the electronic newsroom, Day reviewed productivity issues, quality assurance, employee health, regulation and humanitarian concerns. Day points out training, task management and informed supervision as important aspects in dealing with the work environment impact of technological changes.

Tremblay discussed computerization and the construction of new qualifications in the banking sector. Her studies of the evolution of job structures led to a definition of two main categories of human resource management strategies to handle change in the context of technological innovation. One characterized by pure rationalization and one more oriented towards internal development of qualifications. The latter one being a more "modern" strategy resting on the belief that internal training, information and participation are key elements for success.

When we discuss today the effects and potential of computerization of office work, it is important to consider whether the results of empirical studies can be used to anticipate and predict what will happen in the future. It seems that the rapid development of new technology and the interdependence of technology and job design makes it extremely difficult to identify inherent effects of computerization. This serves to confirm the importance attributed by several of the panelists to the active use of human resource management strategies for achieving desired goals.

A notable aspect of the computer perceived as a tool in the office environment, is that there are strong indications that computer support will serve to increase rather than decrease differences in individual performance and productivity. This is in contrast with traditional automation, which controlled productivity levels and made people more exchangeable. This trend will become even stronger when the tools become more sofisticated and the number of tools increase.

A crucial issue for the future is thus the one of training and competence development. Presently training in the context of computerization often means learning technical details of the systems. It is however reasonable to believe that when the technology to build better user interfaces mature and computer literacy becomes a natural ingredient in every professional workers background, the need for this kind of technical training will decrease if not disappear. Then active training programs for developing professional competence focusing on how to use the computer as an effective tool in a given domain of application, will become a key issue for releasing the full potential of both the human resource and the computer.

Contributed papers:

William S. Solomon: Skills, tasks and technology: Editors and the VDT, (Department of Journalism and Mass Media, Rutgers University, U.S.A).

Donald L. Day: Human factors issues in the electronic newsroom: A briefing guide for media managers, (ibid.).

Virpi Ruohomäki, Matti Vartiainen: Formalization of the activity requirements in an insurance office, (ibid.).

Diane Gabrielle Tremblay: Computerization and the construction of new qualifications in the context of product and process innovation in the banking sector, (ibid.).

Section 5

Feedback and Cooperation

HUMAN JOBS AND COMPUTER INTERFACES
M.I. Nurminen and G.R.S. Weir
Elsevier Science Publishers B.V. (North-Holland)
© 1991 IFIP. All rights reserved.

Computerized Feedback Effects on Feedback Seeking, Performance and Motivation

A. N. Kluger[a], S. Adler[b], and C. Fay[a]

[a]Department of Industrial Relations and Human Resources, Institute of Management and Labor Relations, Rutgers University, Kilmer Campus, New Brunswick, New Jersey 08903-5062, USA

[b]Department of Management, Stevens Institute of Technology, Hoboken, New Jersey 07030, USA

Abstract

Results of two laboratory experiments suggest that: (a) People are very likely to seek feedback from a computer, and very unlikely to seek similar feedback from another person (b) both human and computer outcome feedback may have no effect or even negative effect on performance and motivation in comparison to a no-feedback control group. The latter results seem to be independent of whether feedback was requested or given automatically and whether it was intra-individual (correct/incorrect) or normative (relative to others).

1. INTRODUCTION

In many jobs and educational settings the provision of virtually continuous and accurate computerized performance feedback is technically feasible (U.S. Congress, OTA, 1987). This feasibility has led to much discussion concerning the merits of computer-mediated performance feedback (cf. Lepper & Chabay, 1985) but little experimental research. The benefits of computer-mediated performance feedback may include, but are not limited to, a higher likelihood that people will seek feedback (if it is optional), increased motivation, and superior performance. In this paper we report experimental comparisons of the relative benefits of computer-mediated performance feedback to (a) person-mediated performance feedback and to (b) no feedback. These comparisons will answer two questions: (a) Is computerized feedback superior to human feedback and (b) should computerized feedback be provided at all? Answering these questions may serve to guide software programmers, both in education and work settings, in implementing feedback features into computer programs.

We distinguish between performance feedback and other types of feedback such as personal feedback (e.g., "he doesn't like you"), and task feedback (e.g., a beep sound from the computer when the user hit an illegal key). This paper addresses only the issue of performance feedback. However, for the sake of brevity the term feedback is used throughout this paper.

Ashford and Cummings (1983) argued that people tend to avoid directly seeking feedback from others even if the feedback is important to oneself. This avoidance is caused by fear of "loss of face". Of course, when one deems the value of the information more important than the risk of loss of face, one will overcome this fear and will seek feedback. However, self-generated feedback or task-generated feedback-- which do not involve potential loss of face-- are both preferred to feedback provided by others (Greller, 1980; Herold, Liden & Leatherwood, 1987).

Computers may not be perceived as a threat to ones' "face": The inanimate computer is not evaluating the person, and therefore people may not find computer feedback as aversive as they may find feedback from another person. Thus, one advantage of computers over humans is that they may be more likely to elicit feedback seeking.

A study by Karabenick and Knapp (1988) indirectly supports this prediction. Subjects were given the option of requesting corrective information after each failure on several trials of a construct formation task. While 86% of subjects asked for help from a computer, only 36% asked for help from the computer when they believed that another person was giving them help through a computer network. In the Karabenick and Knapp study, the opportunity to seek help was available only after feedback about success or failure had already been given by the computer. It is still not clear if the preference for computer-mediated *help* found in their study will generalize to the search for performance *feedback* itself. Furthermore, in the Karabenick and Knapp study the person-mediated help was provided through the computer network by an invisible, anonymous person. It has been reported that an "unseen audience" (Criddle, 1971) has more negative effects on decision-making performance than the presence of a "seen audience". It may well be that the inhibited help-seeking effect observed by Karabenick and Knapp (1988) was a result of the invisibility of the person who "helped" and not solely due to fact that it was a person. Thus, in this study feedback was made available directly from a person, and it was hypothesized that:

H_1. *Subjects given the opportunity to request feedback from a computer will chose to do so more often than will subjects given the opportunity to request feedback from a person.*

A second advantage of computer-mediated feedback over person-mediated feedback may be improved performance. Indeed, Earley (1988) found that computerized feedback was more trusted, led to a higher feeling of self-efficacy, and to better performance than identical feedback from the manager in a mail order processing job. We sought to determine whether the beneficial effect of computer-mediated feedback on (motivation and) performance will be replicated when the feedback is given automatically without the user's request and to extend Earley's finding regrading performance to a different task and environment. Accordingly our second hypothesis was:

H_2. *The motivation and performance of subjects receiving feedback from a computer will be higher than the motivation and performance of subjects receiving feedback from a person.*

Although the little empirical evidence available suggests that computer-mediated feedback has superior effects to person-mediated feedback, it is not clear at all that the provision of any feedback is always desirable. Kroll, Levy, and Rapoport (1988) reported that subjects engaged in stock-portfolio management simulation sought hundreds of pieces of information (outcome feedback) from the computer. They did so in spite of the warning that the information they retrieved was a "random walk" of stocks and that they lost time for each piece of information retrieved. Jacoby, Mazursky, Troutman and Kuss (1984) found in a computerized simulation of the security analyst job employing security analysts as subjects, that better performers were *less* likely to search outcome feedback from a computer than poorer decision makers. Although Jacoby et al.'s design was correlational, their data suggest that outcome feedback may impede performance.

Indeed, while most research has shown that performance can be improved by specific and task-relevant feedback (Ammons, 1956; Ilgen, Fisher & Taylor, 1979; and Kopelman, 1986), there is evidence that outcome feedback (i.e., correct/incorrect), in contrast to process feedback, may have negative effects on the learning and performance of complex tasks (Azuma & Cronbach, 1964; Hammond & Summers, 1972; and Hammond Summers and Deane, 1973; for a recent review see Balzer, Doherty, & O'Connor, 1989). In fact, most of these experiments showing negative effects for outcome feedback used computerized feedback. Furthermore, investigators of Computer Aided Instruction (Carroll & Kay, 1988; and Lepper & Gurtner, 1989) have suggested that CAI programs that provide feedback lead to inferior learning in comparison to CAI programs which do not provide feedback.

In a recent study (Kluger, Adler & Reilly, 1989), subjects who were solving advanced mathematical questions showed lower performance when given computerized outcome feedback, relative to subjects who worked on the same task but were given no feedback. In an attempt to replicate this finding, the same experimental task was used in the present study. Note that the task-- solving mathematical questions --is complex, and that the feedback provided was on outcome, i.e., correct/incorrect. Both task complexity and outcome feedback may be responsible for the negative feedback effects observed. Task complexity was suggested as a moderator of feedback effects (e.g., Hammond & Summers, 1972) but was not directly manipulated. In addition, other motivational interventions such as incentives (Eysenck, 1982) and goal setting (Kanfer & Ackerman, 1989) have been shown to have negative effects when applied to complex tasks. The goal of this study is to test the hypothesis that outcome feedback will have negative effects on a complex task.

Based on the above discussion and previous findings (Kluger et al., 1989), it was predicted that:

H_3. *Outcome feedback will have a negative effect on motivation and performance.*

In the present paper we report results of two studies. In both studies we compared the effects of computer-mediated feedback to person-mediated feedback, and the effects of feedback to conditions of no feedback. However, in each study feedback was manipulated in two ways. In Study 1 we manipulated feedback format and contrasted the effects of offering the subjects the opportunity to request feedback to the effects of receiving automatic feedback. Using the automatic feedback condition allowed us to assess whether control over the receipt of feedback is an important determinant of motivation and performance (Ryan, 1982). The results did not show any meaningful difference between the effects of requested feedback and automatic feedback. In Study 2 we manipulated the content of *requested* feedback and contrasted the effect of feedback which only provided corrective outcome (as in Study 1) to feedback that provided information on both outcome and normative feedback (comparison to others). The inclusion of two types of feedback manipulation in each study, permitted us to generalize the results beyond a specific feedback operationalization. In addition, Study 2 allowed us to replicate the results of Study 1 with a different task and subjects population.

2. METHOD: STUDY 1

2.1 subjects
Ninety seven undergraduate engineering students participated in the experiment. They were paid $6.00 each for their participation.

2.2 Setting
The experiment was conducted in a computer laboratory. Dividers were placed between computer work stations so that subjects could not observe each other. Instructions, the experimental task, and dependent measures were all administered on the computer.

2.3 Dependent variables
The experimental task consisted of questions extracted from retired Advanced Graduate Record Examinations (GRE) in Mathematics. Seven questions were chosen to serve as the initial task. Based on pre-testing, the probability of answering a question correctly ranged from .09 to .62. Items were selected within this difficulty range so that performance on the initial task would have an approximately normal distribution. In the pretest sample, the mean performance was 3.13 (*sd*=1.86) items correct out of seven items. The number of items correct was the performance measure.

In this study we provided accurate performance feedback. Most subjects accordingly received a mix of correct (positive) and incorrect (negative) feedback messages. Although feedback sign is a potent variable in determining the effect of feedback on motivation, its effects are complex: (a) under some circumstances positive feedback may have negative effects on motivation (Koestner, Zuckerman, & Koestner, 1987; Deci & Ryan, 1985), and on skilled performance (Baumeister, Hutton, & Cairns, 1990) (b) negative feedback may have more beneficial effects on motivation than positive feedback (Podsakoff & Farh, 1987; and Mikulincer, 1988). However, the difficulty of the experimental task was such that for most subjects the overall feedback sign was neither extremely positive nor extremely negative. Therefore, contamination of the results by feedback sign was minimized.

Twenty-three additional mathematical questions taken from the same set of GRE examinations were used to capture intrinsic task motivation behaviorally. Once the initial seven-item experimental task was completed, subjects were given the opportunity to quit or to work on additional mathematical questions drawn from the pool of these 23 questions. After completing each additional question, subjects were given the opportunity to work on additional questions or to withdraw. Three behavioral measures of task motivation were computed: (1) Whether subjects chose to persist and complete any optional questions at all or withdraw immediately; (2) the total number of optional questions attempted; and (3) the total amount of time that the subject spent on the optional questions.

2.4 procedure

Two factors were manipulated in a 2x3 experimental design. Upon arrival at the laboratory for the experiment, subjects were randomly assigned to either the computer-mediated or person-mediated feedback source condition. Each subject was then randomly assigned to one of three feedback conditions: feedback only upon request; automatic feedback after every trial; or no feedback.

One third of the subjects were assigned to the condition in which feedback was provided only upon request. These subjects received a message on their computer screen after each response asking: "Would you like to see if your answer to the previous question was correct?" Depending on the feedback source condition to which they were assigned, they could then either hit a key on the computer or raise their hand in order to receive feedback. In the computer condition, if feedback was requested, a CORRECT! or INCORRECT! message appeared in the middle of a new screen . In the human condition, if feedback was requested a screen with the answer the subject had entered appeared (e.g., "1. d") and an experimenter compared the response on the screen to a scoring sheet and said "Correct" or "Incorrect". In all cases, feedback was accurate. H_1 was tested in this feedback upon request condition by comparing the rate of feedback requests in the two feedback source (computer/person) conditions.

One third of the subjects were provided performance feedback automatically after each item. The automatic feedback condition was needed to assure that differences between the feedback condition and the no feedback condition were not a function of the control over the feedback, or the amount of feedback available if some subjects declined to review their feedback. If the subject in the automatic feedback condition was assigned to receive computer-mediated feedback, every time that subject entered his or her response to an item, the feedback message - CORRECT! or INCORRECT! automatically appeared in the middle of a new screen. Subjects assigned to receive automatic person-mediated feedback were automatically instructed by the computer, after keying their response, to raise their hand and to wait for the experimenter who then checked the response on the screen and gave the "Correct" or "Incorrect" feedback message.

The remaining third of the subjects served as a control for the feedback manipulations. Two control groups were needed because the appropriate control for human feedback is a person who is present but does not give feedback. Subjects in the person/no feedback condition received a message asking them to raise their hand to call the experimenter after each response so that the experimenter could key a new item. Subjects in the computer/no feedback group received a new item upon keying their answer to each question, and worked alone just like the subjects in the computer-mediated feedback conditions.

Two characteristics of the task are worth noting. First, subjects receiving no feedback were asked to estimate the number of items they answered correctly; A correlation of .74 (n=29; p < .01) was found between their estimate and the actual number of items these subjects answered correctly, suggesting that the task used here contained high task based feedback. However, these subjects overestimated their performance by an average of 1.5 items (out of seven). Second, the items varied in content such that knowledge of results (correct or incorrect) on one item could not help the subjects to better answer any other item.

After answering the seven items comprising the initial experimental task, subjects were informed that the test was over but that they could continue to work on additional items. After each optional item, subjects were given the opportunity to continue or withdraw. Subject who persisted received feedback for the optional items consistent with their experimental assignment and in the same manner in which they had received feedback for the initial task.

3. RESULTS: STUDY 1

Hypothesis 1, which predicted greater feedback seeking when feedback is available upon request from a computer rather than a person, received strong support. Of the 14 subjects given the opportunity to receive person-mediated feedback, only one subject (7%) ever asked for feedback on the initial task and that subject only requested feedback on two out of the seven experimental items. In sharp contrast, 20 of the 21 (95%) of the subjects given the opportunity to receive computer-mediated feedback asked for feedback during the initial task, and these 20 subjects requested feedback on at least three of the seven items. Fifteen of these subjects (71%) asked for feedback on all seven items. The phi coefficient for the relationship between source of feedback and a dichotomous criterion of asking for feedback at least once was .88 ($p < .001$). In sum, the results strongly suggest that people are inhibited in seeking feedback from a person, while they are inclined to seek feedback from a computer.

The data for testing H_1 is derived from the experimental groups that received the option to request feedback. In contrast, testing H_2 and H_3 was based on data from all experimental groups. The intercorrelations among the dependent measures are given in Table 1. The intercorrelations among the measures of persistence, optional items attempted and optional time spent are inflated since all subjects who withdrew immediately received a score of zero on the remaining two motivational measures.

TABLE 1
Intercorrelations of the Dependent Variables

Variable	2	3	4
Performance	.11	.14	.07
Persistence	--	.76*	.68*
Optional time		--	.81**
Optional items			--

*$p < .05$. ** $p < .01$.

Prior to testing the hypotheses, we tested whether there were any differences between the automatic feedback and the feedback upon request condition, using an apriori contrast. No differences emerged on any of the dependent measures between these conditions (see means in Table 2). Therefore, the data from these conditions were collapsed into one feedback contrast.

Hypothesis H_2, predicting that computer-mediated feedback will yield higher motivation and performance than person-mediated feedback, was not supported. A series of t-tests indicated that none of the dependent variable means in the computer-mediated feedback condition were significantly higher than those in the person-mediated feedback condition. Furthermore, some means were in the direction opposite to the one predicted.

Table 3 shows 2 x 2 ANOVA results with feedback contrast (yes/no) as one factor, and source (computer/person) as the other factor. It indicates that H_3, which predicted negative performance and motivational effects of feedback, received mixed support. Subjects receiving feedback showed significantly lower motivation as measured by time spent on the optional items, compared to no feedback controls (see Table 3). Also, the marginal means for all dependent variables in the feedback conditions are all lower than they are in the control conditions. Finally, a significant feedback by source interaction was found for the performance measure ($F(1,95) = 5.82$, $p<.05$). A simple effects of feedback within the two feedback source conditions revealed that person-mediated feedback caused a decline in performance relative to no feedback controls, ($t(40) = 2.34$ $p<.05$), but that computer-mediated feedback caused no similar decline ($t(53) = -.85$. *n.s.*). In other words, feedback had a negative effect on performance only when the source of feedback was a person.

TABLE 2
Means and Standard Deviation by Experimental Groups

Variables	No Feedback		Requested FB		Automatic FB		Total	
	M	SD	M	SD	M	SD	M	SD
			Computer Feedback					
	N=16		N=21		N=18		N=55	
Perform	2.25	1.65	2.38	1.71	3.00	1.53	2.54	1.64
Persist	0.37	0.50	0.23	0.43	0.33	0.48	0.31	0.46
Time	449.31	666.86	65.90	189.52	141.22	266.05	202.09	430.89
Items	3.62	6.02	0.57	1.77	0.72	1.31	1.20	2.94
			Human Feedback					
	N=13		N=14		N=15		N=42	
Perform	4.53	1.80	3.35	1.59	2.80	2.17	3.52	1.97
Persist	0.46	0.51	0.21	0.42	0.33	0.48	0.33	0.47
Time	339.69	515.92	354.28	824.17	239.46	429.32	245.46	442.12
Items	1.30	2.09	1.42	3.61	1.93	3.30	1.57	3.03
			Total					
	N=29		N=35		N=33		N=97	
Perform	3.27	2.05	2.72	1.71	2.91	1.82	2.97	1.85
Persist	0.41	0.50	0.23	0.42	0.33	0.48	0.32	0.47
Time	400.17	596.15	101.17	281.55	185.87	347.33	220.61	433.95
Items	2.03	3.79	0.91	2.65	1.27	2.46	1.36	2.98

Note. FB = Feedback; Perform = Performance; Persist = Persistence; Time = Optional time in seconds; and Items = Optional items attempted.

4. DISCUSSION

The results of this study suggest two conclusions. First, as predicted, subjects sought more feedback from a computer than from a person. Second, this study suggests that feedback may debilitate motivation and performance.

People presented with the option of requesting feedback from a person almost never did, while most of the subjects given this option with a computer requested feedback most of the time. These results are even stronger than those reported recently by Karabenick and Knapp (1988) regarding help seeking from a person versus help seeking from a computer, perhaps because in the present study the person was physically present in the room with the subject and not invisibly communicating through a computer. This results lend strong support to H_1.

TABLE 3
ANOVAs (F values) for the experimental effects and their interaction

| | Dependent Variables | | | |
| | Perform | Persist | Items | Time |
Source				
Feedback	1.27	1.65	2.06	7.56**
Source	7.32**	0.05	0.31	0.18
Interaction	5.82*	0.19	3.30	1.25

$* p< .05. ** p< .01.$

Hypothesis 2 predicting performance and motivational superiority of computer-mediated feedback was not supported. While Earley (1987) found that computer-mediated feedback led to a higher performance than person-mediated feedback, we found no evidence for such an advantage. Several differences between this study and his may be responsible for the inconsistency. The task that Earley used was such that (a) subjects did not have a good performance estimate without feedback (b) it was relatively simple. In addition, (c) Earley's feedback was introduced while a goal setting program was in effect, and (d) the personal involvement of his subjects who working on their regular jobs may have been higher. Furthermore, since (e) Earley's subjects were co-workers, it is very likely that they considered not only how well they performed relative to their goals, but also how well they performed relative to their peers. These differences deserve future investigation as potential moderators of computer-vs. person-mediated feedback effects.

In Study 2 we investigated the latter possibility i.e., negative person-mediated feedback effects will be found when the comparison to others is salient. When comparison to others is salient the potential for loss of face is high and ego involvement is likely. Therefore, feedback messages that cue the receiver to make comparison to others may induce motivational deficits. Butler (1987) compared the effects of comments, grades, praise, and no feedback on multiple outcomes in an educational setting (children). Her data suggest that praise and grades (normative feedback) increases ego involvement attributions (sample item: "desire to avoid doing worse than others") relative to receiving comments and no feedback. Butler's (1987) results showed that the performance of those who received grades, praise, or no feedback declined while the performance of those who received comments improved. Other studies by Harackiewicz and her colleagues (Harackiewicz, Manderlink & Sansone, 1984; Harackiewicz, Abrahams, & Wageman, 1987) suggest that ego consideration and evaluation apprehension play an important role in the reaction to feedback. Unfortunately, these studies did not include a no feedback control group, so that it is hard to know if ego involving feedback impaired motivation and performance. In Study 2, we tested the effect of normative feedback relative to correct/incorrect outcome feedback. We further explored the possibility that negative effects of normative feedback will be found primarily among subjects who received person-mediated feedback. We predicted that:

H_4. *Normative feedback will decrease motivation and performance relative to correct/incorrect feedback. This effect will be stronger in the person-mediated feedback condition than in the computer-mediated feedback condition.*

Hypothesis 3 predicting negative feedback effects received mixed support in Study 1. Negative feedback effects were found for the performance measure in the person feedback condition, but the computer-mediated feedback effects on performance were not significant in this study in contrast with the Kluger et al. (1989) study. A negative effect on motivation was also observed with a measure of optional time spent on extra trials. Taken together, these studies indicate that feedback may have some negative consequences. These findings are very important in light of the voluminous literature recommending the use of feedback across a variety of applied settings (Pritchard et al., 1988). Therefore, we attempted to replicate these findings in Study 2.

In sum, Study 2 was designed to test H_4 and to replicate the findings of Study 1 on a slightly different subject population and slightly different task. Specifically, we sought to replicate (a) the beneficial effect of computer-mediated feedback on feedback seeking, and (b) the negative effects of any (outcome) feedback on performance and motivation.

5. METHOD: STUDY 2

5.1. Subjects
Sixty-nine undergraduate business students participated in the experiment. They were paid $10.00 each for their participation.

5.2 Setting
The experiment was conducted in a computer laboratory in a similar setting to Study 1.

5.3 Dependent variables
The experimental task consisted of questions extracted from retired Graduate Management Admission Tests (GMAT). Ten questions were chosen to serve as the initial task. Thirty additional GMAT questions taken from the same set of examinations were used to capture intrinsic task motivation behaviorally, in a similar way to Study 1. All other scores were calculated as in Study 1.

5.4 Procedure
Two factors were manipulated in a 2x3 experimental design. Upon arrival at the laboratory for the experiment, subjects were randomly assigned to either the

computer-mediated or person-mediated feedback condition. Each subject was then randomly assigned to one of three feedback conditions: intra-individual feedback (correct/incorrect); normative feedback; or no feedback. Both feedback conditions were similar to the "feedback upon request" condition in Study 1. In the normative feedback condition subjects were told both if they were correct/incorrect and "XX% of students like you solved this question correctly". The value of XX was an arbitrary number between 39 and 71.

In a debriefing, none of the subjects guessed the experimental hypothesis or suspected any of the manipulations.

6. RESULTS

Of the 45 subjects that received feedback 21 were in the person-mediated feedback condition and 24 in the computer-mediated feedback condition. Only one (4.7%) of the subjects in the person condition asked for feedback (on 6 out of the 10 trials), while all but one of the subjects (95.8%) in the computer condition sought feedback. Out of the 24 subjects in the computer condition 78% sought feedback on all 10 trials. A dichotomous variable representing feedback seeking (at least once or never) yielded a phi coefficient of .91 with feedback source ($p<$ .0001) replicating the finding of Study 1. No other effect reached significance. Thus the other findings of Study 1 were not replicated and H_4 was not supported.

7. GENERAL DISCUSSION

On the base of Study 1, Study 2, and Karabenick and Knapp (1988), it can be safely concluded that a computer is more likely to be consulted as a source for feedback than a person. An implication of this finding is that in situations in which feedback and information seeking is important for learning, accurate performance, and safe behavior, and in situations in which lack of this information might be detrimental either to the individual or to others -- computerized rather than human feedback should be provided. However, feedback should not always be made available even through computers because it may have negative consequences.

The lack of any other effect in Study 2 suggests that our earlier findings of negative feedback effects may have been spurious. It may be that feedback has no effect on motivation and performance on complex (cognitive ability) tasks of the sorts we used here. Indeed, Eysenck (1982) suggested that performance of cognitive ability tasks are unaffected by manipulations devised to boost motivation such as incentives. On the other hand, it may well be that feedback has a small negative effect on performance of cognitive ability tests. Small effect sizes are not likely to be systematically observed in a every single typical laboratory study. Therefore, a large sample study or a meta-analysis is needed to determine whether feedback has no effect or small negative effect on performance of complex tasks similar to those we used.

While the role of task complexity as a moderator of feedback effects deserves further study, the results of this study suggests caution in implementing feedback in field settings. Computer programmers should not assume that offering the user feedback is always beneficial. Some researchers noted negative feedback effect even in the context of computer aided instruction (e.g., Carroll & Kay, 1988). We did not find any consistent evidence for negative effect. However, even if feedback has no direct effect on performance, it may still have negative utility. As Kroll et al. (1988) noted subjects will seek feedback from the computer hundreds of times even if it can not improve their performance. The seeking of useless feedback is bound to have negative utility i.e., that time and energy could have been devoted to a more productive course of action.

In lieu of the complexity of feedback effect on performance reviewed here, our practical recommendation to programmers designing software for education and for job monitoring is to test the effect of feedback on their users prior to the finalization of the software. We believe that for some tasks feedback will be beneficial, for some it will have no effect and therefore may have negative utility, and yet for some others it may have direct negative effects. Specifying the conditions which determine each of these outcomes is a challenge for future research.

8. AUTHOR NOTES

Study 1 was supported by a grant from the Gaudet Fund at Stevens Institute of Technology. Study 2 was conducted in a computer laboratory donated by IBM to the Department of Industrial Relations and Human Resources, Rutgers University. Portions of this paper were presented at Fifth Annual Convention of the Society of Industrial and Organizational Psychology in Miami Beach, Florida (April, 1990).

9. REFERENCES

Azuma, H. & Cronbach, L. J. (1966). Cue-response correlations in the attainment of a scalar concept. *American Journal of Psychology, 79,* 38-49.

Ammons, R. B. (1956). Effects of knowledge of performance: A survey and tentative theoretical formulation. *The Journal of General Psychology, 54,* 279-299.

Ashford, S. J., & Cummings, L. L. (1983). Feedback as an individual resource: Personal Strategies of creating information. *Organizational Behavior and Human Performance, 32,* 370-398.

Balzer, W. K., Doherty, M. E., & O'Connor, Jr. R. (1989). Effects of cognitive feedback on performance. *Psychological Bulletin, 106,* 410-433.

Baumeister, R. F., Hutton, D. G., & Cairns, K. J. (1990). Negative effects of praise on skilled performance. *Basic and Applied Social Psychology, 11,* 131-148.

Butler, R. (1987). Task-involving and ego-involving properties of evaluation: Effects of different feedback conditions on motivational perceptions, interest, and performance. *Journal of Educational Psychology, 79,* 474-482.

Carroll, J. M., & Kay, D. S. (1988). Prompting, feedback and error correction in the design of a scenario machine. *International Journal of Man-Machine Studies, 28,* 11-27.

Deci, E. L., & Ryan, R. M. (1985). *Intrinsic motivation and self-determination in human behavior.* New York: Plenum Press.

Earley, P. C. (1988). Computer-generated performance feedback in the magazine-subscription industry. *Organizational Behavior and Human Decision Processes, 41,* 50-64.

Eysenck, M. W. (1982). *Attention and Arousal: Cognition and Performance.* Berlin: Springer-Verlag.

Greller, M. M. (1980). Evaluation of feedback source as a function of role and organization level. *Journal of Applied Psychology, 65,* 24-27.

Hammond, K. R. & Summers, D. A. (1972). Cognitive control. *Psychological Review, 79,* 58-67.

Hammond, K. R., Summers, D. A., & Deane, D. H. (1973). Negative effects of outcome-feedback in multiple-cue probability learning. *Organizational Behavior and Human Performance, 9,* 30-34.

Harackiewicz, W. C., Abrahams, S., and Wageman, R. (1987). Performance evaluations and intrinsic motivation: The effects of evaluative focus, rewards, and achievement orientation. *Journal of Personality and Social Psychology, 53,* 1015-1023.

Harackiewicz, W. C., Manderlink, G., & Sansone, C. (1984). Rewarding Pinball Wizardy: Effects on evaluation and cue value on intrinsic motivation. *Journal of Personality and Social Psychology, 47,* 289-300.

Herold, D. M., Liden, R. C., & Leatherwood, M. L. (1987). Using multiple attributes to assess sources of performance feedback. *Academy of Management Journal, 30,* 826-835.

Ilgen, D. R., Fisher, C. D., & Taylor M. S. (1979). Consequences of individual feedback on behavior in organization. *Journal of Applied Psychology, 64,* 349-361.

Jacoby, J., Mazursky, D., Troutman, T. & Kuss, A. (1984). When feedback is ignored: Disutility of outcome feedback. *Journal of Applied Psychology, 69,* 531-545.

Kanfer, R., & Ackerman, P. L. (1989). Motivation and cognitive abilities: An integrative/aptitude-treatment interaction approach to skill acquisition. [Monograph]. *Journal of Applied Psychology, 74,* 657-690.

Karabenick, S. A. & Knapp, J. R. (1988). Effects of computer privacy on help seeking. *Journal of Applied Social Psychology, 16,* 461-472.

Kluger, A. N., Adler, S. & Reilly R. R. (1989). *Negative effects of feedback on motivation: The role of control and individual differences.* Unpublished Manuscript.

Koestner, R., Zuckerman, M. & Koestner, J. (1987). Praise, involvement, and intrinsic motivation. *Journal of Personality and Social Psychology, 53,* 383-390.

Kopelman, R. (1986). Objective feedback. In E. A. Locke (Ed.). *Generalizing from the Laboratory to Field Setting.* Lexington Books, Lexington, Massachusetts.

Kroll, Y., Levy, H., & Rapoport, A. (1988). Experimental tests of the separation theorem and the capital asset pricing model. *American Economic Review, 78,* 500-519.

Lepper, M., & Chabay, R. W. (1985). Intrinsic motivation and instruction: Conflicting views on the role of motivational processes in computer-based education. *Educational Psychologists, 20,* 217-230.

Lepper, M., & Gurtner, J. L. (1989). Children and computers: approaching the twenty first century. *American Psychologists, 44,* 170-178.

Mikulincer, M. (1988). Reactance and helplessness following exposure to unsolvable problems: The effects of attributional style. *Journal of Personality and Social Psychology, 54,* 679-686.

Podsakoff, P. M., & Farh, J. H. (1989). Effects of feedback sign and credibility on goal setting and task performance. *Organizational Behavior and Human Decision Processes, 44,* 45-67.

Pritchard, R. D., Jones, S. D., Roth, P. L., Stuebing, K. K., & Ekeberg, S. E. (1988). Effects of group feedback, goal setting, and incentives on organizational productivity. [Monograph]. *Journal of Applied Psychology, 73,* 337-358.

Ryan, R. M. (1982). Control and information in the intraperosnal sphere: An extension of cognitive evaluation theory. *Journal of Personality and Social Psychology, 43*, 450-461.

U.S. Congress, Office of Technology Assessment (1987). *The Electronic Supervisor: New Technology, New Tensions*. (OTA- CIT-333), Washington, DC: U.S. Government Printing Office.

HUMAN JOBS AND COMPUTER INTERFACES
M.I. Nurminen and G.R.S. Weir
Elsevier Science Publishers B.V. (North-Holland)   147
© 1991 IFIP. All rights reserved.

Building expectations from context in on-line conferencing: a review

John C. McCarthy, Victoria C. Miles, Andrew F. Monk, and Michael D. Harrison.

Human Computer Interaction Group, Departments of Psychology and Computer Science, University of York, Heslington, York YO1 5DD, United Kingdom.

Abstract

Accurate expectations are formed in communication when participants are able to build a close relationship between the text of the communication and its context. In this paper we analyse strategies for the presentation of text and context in text-based interactive conferencing. Although transparency is widely believed to be the optimum strategy for synchronous systems there are problems with both its realisation and use. On the other hand asynchronous systems use a strategy which initially separates text and context and then reconstructs them at the interface. This strategy can be usefully employed in synchronous systems to support the user in keeping track of changing context. Some of the ways in which this can be done are illustrated using examples from text-based on-line conferencing.

1. INTRODUCTION

The job for users of CSCW systems is by definition a group one; they are using their system to cooperate with each other in the execution of some task. Consequently successful communication is of prime importance, especially when the job is undertaken simultaneously by all participants. It is suggested in literatures covering topics as diverse as face-to-face interaction and text processing that expectations derived from context play a significant part in ensuring successful communication. In this paper we apply insights from the multi-disciplinary literature on language use to an analysis of the role of context in on-line, text-based conferencing.

One approach designers have taken to support synchronous, distributed communication is to employ high bandwidth communication, which supplements the textual computer link with auditory and video links (see for example, Buxton and Moran [2]). Our approach is different. Our aim is to develop a system which employs textual communication only and still supports synchronous distributed communication. There are both practical and theoretical arguments in favour of this approach.

The practical arguments centre on availability. With the widespread availability of electronic mail, synchronous textual communication may precede broad bandwidth technologies in receiving widespread acceptance (see Egido [7] for a review of videoconferencing) and may well prove more useful and practicable than high bandwidth systems, such as Colab, which require very high resource commitment.

The theoretical argument is that text-only communication may reveal fundamental communication processes and mechanisms which would otherwise remain concealed by the presence of alternative channels of communication. These basic findings could then be applied in high bandwidth systems. Moreover, the same argument makes text-based on-line conferencing an unusual and therefore interesting testing ground for models of text/discourse processing.

In an earlier paper we considered the technical aspect of text-based communication [18]; that is, how to achieve the bandwidth required for basic information exchange without using audio and video links. We argued there that system bandwidth can be enhanced by enriching interface structure so as to introduce new virtual channels. But communication is more than information exchange. Even when people are perfectly capable of exchanging information they often misunderstand each other. We take achieving mutual understanding to be part of the task of communication. Therefore, in this paper we want to go beyond consideration of "the technical problem with communication" (Shannon and Weaver, [21]) to look at the issue of mutual understanding applied to textual electronic conferencing. Again, our broad approach is to consider the problem of understanding within the solely textual domain.

In the next section, we will discuss the role of expectation in facilitating successful communication. We will then apply evidence from the literature on language use and from our own studies to classify the kinds of contextual information which are required if participants in a computer-mediated conversation are to develop accurate expectations. Having identified the classes of information which need to be shared, we will go on to discuss design issues relating to the presentation of text and context in text-based on-line conferencing. Throughout the paper arguments will be illustrated with reference to text-based conferencing and other groupware applications.

2. EXPECTATION AND CONTEXT

Successful group interaction depends on participants' ability to understand each other. This is not a simple matter, for two reasons. One is linguistic: language alone can lack precision. For instance, indexicals, such as 'we', 'it', and 'that' do not refer to particular entities but are variables for entities specified by the context [16]. This imprecision allows language to express local needs efficiently and its meaning to be specified by local action. The other is metaphysical: understanding is not a function of shared meanings derived from fixed external realities, rather it is a relation of "fit" [28]. We feel we are understood when others react in accordance with our expectations, and we interpret the words and actions of others in accordance with the model of their thinking and acting we have built up in the course of our interaction with them.

Nonetheless, most communication is successful; people do understand each other. Although explanations of such understanding differ in many respects they tend to agree that an underlying mechanism is, what we call, expectation. Halliday and Hasan [11] argue that people understand a text by making predictions about the text from the context. Grice [8] talks about participants in a conversation operating under the assumption that other participants try to be cooperative; and Sperber and Wilson [23] suggest that we can assume that those other participants are being relevant. Sacks, Schegloff, and Jefferson [20] argue that when a participant asks a question this sets up an expectation for an answer. Finally the psycholinguists talk about expectations developing as the sentence is read or the utterance is heard, that is on hearing the words "The boy hit the ....", the listener forms an expectation of the kind of thing which will be referred to next.

In each of these cases it is *the close interrelationship between text and context* that supports the development of accurate expectations. That is to say, it is the words already heard, the question already asked, models of the other participants, the situation in which the conversation takes place, and even conventions about conversation itself which drive the expectations developed. Expectations derived from the context constrain the set of viable constructions available in processing further communicative events. As communication is successful most of the time it seems that expectations are accurate most of the time. This leaves us with two questions: what kinds of contextual information are required for such accurate expectation; and how can these information requirements be supported in the design of on-line conferencing systems.

2.1. Contextual information requirements

Although a number of disciplines, including anthropology, linguistics, and psychology converge upon a set of information requirements for understanding an utterance, such as the speaker's background and the history of the interaction, most research has centred on face-to-face communication. Bearing in mind the work of Krauss (see for example, Krauss, Apple, Morency, Wenzel, and Winton, [14]), Chapanis [3], and the London Communication Group (see for example, Short, [22]), which found differences in the communication process depending on the medium of communication, caution is recommended in adopting these requirements for media other than face-to-face. Therefore, rather than readily accepting them, we have looked at the use of our text-based conferencing system, Conferencer [18], to identify the contextual information necessary to support accurate expectations. Our conclusions are illustrated with reference to the task of remote joint authoring.

Imagine an application which allows two remotely situated users to jointly author a document. In this illustration, communication is via the computer only, and in addition to a task space for the document both users are presented with a 'conversation area', which allows them to converse in an informal way about the task, and which maintains a transcript of their conversation. In the next section we will outline the types of contextual information they require to carry out their task.

3. TYPES OF CONTEXT

It is not easy to define context. The best we can do at this stage is provide a taxonomy of the kinds of contextual information which are required to facilitate mutual understanding in the setting described above. This list can be considered to be the basis for an extensional definition of context, at least in remote joint authoring. Although this approach to context may not apply in full to all forms of groupware, the taxonomy is indicative of the kinds of contextual information required in all forms of conversation.

• *Co-text of conversation*

By incorporating a 'conversation area' into a description of a joint authoring application, we emphasise the relationship between text and context. Linguistic text is a primary communicative resource [11, 26] and as such can play a key role in creating or renewing the context [13]. If the 'conversation area' is used to discuss the task, then the conversation transcript presents a common ground between authors. Clark [4, 5] argues that mutual understanding can only occur when people can assume that the conversation to date is common ground.

• *The identity of participants*

If we take Von Glasersfeld's view [28] that expectations of people are built up with communication, and that on the basis of these expectations evaluation of success in being understood is made, and further, if we agree with Clark and Marshall [4] that messages are tailored to the common ground shared with others, then to identify participants is a fundamental requirement. Thus in the joint authoring application mutual understanding would be supported by identifying who said what in the 'conversation area' and who wrote which parts of the joint document.

• *Participant and system status*

To understand a person's ideas and feelings, others need information which will situate that person's utterance or text [4, 26]. Moreover each participant requires information on the current status of the other participants and of the communication system itself. Suchman has noted that silence in a conversation can be taken as a message with a particular meaning. When communication is mediated electronically there is the added possibility that silence signifies physical breakdown.

Taking the example of the joint authoring application, knowledge of participant status may help avoid a period of unnecessary inactivity, where each author falsely expects that the other is about to start some task activity: appropriate system status information would ensure that such a silence was not construed as system malfunction. Similarly, participant status information that one author is currently editing the joint document, and system status information that a particular section of text is under edit, will ensure that attempted simultaneous text editing is avoided.

• *Task objects*

In task related communication the structure of the interaction and therefore its coherence is closely related to the structure of the task [9]. Thus task objects, such as versions of a document, and task relevant information, such as changes made to a version of a document, should be commonly available. The value of the task object is obvious in the joint authoring application where that shared document ensures a common focus of attention. We have seen in our own studies that the process of forming accurate expectations and consequently of achieving mutual understanding is hampered when task objects are not available to all [19]. For example, problems might be expected to arise if each participant has a privately held version of the document.

• *Relevant expertise and goals*

Accurate expectation is also facilitated by the availability of relevant information on the expertise and goals of fellow participants [12]. Looking again at the joint authoring application, the process of mutual understanding will be supported and coloured by the authors knowing that one has a background in psychology and the other in computer science. Failure to share information about background knowledge may result in inaccurate expectations about the skill level of the participants and comprehension problems with regard to knowledge or ideas.

These are the kinds of contextual information required to facilitate the development of accurate expectations in text-based on-line conferencing. This taxonomy is really an attempt to define one subset of context that is, the local context. Other kinds of information, such as what was said the last time these participants discussed their document over coffee, are not addressed here. Our aim is the very modest one of exploring the role of context in those parts of the joint authoring process for which the authors decide to use the conferencing system.

However there is more to supporting the development of accurate expectation than merely providing approporiate contextual information. As the development of these expectations depends largely on the relationship between text and context, this relationship must be accurately reflected in the way in which text and context relate to each other at the interface. In the following sections we will explore some of the issues which should inform a strategy for presenting text and context.

4. PRESENTING TEXT AND CONTEXT

Our main aim in developing an appropriate presentation strategy for text and context is to accurately reflect the "connectivity" [6] between communication events which gives them coherence. In this section we will first examine a number of strategies which are embodied in some existing systems. We will then illustrate some of these strategies using examples from text-based on-line conferencing.

4.1. Transparency

Some existing synchronous communication systems adopt the approach that the intrinsic connectivity or seamlessness of communication can be preserved by making communicative behaviour transparent. While this may be a valuable principle there are problems with its application.

Transparency in principle

Intuitively a transparent interface seems to be the optimum presentation strategy for the development of accurate expectations. In this case all relevant contextual information is available to all participants and temporal relations between the different types of context and text are preserved. Face-to-face communication is an example of such a system. In face-to-face interaction each of the contextual information requirements outlined in section 3 is available. This contextual information may be conveyed by the surface features of the vocal text [10] and/or by the non-verbal signals surrounding it [29]. The identity of the participants, their non-verbal behaviour, the place in which the interaction is taking place, and the purpose of the conversation are all informative in this regard, and are all available to each of the participants. Thus if the joint authoring is undertaken face-to-face, the contextual information, from which expectations about the text of the interaction are derived, is maximally available to both participants. In Suchman's terms they have a shared context [26]. Some interactive textual communication systems have tried to emulate this situation.

In Colab, for instance, the design principle WYSIWIS (What You See Is What I See) has been suggested as a suitable abstraction for tools which are shared [24, 25]. The idea is that all participants see exactly the same objects and they also see where other participants are pointing. The authors suggest that such a shared image or whiteboard is a sound basis for shared focus. However, the WYSIWIS principle has not been fully realised in any of the Colab applications.

Transparency in practice

In practice, WYSIWIS principles have had to be relaxed. For instance, Colab provides private windows to complement the public windows; provides pointer visibility on request only; greys out busy items; and changes display only on completion of an act (e.g. editing). We will illustrate the degree to which 'transparency' has been realised using our own prototype system, Conferencer [18], which operates on similar principles to Colab.

Figure 1 shows the interface to the current version of Conferencer. As with Colab, some features do not operate on a WYSIWIS basis. This means that some of the contextual information requirements discussed in section 3 are not fully available For example, while a wholly transparent system provides full information on the current status of participants and of the system, such information is limited here. The composition box is always private and the cards on the pinboard are private while they are being edited or moved. Therefore participants cannot see another person's message while it is being composed. Neither can they see the changes being made to a card until the person editing it is finished. However some information on the current activities of other participants can be gleaned by using the status flags provided

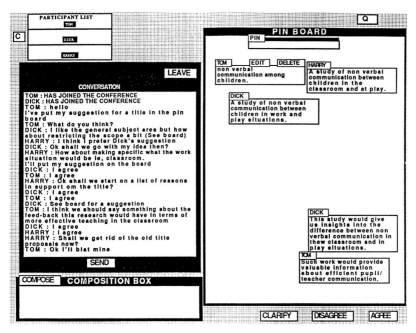

Figure 1: Current version of the 'Conferencer' prototype.

in the top left hand corner. Using these, it can be seen that another person is composing a message or editing a card. In both of these cases a trade-off between the participants need for privacy and his need for *status information* led to this formulation. Many of the other types of contextual information are still available in this system. As people can enter and leave the conference, *the identity of participants* is revealed in the participant list here. A permanent record of the *text of the conversation* is available in the conversation area (WYSIWIS is again relaxed here when a person is scrolling through the record). Finally, *task objects* are shared in the public pinboard. This is where joint authors would actually generate their document.

Clearly there are practical obstacles to the realisation of a fully transparent system. However, even if such a system could be implemented, there is also a serious problem with its use.

A usability problem

In a transparent system the context of the message is revealed through the behaviour of the participants. Seeing that author A has been working on the document in the public pinboard, and that he has stopped and is now composing a message, sets up an expectation for author B that the topic of the message will have to do with the part of the document A has just been working on. Further, if there has already been some discussion about this part of the document, the record of the conversation may be consulted to add to the contextual information available. Clearly, the onus is on users to keep track of an ever-changing context. Our experience, from studies with Conferencer, is that this may be too much to expect, as attention is often diverted away from the screen.

Consider again the joint authors: while author A has been working on the document, author B has been composing a message. Consequently when B receives the message from A he has no indication of the context within which that message was created. Typing messages takes time and distracts attention away from the screen: it creates a gap between a message arriving and being read, during which time the context may have changed. As a consequence of this time lag the connectivity between communicative events may be reflected ambiguously in so called 'transparent' displays.

Comments

There are two problems with relying on transparency to present text and context in text-based on-line communication. One is that control constraints have typically led to the relaxation of the WYSIWIS principle and therefore full transparency is more an aspiration than a reality. The other is that even if full transparency was a reality the designer cannot depend on users to keep track of an ever changing context. Consequently the key presentation issue is one of reinstating the context in which a message was created for the person receiving it. In asynchronous message sending systems, where time lags between communication events are large, this has been an issue for some time. Therefore design decisions taken in the asynchronous setting may be informative for the design of synchronous systems. In several such systems the separation of textual and contextual aspects of a message is made explicit.

4.2. Separating context and text

As with transparent systems all the contextual information outlined in section 3 can be presented in an asynchronous system, although categories such as participant status will take on a slightly different meaning to reflect the slow pace of the interaction. That is to say, while knowledge of the moment to moment activity of a fellow participant may not be required, more detailed knowledge of his behaviour and intentions at the time he composed the message may be required. In contrast with the transparent system, although all the appropriate contextual information may be available here, the temporal relationship between text and context may not be preserved. It is easy to imagine how, say, the inappropriate ordering of the conversation record would lead to the development of inaccurate expectations.

Asynchronous systems start from the assumption that the time lag between messages puts context and text out of joint. These systems separate the context and the text of a message and present them in a spatial relationship with each other, in order to express their conceptual relationships. For instance the templates used in the Lens system [17] and the frames used in KMS [30] may provide information about the subject matter of the message, the identity of other participants in this conversation, and so on. In either case the template or frame surrounds the message. Thus the message is embedded within its broader context.

There are two parts to a frame or template; the non-linguistic border which normally consists of a box within which the message is contained and the linguistic header. Consider the possibilities for conveying contextual information using the border alone. If different borders are used for different message types, for instance, one for a request and another for a reply, a great deal of contextual information can be conveyed before any header information is written. Lai and Malone [15] have talked about embedding messages within a series of borders. Thus a message may be framed as an action request (border 1) relevant to, say, a seminar programme or the CSCW research project (border 2). The border can be used in this way to cue the receiver to the context in which the message was created. More detailed contextual information can be presented in the header: the sender's name, the identity of other people to whom the message is being copied, the subject matter of the message, the required response, and so on. This allows the receiver to develop more precise expectations before reading the message. Finally, a freeform message can be presented within the frame and below the header. This strategy supports the reconstruction of the sender's context by the receiver prior to him reading the text.

Let us illustrate how contextual information is presented in asynchronous systems with reference to the Lens system, a template from which is reproduced in figure 2.

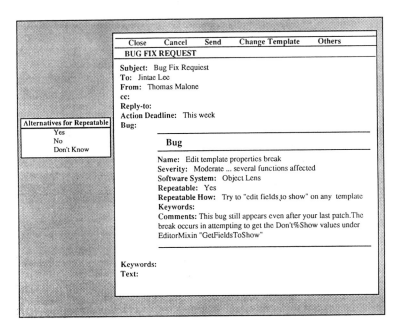

Figure 2: Embedded templates from the Lens system.

Figure 2 shows a template embedded within another template. The participants in the conversation are talking about a bug which needs to be fixed. The sender creates a template for the 'Bug Object' itself and embeds it within the template 'Bug Fix Request'. In doing this, he ensures that the *task object(s)* are available to the receiver. The header information and the 'Bug Object' template establishes the *identity of the participants* and the *current state of the conversation*. With reference to other contextual information requirements already identified: *participant status* is not important in this case as the interaction is asynchronous; and, although *relevant expertise* is not explicitly represented, the semi-structured nature of the interaction makes it possible for the system to monitor and comment on it [1]. As the contextual information is presented above the text it is likely to be read first thereby facilitating the development of accurate expectations which inform subsequent reading of the text.

Two aspects of the design of asynchronous communication systems can be usefully applied to the design of synchronous systems, and both emerge from the fact that text and context can be at least partially separated. The first is that once separation is accepted a range of non-linguistic signals, such as icons, flags, and frames, become available for the presentation of contextual information. The second is that separation also facilitates the reinstatement of the composition context of a message for the reader. That is to say that the history of a message can be maintained independently of the text of the message. Thus the logical separation of text and context increases the designer's options when considering the presentation of text and context. In the next section we will explore the application of these ideas in structuring the interface of an on-line conferencing system to orientate the participants towards the appropriate context of a message.

4.3. Orientating toward context in on-line conferencing

We argued earlier that in synchronous or on-line communication a transparent interface is the optimum situation for the development of accurate expectations which are necessary for mutual understanding. This is because transparency makes the contextual information outlined in section 3 available to all participants and preserves temporal relations. We have also seen that transparency is not yet a realistic option and that even if it were users' lapses of attention or parallel work would always lead to some asynchrony. However we have learned from the way in which some asynchronous systems treat text and context that the designer of a synchronous system has a great many options available to him in presenting text and context. An appropriate presentation strategy can be used to orientate the user to the historical context of the message, again facilitating the development of accurate expectation. Participants may need information to orientate them to the state of the system when a message was sent, when a message was started, or at other key points in the communication process. In our system, and in others that rely on 'transparency', the users have a lot of information on the current state of the interaction but none on the historical context of the interaction. In this section we will explore some of the presentation options available to the designer by describing two areas in our system in which we are currently investigating ways of presenting some of the history of the interaction.

Example 1: The Conversation Record

We have implemented a number of features in our prototype conferencing system to support shared context, including a permanent record of contributions. Contributions are presented in the order in which they are sent. Considering some of the arguments already made regarding the differences between sender's and receiver's context, participants may be more interested in information other than the order in which they were sent. Take the joint authoring case again, and assume there are three authors. The conference has been proceeding for some time. The participants have been discussing topic X. Author A begins to compose a contribution which continues with the discussion of X. Having seen A's contribution, author C begins to compose a request for clarification from A. An instant later author B begins to compose a contribution which mainly agrees with A. As contributions are presented in the order in which they are sent, and as B sent his message before C, the contributions appear as follows:

A: Surely we could use X to ....

B: I agree with most of that

C: Please clarify what you mean

Although C intended to ask A for clarification, it would appear from this sequence that he intended to ask B. His contribution was a response to the state of the conferencing system after A had made his contribution but appears to the others to be a response to the state of the system after B had made his contribution; highlighting the time-critical nature of the process of communication. We argued in section 2 that it is the close interrelationship between text and context which supports the development of accurate expectations, but we must be aware that context is dynamic, changing with each new textual contribution [13]. Therefore the context in which the participant composed his contribution needs to be reflected in the display, as this is the context in which it should be interpreted.

In this specific case, presenting the contributions in the order in which they are initiated would be more appropriate. This would present participants with an accurate composition history. On adopting such a strategy for presenting contributions, instances where the former strategy would more accurately reflect the relationship between context and text would be revealed. A more flexible approach would be to allow senders to select the most appropriate place in the conversation space for their contributions. In both cases some method of highlighting new contributions, previously signalled by them being at the end of the sequence, would be required.

Example 2: Participant Status Flags

In attempting to orientate towards the context of a contribution, our considerations must go beyond the sequence of contributions themselves. Arguments similar to those for sequencing contributions can be applied to the status flags. When a participant joins a conference his or her name is appended to a participant list, which is constantly displayed. When a participant begins to compose a contribution, a flag containing the letter C is displayed to the left of his name on this list. When he is creating a new card on the pinboard, a flag containing the letter P is displayed to the right of his name. Analysis of use of the system has highlighted a number of problems with this implementation of status flags, which tend to converge on the notion of representing the temporal relationship between text and context [18].

At present these flags are presented when the user activates a particular area and withdrawn when the user activates another area. Thus this implementation gives no history of activity: only the current activity status is indicated. In such a system if the user is not attending when a message arrives he has no clue as to the connectivity of communication events.

In the example outlined above, C's contribution is ambiguous: it is not clear whether he is looking for clarification from A or B. Knowing from the status flags that C was working in his private area, and had begun to compose his contribution after A's contribution had arrived but before B's had arrived, would probably be enough to disambiguate the referent. That is, on seeing that C had begun to compose after he had received A's contribution, the others would probably correctly expect his contribution to be a reply to A's. The problem is that as A and B are also busy composing their next contributions they are unlikely to be looking at the screen when C starts to compose. Thus the 'connectivity' between the three communicative events is inaccurately presented at the interface.

To deal with this case, two modifications of our current status flag arrangement are required:

• the temporal relationship between different participants' status flags must be shown

• the start and finish of each communicative event must be shown

The diagram in figure 3, which is intended to clarify the required modifications rather than suggest an implementation, illustrates how this might work.

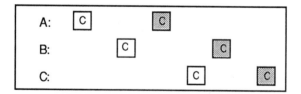

Figure 3: Modified participant status flags

In Figure 3, A, B, and C represent the three participants in the conference and the flags represent the most recent participant event (composition, pinboard, etc.). The white box indicates the start point of the event (starting to compose) and the shaded box indicates its termination (sending the composed message). The time course of events is represented as moving from left to right. The configuration displayed represents the series of events described in the case of ambiguous communication between A, B, and C outlined above. It is clear from this configuration that C started composing after A's contribution had arrived but before B's had arrived; precisely the information required to disambiguate the referent of C's agreement. It is felt that rendering the start and termination of significant events in this way and rendering the temporal relationship between these events for different participants will resolve many instances of ambiguous communication.

Summary

This brief analysis of a single case illustrates the problem of supporting accurate expectation, and therefore interpretation, in a time-critical communication system, where the text and context of a message are even slightly out of joint. The solutions offered here are indicative of the kinds of solutions currently being examined on our own prototype: they are not intended to be definitive. Indeed future analysis of the system with these solutions implemented may merely point to further problems with rendering the connectivity between text and context in synchronous systems. If this leads to a more complete understanding of the problem it will have been a worthwhile exercise.

5. CONCLUSIONS

In this paper we have argued, from both research and application perspectives, for the development of text-based, synchronous communication systems. We have suggested that the development of accurate expectation, a mechanism which supports understanding, is dependent on the availability of contextual information. Applying the multi-disciplinary literature on the use of language and the results from our own studies we have identified the kinds of contextual information which would be required to facilitate the development of accurate expectations in textual, synchronous conversation. Finally we have looked at some issues relevant to the presentation of text and context in such systems.

The inevitability of asynchrony even in on-line systems led us to consider some of the design strategies adopted in asynchronous systems. The separation of text and context, which is typical of asynchronous systems, if adopted in the design of synchronous systems would offer the designer a range of options not otherwise available. An appropriate use of this separation strategy can facilitate the presentation of an accurate interaction history. This has been illustrated with reference to text-based on-line conferencing.

In the introduction we argued that the results of an analysis of text-based communication could be applied to other media. The validity of this claim depends on the extent to which our analysis generalises.

The potential for mismatch between sender's and receiver's contexts is universal. In text-based systems mismatch arises because of the time taken to type or write a message. In face-to-face communication the same problem arises but the source of the problem is the transience of the interaction history. This can be most clearly seen in the case of discourse deixis where one participant refers back to something which happened earlier in the conversation and listeners don't remember the event referred to. There is no 'text of conversation', as described in section 3, to refer back to. The telephone case is even more difficult as the sender's and receiver's contexts are not mutually available. Something can happen in the sender's room, which effects what he is saying or how he is saying it, which is not available to the receiver. That is to say that the receiver has no information on the status on the sender, and for example could be unaware of the identity or even presence of a third participant in the conversation. Finally in multi media communication the inappropriate interleaving of textual, vocal, and non-verbal contributions can lead to mismatched contexts in much the same way as that identified in the conversation record example in section 4.3. The interleaving of communicative events is always critical; the only difference between the multi media and text cases is the nature of the events.

Although our analysis of the problem has widespread applicability, our analysis of strategies for solving the problem may have more limited application. The solutions we have suggested involve exploiting asynchrony by separating representations of text and context. We have shown how this would apply to text-based conferencing; it could also apply to multi media communication. The difference between the textual and multi media situation is one of degree of complexity. In the text-based system we are concerned with relationships between text, icons, and flags. In multi media systems vocal and visual contributions form part of the interaction history. They can be separated and reconstructed in much the same way as verbal text and icons were in the text-based examples. We will illustrate this generalisation with reference to the electronic multi media system Colab, though of course the principle also applies to multi media systems such as face-to-face with paper or whiteboard.

Tatar, Foster, and Bobrow [27] have observed a number of communication problems with a Colab application. According to their analysis the following design characteristics are responsible: screen displays can be inconsistent between participants; individual actions on Colab objects can be private; and contributions can be made anonymously. Their solution is to make as much of the context as possible available; that is to minimise privacy, inconsistency, and anonymity. Following our analysis this is necessary but not sufficient; they need to go beyond this and consider the relationship between text and context in their redesign. In principle they could adopt some of the strategies discussed in section 4.3 to orientate the receiver to the sender's context. That is they could present cues to the state of the system (who was doing what, or saying what, or pointing where) when the text was composed. In practice this might be easier to achieve with distributed multi media systems where there is already some system support for the storage and presentation of vocal and visual contributions.

In conclusion, if computer mediated communication systems are to support group work they must support mutual understanding. Rich interface structuring, which affords participants the opportunity to express themselves in a variety of ways, is a first step. However this merely makes technical communication, the transmission and reception of the message, possible. What we have argued here is that the designer must go beyond the message to consider ways of communicating the message in its context, as the connectivity of context and text is a necessary resource for achieving mutual understanding.

6. REFERENCES

1. Bignole, C. and Simone, C. AI techniques for supporting human to human communication in CHAOS. Proceeding of the European Conference on Computer Supported Cooperative Work, 1989.

2. Buxton, B. and Moran, T. Europarc's integrated interactive intermedia facility (IIIF): early experiences. In Gibbs, S. and Verrijn-Stuart, A. (Eds.). Multi-user interfaces and applications. North Holland, Amsterdam, 1990.

3. Chapanis, A. Interactive human communication. In Greif, I. (Ed.). Computer supported cooperative work: a book of readings. San Mateo, California: Morgan Kaufman Publishers, Inc., 1988.

4. Clark, H.H. and Marshall, C.R. Definite reference and mutual knowledge. In Joshi, A.K., Sag, I., and Webber, B. (Eds.). Elements of discourse understanding. Cambridge University Press, Cambridge, 1981.

5. Clark, H.H. and Carlson, T.T. Speech acts and hearers beliefs. In Smith, N.V. (Ed.) Mutual Understanding. Academic Press, London, 1982.

6. De Beaugrande, R. Text, discourse, and process: towards a multi-disciplinary science of texts. Ablex Publishing Corporation, 1980.

7. Egido, C. Video conferencing as a technology to support group work: a review of its failures. Proceeding of the Conference on Computer Supported Cooperative Work. New York: ACM, 1988.

8. Grice, H. Logic and conversation. In Cole, P. and Morgan, J. (Eds.). Syntax and semantics vol. 3: speech acts. Academic Press, New York, 1975.

9. Grosz, B.J. Focusing and description in natural language dialogues. In Joshi, A.K., Webber, B.L., and Sag, I.A. (Eds.). Elements of discourse understanding. Cambridge University Press, Cambridge, 1981.

10. Gumperz, J.J. Discourse strategies. Cambridge University Press, Cambridge, 1982.

11. Halliday, M.A.K. and Hasan, R. Language, context, and text: aspects of language in a social semiotic perspective. Oxford University Press, Oxford, 1989.

12. Haslett, B. Communication: strategic action in context. Lawrence Erlbaum Associates, Hillsdale, New Jersey, 1987.

13. Heritage,, J. Current developments in conversation analysis. In Roger, P. and Bull, P. (Eds.) Conversation: an interdisciplinary perspective. pp. 21-47. Clevedon, Philadelphia: Multilingual Matters Ltd, 1989.

14. Krauss R.M., Apple W., Morency N., Wenzel C., and Winton W. Verbal, vocal, and visible factors in judgments of another's affect. Journal of Personality and Social Psychology, vol. 40, no. 2, 312-320, 1981.

15. Lai, K. and Malone, T.W. Object Lens: a spreadsheet for cooperative work. Proceeding of the Conference on Computer Supported Cooperative Work, 1988.

162

16. Levinson, S.C. Pragmatics. Cambridge University Press, Cambridge, 1983.

17. Malone, T.W., Grant, K.R., Lai, K., Rao, R., and Rosenblitt, D. Semistructured messages are surprisingly useful for computer supported coordination. ACM Transactions on Office Information Systems, Vol 5, No. 2, 115-131, 1987.

18. McCarthy, J.C. and Miles, V.C. Elaborating communication channels in 'Conferencer'. In Gibbs, S. and Verrijn-Stuart, A. (Eds.). Multi-user interfaces and applications. North Holland, Amsterdam, 1990.

19. McCarthy, J.C., Miles, V.C., and Monk, A.F. (1991). An experimental study of common ground in text-based communication. In Robertson, S.P., Olsen, G.M., & Olsen, J.S. (Eds.) Human factors in computing systems: reaching through technology, CHI'91 conference proceedings. New York: ACM Press, pp. 209-215.

20. Sacks, H., Schegloff, E.A., and Jefferson, G.A. A simplest systematics for the organisation of turn-taking for conversation. Language, 50, 697-735, 1974.

21. Shannon, C.E. and Weaver, W. The mathematical theory of communication. University of Illinois Press, Urbana, 1949.

22. Short, J. A. Medium of communication and consensus. Communication Studies Group, paper number E/72210/SH, 1972.

23. Sperber, D. and Wilson, D. Relevance: communication and cognition. Blackwell, Oxford, 1986.

24. Stefik, M., Bobrow, D.G., Lanning, S. and Tatar, D.G. WYSIWIS revisited: early experiences with multi-user interfaces. Proceeding of the Conference on Computer Supported Cooperative Work. New York: ACM, 1986.

25. Stefik, M., Foster, G., Bobrow, D.G., Kahn, K., Lanning, S. & Suchman, L. Beyond the chalkboard: computer support for collaboration and problem solving in meetings. Communications of the ACM, 30, 32-47, 1987.

26. Suchman, L. Plans and situated actions: the problem for human-machine communication. Cambridge: Cambridge University Press, 1987.

27. Tatar, D.G., Foster, G., and Bobrow, D.G. Design for conversation: lessons from Cognoter. International Journal of Man Machine Studies, 34, 185-209, 1991.

28. Von Glasersfeld, E. The reluctance to change a way of thinking. The Irish Journal of Psychology, 9, 83-90, 1988.

29. Watzlawick, P., Beavin, J.H., and Jackson, D.D. Pragmatics of human communication. New York: W.W. Norton, 1967.

30. Yoder, E., Akscyn, R., & McCracken, D. Collaboration in KMS, a shared hypermedia system. Proceedings of CHI'89, pp 37-42. New York: ACM, 1989.

HUMAN JOBS AND COMPUTER INTERFACES
M.I. Nurminen and G.R.S. Weir
Elsevier Science Publishers B.V. (North-Holland)
© 1991 IFIP. All rights reserved.

Feedback and Cooperation: Discussant's Note

Pål Sørgaard

Norwegian Computing Center, P.O. Box 114, N-0314 Oslo, Norway

1   Introduction

The topic of this session, feedback and cooperation, is indeed worthy of a lengthy discussion. Firstly, cooperation cannot take place without some (human) feedback. In the case of computer supported cooperative work (CSCW), some of this feedback may be mediated through a computer system. A trivial example of this is how some systems for electronic mail automatically provide the sender with a confirmation that a message has been read (or viewed) by the receiver.

Secondly, every computer system provides some (computer) feedback to its users. There are wast differences in the kind, amount and appearance of the feedback. The qualities of the feedback have implications for how the system is perceived and used, and this will in its turn have implications for the work, for how the work is organised and for how people cooperate.

We thus have at least two possible interpretations of the theme feedback and cooperation. The two papers in this session can be said to address each their interpretation. For this reason the two papers will be discussed separately.

2   McCarthy et al.

McCarthy et al. address the question of how to relay human feedback between users of a conferencing system, i.e. a special version of the first interpretation of the topic of this session. Their key issue is how to provide the participants in a computer-conference with the appropriate context for understanding the different messages.

The paper differs from many traditional computer science papers by being serious in its attempt to address a problem of real-world importance: roughly half the references address issues like conversation analysis and discourse understanding. It is evident that the authors have undertaken a major effort in studying the nature of the problem they are addressing and for which they are designing support. In this way the paper sets an example for others working with experimental design of computer systems. Hopefully the approach will also result in improved discussions with researchers from other disciplines, and, ultimately, in better designs.

McCarthy et al. use their theoretical insight to propose various mechanisms that can keep track of the activities of the participants in a conference, and that can present information about this to the other participants in a way that aids their understanding of the messages.

Taken to the extreme, the ambition of McCarthy et al. is to develop a system for synchronous, distributed, and text-only conferencing. As they note themselves, even on-line systems are not purely synchronous, and many of the mechanism used in asynchronous conferencing systems may therefore be applicable in their own case. This makes the aim of McCarthy et al.'s research more realistic, but there is still a major issue to be addressed: McCarthy et al. clearly aim at representing the whole context of the conference *in* the system, or at least they consider the system to be the only channel for mediating context. I am very sceptical to this aim and the assumptions behind it. I would claim that in any practical situation there will always be other media in use; before, after, or even during the conference-session. The persons involved may have met face-to-face at many occasions, they use conventional mail to send documents to each other, they may share education, instructions about their work, and cultural background, they pick up the phone, etc.

A major part of the context of the conference will be the nature of the work-assignment they are conferencing about (for example, the topic of a shared paper). What this is depends on the work being performed, and it is therefore very hard to generalise about it. There will, however, always be something "outside the system", and this will have its own manifestations and representations independent of the conferencing system.

A more suitable and practical aim for supporting understanding of the context of a conference would therefore be facilities for maintaining links to other media being used in the same conversation and mechanisms that make it possible to "hook" the conference up to other systems. To come up with a trivial example: I have many conversations that are partially on electronic mail and partially on other media. In my mail-handler I can store the messages as I want to (for example, according to topic), but there is no way of putting in notes about other communicational events that are parts of the same conversation. This is, however, possible with a paper-based mechanism, and thus a paper-based archive is more universal than my mail-handler.

A final issue that needs to be raised when we discuss a paper like McCarthy et al.'s paper, is the question of the extent to which the *use* of a system is determined by its design. Several papers (for example [1]) describe vastly different uses of the same system. Others (for example [6]) argue that use is a more fundamental category than development. In designing conferencing systems we must be aware of this final issue. We cannot foresee exactly how the system will be used nor can we imagine all the possible pitfalls and abuses. This has at least two consequences:

- The qualities of the system may be widely different from one work-context to another. Evaluation must therefore take place in different settings.

- It must be possible for the "users" to build up a clear and valid understanding of the mechanisms that mediate context and feedback between the conference participants. In this way they can use the mechanisms as they want to or choose to ignore them if they appear to be irrelevant.

3 Kluger et al.

Kluger et al. look at the effects of the feedback provided by the computer system, or more accurately, the effects of computerised performance feedback. The paper is based on two laboratory experiments in the tradition of experimental psychology. It is very tempting to criticise the paper for the low relevance of the experiments to the theme of the conference, but such a critique would essentially boil down to a critique of the scientific school from which the paper comes. This is a tradition that with the words of Mason [5] can be said to emphasise scientific control at the expense of wordly relevance.

One of the aims of Kluger et al.'s paper is to contribute to a deeper understanding of the effects of different kinds of computerised feedback. The paper can be seen as an argument against the typical assumption that all feedback is good.

There are different kinds of possible feedback from a computer system: feedback as you type, replies to commands, printouts when you say "print", and computerised performance feedback and also monitoring of the employees' performance (see Day's paper in this volume). Kluger et al. *only* address computerised performance feedback, and this must be kept in mind while reading and interpreting their paper.

In their experiments Kluger et al. find that there is a vast difference between seeking computerised performance feedback and seeking human performance feedback on the experimental task: mathematical exercises. This can probably be used as an argument for including optional performance meters in various systems, a classical example would be a spelling checker: why bother your colleague with trivial spelling errors? It is not evident, however, that this generalises to all kinds of performance feedback. People, as social individuals, rely on the feedback they get on their "social performance". That is the way we learn to behave! This kind of performance feedback is essential in most work-settings, and it is generally hard to computerise. This implies a further restriction of the application-area of the results of this paper.

Psychologists working with motivation often distinguish between intrinsic and extrinsic motivation. Intrinsic motivation is the joy and fun of doing a task, extrinsic motivation has to do with reward structures like competition, pay, and career [3]. It is a well-known experience that evaluative feedback and competition tends to have a negative effect on intrinsic motivation [2]. Hence the attempt by Kluger et al. to test the third hypothesis: "Outcome feedback will have a negative effect on motivation and performance". This hypothesis was not confirmed, however. This issue is also being investigated by Heim and Øiestad, who look at motivation and feedback in computer games [4]. These games are good at giving feedback supporting intrinsic motivation (for some persons): movement, excitement, etc., but they also provide ways to compete, a sort of support for extrinsic motivation that might be in conflict with intrinsic motivation. This does not appear to be a problem for those who like such games. Youth playing such games often state they would not do it if there were no competition.

Clearly this is a field with a number of unanswered questions. It remains to be seen whether the answers will come from experimental psychology or from other research disciplines.

References

[1] Jeanette Blomberg. The variable impact of computer technologies in the organization of work activities. In *Proceedings from the Conference on Computer Supported Cooperative Work*, pages 35–42, Austin, Texas, December 1986. MCC Software Technology Program.

[2] E. L. Deci and R. M. Ryan. *Intrinsic Motivation and Self-Determination in Human Behavior*. Plenum Press, New York, 1985.

[3] G. Eckblad. *Scheme Theory*. Academic Press, London, 1981.

[4] Jan Heim and Guro Øiestad. Motivasjonsappeller i dataspill (appeals for motivation in computer games). Project description, Norwegian Computing Center, May 1990.

[5] Richard O. Mason. Experimentation and knowledge: A pragmatic perspective. *Knowledge: Creation, Diffusion, Utilization*, 10(1):3–24, September 1988.

[6] Markku I. Nurminen, Riitta Kalmi, Pirkko Karhu, and Jukka Niemelä. Use or development of information systems: Which is more fundamental? In Patrick Docherty, Klaus Fuchs-Kittowski, Paul Kolm, and Lars Mathiassen, editors, *System Design for Human Development and Productivity: Participation and Beyond*, pages 187–196, Amsterdam, 1987. North-Holland.

Section 6

Organisational Change

HUMAN JOBS AND COMPUTER INTERFACES
M.I. Nurminen and G.R.S. Weir
Elsevier Science Publishers B.V. (North-Holland)
© 1991 IFIP. All rights reserved.

Groupwork from a Personal Viewpoint

Hiroyoshi Ishibashi, Tetsuyuki Toyofuku*, Kazuo Tanaka and Yoshimasa Goto

Tokyo Information and Communications Research Laboratory, Matsushita Electric Industrial Co.,Ltd., 3-10-1 Higashi-Mita, Tama-ku, Kawasaki 214 JAPAN

*Currently at VLSI Devices Research Laboratory, Semiconductor Research Center, Matsushita Electric Industrial Co.,Ltd.

Abstract

Groupwork is composed of many tasks performed by group members, and its coordination is a big issue in groupware systems. This paper describes a system called *MIZUHO* for coordinating groupwork through personal viewpoints.

MIZUHO is designed on two principles. The first is to support coordinating tasks of groupwork. The second principle is to offer personalized shared environments for groupwork. To these ends, we have developed the View model for designing the system.

With this approach, the *MIZUHO* system for coordinating groupwork benefits each user and supports a wide range of individual work and groupwork, including strict and weak procedures.

1 Introduction

Groupwork is composed of many tasks performed by group members. For example, a project, *publishing manuals* includes several tasks such as *writing drafts*, *drawing figures*, and *printing*. In order to carry out groupwork, people have to coordinate these tasks: ordering and executing tasks. Because tasks are assigned to the group members, the group members interact with each other when they execute tasks. Although computer support for groupwork may include several aspects such as data sharing and schedule management, task coordination and management of interactions between people are basic requirements common in groupwork.

We are developing a system called *MIZUHO* which supports coordinating tasks and managing interactions between people. *MIZUHO* can manage tasks to be done by oneself or by group members because it supports groupwork focusing on task coordination. This paper describes the design and the current stage of development of *MIZUHO* .

The following design principles for the *MIZUHO* system:

- The system must support groupwork focusing on task coordination

  This principle enables the system to support not only *strict procedures* but also *weak procedures*, ill-defined procedures. Strict procedures are composed of tasks which are already planned, we know what to do. Weak procedures are defined at the time that they work on tasks, we don't know how things will work out. Strict procedures are easily supported by computer systems, but the majority of groupwork involves weak procedures [6].

Because *MIZUHO* manages tasks of groupwork, it supports both strict procedures where tasks are predefined and weak procedures where tasks are dynamically defined.

Although the famous system, "Coordinator" [3] supports managing groupwork interactions between group members by using a static communication framework, the *MIZUHO* system coordinates tasks and managing interactions between group members.

- The system must support groupwork through personal viewpoints.

    It has been repeatedly reported that group members do not accept groupware systems that benefit only the boss and not the group members [1] [5].

    Reflecting this, we emphasize a personal viewpoint in addition to a group viewpoint. *MIZUHO* offers a personalized human interface and environment for each member, and treats both groupwork and individual work in the same way.

    A shared environment is a fundamental necessity for groupwork [4]. However, it does not need to be the same for all group members. What each member needs is a personalized shared environment indicating what that member should know.

Based on these principles, the *MIZUHO* system provides a human interface called a Checklist which may be either personalized or general. Through the Checklist each member can see the state of the projects and tasks related to him, and can interact with other members by sending requests or notifications and receiving replies or acknowledgments about tasks.

This paper is organized as follows. Sections 2 and 3 describe models that are realized in the *MIZUHO* system. Section 2 introduces a model for analyzing the relationship between groupwork and members' tasks. Section 3 illustrates a graph called the Task Dependency Model which shows execution flow and dependency of tasks. This model is also depicted in a Checklist which is the human interface with the system. Section 4 illustrates how *MIZUHO* supports task execution and interaction management. Section 5 shows the current stage of system development. Section 6 concludes the paper.

2 View Model for Definitions and Viewpoints of Tasks.

This section introduces a model with two views to analyze groupwork and tasks performed by group members: the *Group View*, which is used in defining and executing tasks from the whole group, and the *Personal View*, which is used in defining and executing tasks from each individual. *MIZUHO* uses these two views to provide the same environment for both groupwork and individual work.

2.1 Personal View and Group View

2.1.1 Viewpoints of Tasks

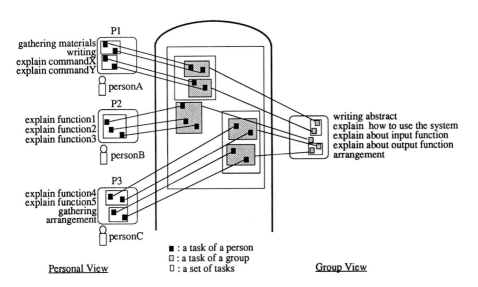

Figure 1: Personal View and Group View

Fig.1 illustrates an example of tasks, the Group View, and the Personal View.

In the Group View, tasks and their task composition, their assignments, and actual actions are agreed on by group members, A, B, and C. Fig.1 shows how the specific project is composed of five tasks and how A, B, and C agree to do them.

On the other hand, the Personal View is a personalized view showing only tasks related to a specific person. Task composition may differ from person to person. In the Personal View of group member A, for example, the task, "writing abstract" is divided into smaller tasks, "gathering materials" and "writing". B and C don't need to know how A executes and manages the tasks; they need only know that A will do it.

The Personal View describes the tasks executed by that person in detail, but need only briefly describe the tasks done by other members. The members do not have to sift through a mountain of information to get to the part that concerns them.

Each member may work through only his Personal View as long as he works on his own tasks, and may access data concerning the whole group project through the Group View.

2.1.2 Defining and Executing Tasks

In order to work out a group project, tasks in a project must be defined and executed. Both the Personal View and the Group View work are used in defining and executing tasks.

In the case of task definition from the Personal View, each member proposes tasks to be done by both himself and the other members, from his own viewpoint. On the other hand, tasks may be defined not from a specific personal viewpoint, but from a viewpoint agreed on by the entire group, the Group View (see Fig. 1). There may be, for example, regulations or rules on writing manuals which define who does which tasks. They are expressed from the Group View of this project.

In many actual cases, however, tasks are defined through a combination of the Personal View and the Group View. For example, task composition and the assignment of the whole group project are agreed on by all the group members, then each member is left to his tasks. The details are discussed in Section 4.

2.1.3 Conflict on Views

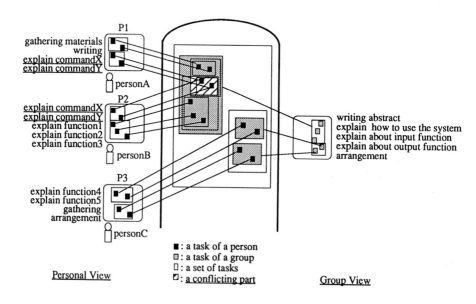

Figure 2: Conflict on Views

Fig. 2 shows a Personal Views conflict about the task "explain how to use the system". In this example, Both A and B define the same tasks, "explain command X" and "explain command Y". But they assign the different person who is to do the task. Even though the system informs that the conflict has occurred, the conflict must be settled by the users.

3   Task Dependency Model and Checklist

This section introduces a graph called the *Task Dependency Model*, which indicates tasks, dependencies between tasks, and execution flow of tasks [2]. The *MIZUHO* system maintains and uses this graph for controlling task execution and interaction between the users. The *Checklist* is *MIZUHO* 's human interface showing the Task Dependency Model. It indicates the current states of tasks: for example, what each user should do and whether a task has been completed or not, and also accepts user input. The users define and execute their tasks and they interact with each other through the Checklist.

3.1   Task Dependency Model

The Task Dependency Model is expressed with nodes and arrows. Nodes correspond to tasks which are any work units to be managed.

Arrows indicate sequences and dependencies between tasks (see Fig. 3).

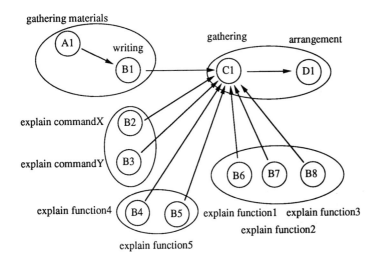

Figure 3: Task Dependency Model

There are the following dependencies between tasks (as illustrated in Fig.4).

(1) Sequence : B1 is executed only after A1 is completed.

(2) Parallel : n tasks, B1 through Bn, are executed only after task A1 is completed.

(3) And : one task B1, is executed only after all of n tasks, A1 through An, are completed.

(4) Selection : one of n tasks B1,..Bn, is executed only after task A1 is completed.

(5) Or : task B1 is executed after one of n tasks B1 through Bn are completed.

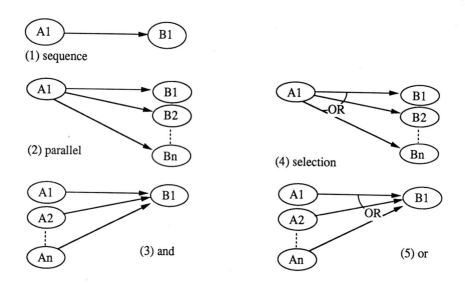

Figure 4: Types of Dependency

Any execution flow and relation of tasks can be expressed by a combination of these five types. Fig. 3, for example, expresses the project "writing a manual" with the Task Dependency Model. As indicated in Fig. 3, a set of several tasks may be handled as one task.

3.2 Checklist

The Checklist is a human interface showing the Task Dependency Model in a format similar to traditional checklists (Fig. 5). We adopted this checklist style for the human interface, because it is easy to understand at a glance, and because it, especially the Personal Checklist, is very useful in managing a person's tasks.

Mapping the Task Dependency Model through the Group View generates the *Group Checklist*, and mapping the Task Dependency Model through the Personal View generates

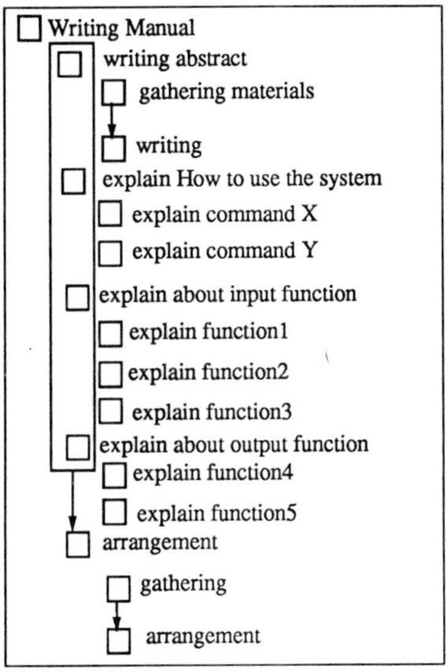

Figure 5: Checklist

the *Personal Checklist* (Fig. 6). The users work on their tasks and interact with each other through the Checklist.

Fig. 5 illustrates the structure of the Checklist. The Checklist is composed of *items* and *check boxes*. Each item corresponds to a task or a set of tasks. The relationships between tasks are expressed in the Checklist as illustrated in Fig. 7. Users can visualize execution flow and task relationships on the Checklist.

Check boxes indicate the current states of tasks. Each user may define the states of tasks for himself. For example, in the case of the task *voting*, a person may define two states, *not yet completed* and *completed*. *Completed* means that all members have voted. Another person may define those two states or another; *agree* which means a majority vote has been counted.

Check boxes accept user input such as *complete*, *reject*, and *request*, and indicate the current state of corresponding tasks such as *not yet completed*, *completed*, and *requested*. The state indicated by the check box in the Personal Checklist may differ from person to person, even though it corresponds to the same task. This is because the meaning of the task state may be different for each user. When Person A asked Person B to do Task X, for example, A's check box indicates *request* and B's check box indicates *requested* for the same task, Task X.

176

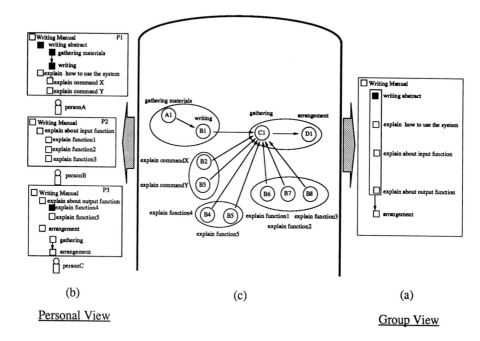

(b)　　　　　　　　　　　　　(c)　　　　　　　　　　　　　(a)

Personal View　　　　　　　　　　　　　　　　　　　Group View

Figure 6: Check Lists: Group View and Personal View

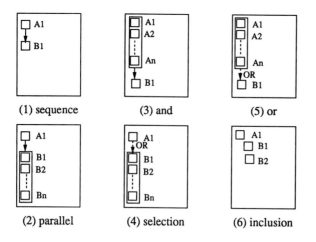

Figure 7: Relations between Tasks on Checklist

To sum up, the Checklists have the following merits:

- Each person may manage tasks using any work unit they like.

- Each person may manage in detail or briefly.

- Each person may define the states of any items.

- Each person may describe the relations between tasks.

4 How MIZUHO Works

This section illustrates how *MIZUHO* coordinates user's activities both for individual work and groupwork.

4.1 Pre-Defined Tasks and Implicit Interactions

This subsection explains how the *MIZUHO* system works in the case where all tasks are pre-defined before task execution. This simplest case includes a strict procedure such as purchase order.

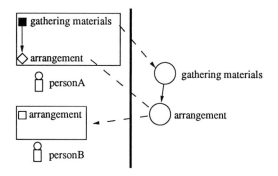

Figure 8: Pre-Defined Tasks and Interactions

Fig. 8 gives an example of execution of pre-defined tasks. Person A updates the check boxes of the item "gathering materials" to *completed*.

Then the check box of the task to be done next, "arrangement", is updated. The change of this state is informed to B, then the check box of the task "arrangement" on B's Checklist indicates *ready* informing B to begin his task.

On the other hand, the check box of the task "arrangement" on A's Checklist indicates *on-going* which indicates that A is waiting for B to complete the task.

This example illustrates task executions and interactions caused by task execution. A and B work together and interact with each other, but their interaction is implicit.

4.2 Dynamically-Defined Tasks and Implicit/Explicit Interactions

In many cases, some tasks for a project are not pre-defined, even though other tasks are already planned. In this case, the users define some tasks one at a time, while they work on other tasks.

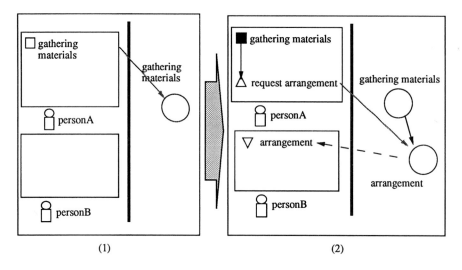

(1)   (2)

Figure 9: Dynamically Defined Tasks and Interactions

Fig. 9 gives an example of execution of dynamically defined tasks. Person A finds a new task "arrangement" which should be done by Person B. Then A creates and defines the new task to be done by Person B on his Personal Checklist. For example, the task "arrangement" is defined as the task to be done next to the task "gathering materials". The *MIZUHO* system adds the new task to the Task Dependency Model and a corresponding item on B's Checklist.

A's check box indicates *request* and B's check box indicates *requested*. If B accepts this new task and finishes it, B's check box changes to *completed*, then A is notified through his check box indicating the current state as now *completed*.

If B does not accept A's request or if they need to discuss the new task, the interaction between them is more explicit. For example, they may communicate through e-mail messages. The *MIZUHO* system does not manage this kind of explicit interaction. It just stores e-mail messages and links them to the related tasks.

4.3 Groupwork and Individual Work

There is no limit to the number of projects each Personal Checklist can manage. Each can accept not only groupwork but also individual work, a project performed by only one user. Each user can manage all of his projects and tasks through his single Personal Checklist with the *MIZUHO* system in the same manner.

5 Current Stage of System Development

This section illustrates the current stage of system development of the *MIZUHO* system. Currently, *MIZUHO* is implemented with the following functions:

- A user of the *MIZUHO* system can manage his tasks with the Checklist.

- Users of the *MIZUHO* system can interact with each other through the Checklists.

Fig 10 shows the Checklist displayed on the monitor.
This Checklist has items such as "Writing Manual" and "Personal Media Project" which a user manages. The Checklist indicates the task states using check boxes for each item. Check boxes indicate the states of the corresponding tasks using the symbols shown in Table 1.

Table 1: Correspondence Between the Check Box Symbol and the Task State

check box symbol	task state
□	not yet complete
■	complete
△	request (asked someone else to do a task)
▽	requested (asked to do a task by someone else)

The Checklist indicates the progress of all the user's projects with items and check boxes. The Checklist has a menu as shown in the right part of Fig. 10. The menu contains selections such as Insert, Edit, Send, Request and Complete.

If a user requests someone else to do a task which is registered in the Checklist, first he moves the cursor to that particular task and then clicks the Send menu selection with the mouse. *MIZUHO* will inform the request to the task to the specified person and will change the state of that task to the *request* state and the state of the corresponding task of the specified person to the *requested* state.

When a user completes the requested task, he moves the cursor to that task and clicks on the Complete menu selection with the mouse. *MIZUHO* will then notify the user who made the request that the task has been completed.

180

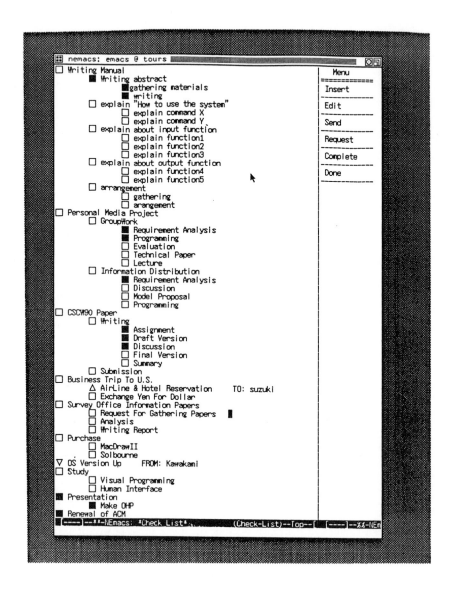

Figure 10: An Example Checklist

MIZUHO is developed on Nemacs (Nihongo Emacs) which is an extension of Gnu Emacs with Japanese ability [7]. *MIZUHO* works on workstations networked on a LAN and equipped with bit-mapped displays.

We are going to complete the *MIZUHO* system soon and will empirically study the *MIZUHO* system in actual use.

6   Conclusion

This paper describes the *MIZUHO* system for groupwork coordination. This system does the following:

- coordinates tasks and manages interaction between users.

- provides personalized shared environments in which each person can see his tasks and his situation.

- supports both groupwork and individual work in the same manner.

- performs both strict and weak procedures.

It does these things from two viewpoints:

1. supporting groupwork focusing on task coordination

2. supporting groupwork through personal viewpoints.

Based on the first viewpoint, the *MIZUHO* system supports a wide range of groupwork. The *MIZUHO* system, however, does not manage every interaction between people such as conversation through e-mail messages. It manages interactions initiated by task execution, or implicit interactions which are necessary for groupwork. This avoids the problem of overcontrol by groupware systems and makes *MIZUHO* acceptable to users.

We have introduced the Personal View and the Group View for designing the *MIZUHO* system. This approach provides a personalized shared environment, a Personal Checklist, and a common shared environment. The Personal View offers a *micro* environment, and the Group View offers a *macro* environment. Because of the Personal Checklist, each user can work in his own way on a group project. Because of the Group View and the Group Checklist, users can resolve conflict between themselves.

We adopted a checklist format for a human interface. This approach enables MIZUHO's good human interface which provides necessary information and hides unnecessary information. Because of the Personal Checklist, and because of managing interaction initiated by task execution, users can work for groupwork in a manner similar to individual work.

At the time we wrote this paper, primitive functions of the *MIZUHO* system had been implemented.

Our future works will include:

- Empirical study in our laboratory:

  We will use the *MIZUHO* system in our actual office work.

- Society model :

  The *MIZUHO* system may need more solid description about human society for coordination. We are constructing a Society Model that can be used by *MIZUHO* .

Acknowledgment

The authors thank S.Motoike, G.Michelitsch, and Dr.K.Kawakami for their valuable help in our research. We also thank A.Ishikawa for drawing the figures.

References

[1] Groupware: Big Breakthrough — or Big Brother. Business Week, June 5 1989, pp.85.

[2] Clarence A. Ellis. Information Control Nets: A Mathematical Model of Office Information Flow. In *Conference on Simulation, Measurement and Modeling of Computer Systems*, 1979.

[3] Fernando Flores, Michael Graves, Brad Hartfield and Terry Winograd. Computer Systems and the Design of Organizational Interaction. *ACM Transactions on Office Information Systems*, Vol.6, No.2, April 1988, pp.153-172.

[4] Simon J. Gibbs. LIZA: An Extensible Groupware Toolkit. *Proceedings of CHI'89*, Austin, TX, April 1989, pp.29-35.

[5] Jonathan Grudin. Why CSCW Applications Fail: Problems in the Design and Evaluation of Organizational Interfaces. *Proceedings of CSCW'88*, Portland, Oregon, 1988, pp.85-93.

[6] Hiroshi Ishii. Cooperative Work Models and Groupware. In *Friend21 International Symposium on Next Generation Human Technologies*, September 1989.

[7] Richard Stallman. *Gnu Emacs Manual.* Free Software Foundation, Inc., 1987.

HUMAN JOBS AND COMPUTER INTERFACES
M.I. Nurminen and G.R.S. Weir
Elsevier Science Publishers B.V. (North-Holland)
© 1991 IFIP. All rights reserved.

Electronic Mail & Post Modern Organisation

Mike Robinson

Centre for Innovation & Cooperative Technology, University of Amsterdam,
Grote Bickerstraat 72, KS 1013 Amsterdam, The Netherlands
E-mail: mike@ooc.uva.nl

Abstract

A brief story is told of a large company that experiences major staff loss despite excellent wages and working conditions. It is suggested that underlying structural factors are changes in the nature of communication media, and changes in the nature of work organisation. Both lead to informal associations, and change the ground on which people operate. It appears that this problem cannot be resolved without new conceptions of corporate boundaries and of managing cooperation.

Introduction

The following story was obtained through the Trojan Door[1] of consultancy. There are few grounds for thinking it is unique. It is about a very large and successful US company. As a matter of policy, the company pays above average salaries. It targets the upper 25% of comparable salary ranges in the Fortune 500 list for its employees. It provides excellent career opportunities and internal promotion prospects. As a matter of enlightened self interest, it encourages technical and managerial employees to keep up with the latest developments in their field through training and contact with professional and scientific organisations.

So far so good. In theory, all this should generate contented and loyal staff, with a corporate career orientation, who add to competitiveness and efficiency through awareness of the latest developments and thinking. In practice, the company is suffering a loss rate on its most "promising" staff of more than 30 percent per annum. In computing departments, this leads to a serious lack of continuity. There can be up to a 300% turnover of staff within a project.[2] The problem extends to all technical and managerial staff. The loss rate is such that those who had previously been expected to pursue career ladders into senior management never get there. The spectre has arisen of a company with no reliable long-term internal (or for that matter, external) candidates for senior managerial positions. This is in addition to the security and confidentiality issues posed by such a flux of people through the organisation.

---

[1] A nice phrase due to John King in an Invited Talk at the 13th IRIS, Åbo Akademi, Finland, June 1990.

[2] Similar phenomena have been widely noted as a major problem for defence and safety-critical applications, one result being a worldwide push for structured design and programming methods to support continuity despite staff turnover.

An underlying mechanism was suggested by a Board Member. Because of the need to "stay ahead" in their fields, employees are increasingly involved with their professional and scientific associations, and with networks of peers. The networks form their own agendas. If these are blocked, the networks carry news of other job opportunities. The result is not just increased mobility. It is loyalty to networks and associations over and above loyalty to any particular company. A comparison was even made with the former East German DDR. On the outside it looked stable. In fact, it was on the point of collapse: people were voting with their feet.

The paper will suggest two underlying structural features of this problem: changes in the medium of communication; and changes in the form of industrial organisation. It will also be suggested that, since the underlying structural features are general, the problem is likely to be widespread. This in turn leads to a need to reconceptualise our fundamental image of what an organisation is, and to speculate on what a post modern organisation might look like.

Electronic Mail

Electronic mail is singled out from other communications media like phones and fax which are more ubiquitous. This is not to assert that e-mail has more consequences for inter-organisational connectivity. In fact recent studies (Reder & Schwab, 1990) show that much office communication relies on switching between many media. E-mail is singled out because it is computer based, and is likely to foreshadow the next generation of multi-media applications. It also has several features that distinguish it from other media, which are of special interest for current purposes.

The success of a user unfriendly application

Electronic mail appeared with the ARPANET in 1966 -- almost in electronic pre-history when many still thought of the computer as a "number cruncher" rather than a communication and information medium. The ARPANET linked industrial research centres and universities involved in DARPA[3] contracts throughout the US, with connections in the UK, Norway, and Hawaii. It allowed access to remote computer facilities; file transfer between sites; bulletin boards; and electronic mail exchanges between individuals and memo groups at different sites. The e-mail function "was not given much attention in the initial design of the net, yet it became one of the most valued services provided" (Bannon, 1985:16). This favourable valuation was made despite technical inadequacy of the facility, as the following comment on the use of cumbersome computer systems in general shows.

> "people .... that, only a few years ago wouldn't have thought about sharing data, findings, and working cooperatively are, in fact, doing that now. All despite the fact that we have a less-than-rudimentary electronic mail system, and none of the nifty tools that supposedly provide for handy electronic interaction"
>
> (Bannon, 1985: 18)

In more than two decades since the ARPANET, e-mail has remained popular with vastly increasing numbers of users and systems. One estimate puts the number of messages

---

[3]The US Department of Defence Advanced Research Projects Agency

sent in the US in 1985 at 500,000,000 (Snyders, 1987). Yet surprisingly, e-mail is still technically unfriendly, and is "not given much attention in the initial design" of applications. There is recent evidence that many highly sophisticated, multi-function, work-oriented, group-supporting software packages are accepted precisely because they offer e-mail facilities. Interviews with 223 people who used advanced groupware systems in 25 large and very large enterprises found:

> "The functionality for sending and receiving electronic messages, available in all the products we studied, was by far the function most heavily used and universally stated as valuable. ...... People quickly learned the electronic messaging functions, and this contrasted with their failure to use many of the other functions available in these systems. Messaging was used extensively regardless of its user interface design, ease of access, or sophistication of function.
>
> (Bullen & Bennett,1990:293)

Amongst other systems, Bullen and Bennett discuss the interface provided by the The Coordinator, based on speech act theory (Searle, 1969). The functionality supports requests, promises, "free form", etc. The authors found people consistently sending each other 'requests' regardless of the content of the message. Not surprisingly, 'request' was the first menu choice, where the cursor fell by default. Many of those interviewed reported that they ignored the choices, and just 'hit enter' to send a message. It was concluded that " messaging overshadows other system based functions ..... electronic messaging support is what is most needed."

In other systems, failure to use functions such as electronic calendars, project tracking, reminders, directories, and expense tracking, is explained by many factors. Isolated tools require extra work to transfer control or data; some tools require users to spend time on activities they do not normally carry out; some tools create inequality between those doing the work and those benefiting from it (Grudin,1988). In addition, there can be lack of commitment from management; unclear initial expectations; lack of, or only mechanical "what keys to push" training; and a "plateau of competence" -- lack of interest in features or functions that are not immediately useful (Rosson:1985).

The contrasting success of e-mail has still to be convincingly explained. It suffers from many of the above problems. It is common for installed e-mail systems not be be used at all, or to be used very partially. This can be traced to technical problems, and to lack of a "critical mass" of people to communicate with (Leroy & Robinson, 1987). It can also be traced to a range of user interfaces that range from the user-unfriendly to the downright hostile. Don Norman's (1981) remarks about UNIX seem to apply perfectly to e-mail. ".... a disaster for the casual user. It fails both on the scientific principles of human engineering, and even in just plain common sense." One can note specific failures. A projected, ideal use of e-mail was the linking of regional trades union offices throughout Europe (TURN, 1990). In practice, many "customers" prefered fax -- an easy to use, less technical alternative for officials used to secretaries, and often without computer or keyboard skills.

Nevertheless, Bullen & Bennett make a statement consistent with Bannon (1985) which contradicts almost all known wisdom on the design of computer interfaces: *"Messaging was used extensively regardless of its user interface design, ease of access, or sophistication of function."* An anthropological study by Constance Perin (1989) provides clues about the success of e-mail despite its user unfriendliness.

E-mail & Electronic Social Fields

Perin starts by observing that, with computer support, workers can communicate directly with each other at any time of day or night; can control the times and places they receive and send messages; and can effectively carry out certain tasks away from their offices. But she goes on to point out that this flexibility is not unproblematic:

> "These alternatives are seen both negatively and positively: on the one hand, in deconstructing the traditional relationship between organisational authority and space-time norms, they are seen as subverting legitimated organisational structures: on the other hand, such spatial and temporal alternatives appear to meet many of the criteria said to be conducive to innovation and productivity in bureaucratic organisations. .... I propose that these electronic social formations represent new sources of industrial conflict, *raising questions about conventional relationships of space and time to industrial discipline and control.*"

(Perin, 1989: 1/2, my emphasis)

Perin's analysis revolves around the notion of "social fields". She defines these as semi-autonomous, self-regulating, ambiguous, self-constituting, and "conceptual". They are less self-aware, less concrete, and less legitimated than work groups or organisations, and are not co-extensive with them. They are socially real to their members, who are governed by the rules, norms, and meanings that evolve within the fields. There is a potential contradiction between structuring principles of "self-management" and "self-regulation" and the "hierarchical and authoritarian principles associated with organisation-work".

> "Electronic social fields are premised on the value of disclosure, sharing, cooperation, and mutual assistance, which often run counter to the competitive and hierarchical values organisations are structured to maximize. .... "It seems that in computer mediated groups, where there are no salient reminders of status differences, communication is less closely regulated. Increasing the pool of information and at the same time mitigating the effects of status could contribute to organizational strength. It may also contribute to organizational instability" (Kiesler 1986: 54)."

(ibid:5)

Nevertheless, Perin states that social fields are *"less a political force than a formation which organizations inadequately or inexplicitly recognise"*. This is an interesting observation. If electronic social fields provide a resource from which individual and collective actions can emerge, then why are these actions not seen as political? Traditionally, it was relatively easy to classify the activities of workers. Either they were pursuing an individual agenda which was in most cases blameworthy, and to be checked; or they were pursuing an oppositional agenda, often via trades unions, and seen as political; or they were pursuing the organisational agenda, which even if misguided, called for support rather than correction.

There are considerable differences between traditional and electronic social fields. First, traditional social communication, especially trades union meetings, but including conversations and phone calls, are visible to management. Electronic social fields may be invisible. Communication via a keyboard looks like work[4]. Secondly, electronic fields give a far wider choice about who to "associate" with. In particular, it is just as easy to communicate with people outside as inside a company. Consequently, there is a far wider range of available contacts around which association can revolve. Additionally, e-mail fosters a lack

---

[4]And fairly simple measures, utilising overlaid "windows" and "screen savers" can be taken to maintain that appearance, even in hostile environments.

of status distinctions; a blurring of the distinction between home and office, and between work and nonwork; and a tendency to produce uninhibited and nonconforming behaviour, coupled with strong internal conventions on acceptable abbreviations, styles, etc. (Sproull & Kiesler, 1988). These latter factors are associated with strong group cohesion.

From these considerations it seems likely that Perin's social fields are forms of association that can create their own agendas -- but these are largely independent of, or only contingently connected with any corporate agenda. In contrast, a classic trades union agenda usually operates on, or contests the same ground as management, and is thus seen as political. Nevertheless, an organisation where a multiplicity of invisible *collective* agendas[5] are being activated will face "new sources of industrial conflict, ... questions about conventional relationships of space and time to industrial discipline and control".

The role of different "agendas" in understanding both e-mail, and the nature of cooperation will be expanded later. For the moment it is worth noting that Perin's points are very similar to the informal observations made by the Board Member is the initial story. Social fields (or networks) may command more allegiance and loyalty than the company itself. It is now of interest to look at one attempt to make sense of the burgeoning use of electronic communication from a managerial point of view.

Organisations with "minds of their own"

Fenton Robb, a former Deputy Chairman of Scottish Gas in the UK, has speculated on the meaning of these new electronic social fields. He challenges the myth of managerial control -- the assumptions that organisations are in principle comprehensible, and that managers can intervene from a meta-level, as if they were outside or "above" them. He identifies new difficulties originating in the exponential growth of inter-organisational communication.

> "The rapid growth of innovative technology which interconnects already established human organisations is taking place without any purposeful overall design. Connections are established and maintained vicariously. Once connections are made there is a rapid increase in channel capacity and little control over what is communicated through those channels. *Communications are emerging as metaprocesses to the organisations which they serve.*"

(Robb, 1989a: 203)

A similar point is made in a later paper:

> "To the human observer, the operations of such a metaprocess, if they are at all observable and attributable, will appear chaotic and unrelated to any human organisational purpose. They will also be highly resistant to intervention. A man-made organisation in the grip of such a metaprocess may be perceived as "having a mind of its own" in a most literal sense. It may continue to preserve itself, but it may do so at great cost to the humans and their organisations."

(Robb, 1989b)

While Robb's idea of "supra-human organisations" has a science fiction flavour, the response of the "human observer" (ie. manager) that something is going on that has a "mind of its own" is very real. It seems likely that inter-organisational communication technologies have resulted in metaprocesses that are managerially incomprehensible. This is because social fields have been created that can develop their own agendas -- and these cannot be grasped within individual, trades union, or corporate schemas. These new social

---

[5]As opposed to the multiplicity of individual "hidden agendas" that are common in most organisations.

fields have a tendency to recreate their own structure, but they are not cyborgs. They are simply a dimension of human action -- an instance of the political concept of "free association" -- that has found a new channel through which to express and organise itself. In this context it is not so surprising that "messaging was used extensively regardless of its user interface design, ease of access, or sophistication of function." Nor is it surprising that it is seen as seen as "subverting legitimated organisational structures".

E-mail and the nature of work

The preceding sections have explored the organisational contradictions and the popularity of an "unfriendly" computer application -- electronic mail[6]. They illustrate the first structural feature in the analysis of the initial anecdote. *Changes in the nature of communication media have given rise to "social fields", networks, and forms of association that are outside the possibility of management inspection and control.* Quite literally, a new ground has been created on which people can operate. All this is an unintended side-effect of the introduction of a functional medium. An explanation of how the side-effect could become central introduces the second structural feature: changes in the nature of work and form of industrial organisation

The last decade has seen some important advances in the understanding of work, many of which have come from the field of Computer Supported Cooperative Work. Hughes, Randall, and Shapiro (1991) even claim the emergence of a new paradigm. Kling (1980, 1988) and Hirschheim (1985: Chap. 6) give excellent accounts of the various theoretical perspectives on computer support. Central to CSCW are the related ideas that negotiation and interpretation are crucial to work at all levels, and there is no such thing as an external, "objective" overview of work process (Sheil, 1983; Orlikowski, 1989). Probably the best known exposition is Suchman's (1987) "Plans and Situated Actions", which effectively postulates an impossibility theorum: there is an indeterminate relationship between any plan and its execution. Work cannot be specified in requisite detail in advance and externally to the concrete situation[7]. Closely related concepts are "articulation work" (Gerson & Star,1986); "shared information space" (Thompson, 1984; Bannon, 1989); "double level language" and "mutual influence" (Robinson, 1991); "shared material" (Sorgaard, 1989); and "equality" (Grudin, 1988)[8]. The "Scandinavian School"[9] has made a major contribution in demonstrating and researching the close links between specific understandings of particular work processes and successful system design (see for instance Bjerknes, Ehn, & Kyng, 1987; Bjerknes, Dahlbom, et al., 1990).

All this supports the notion that work has to be understood as situated and artful, negotiated and constructed as it goes along. In the next sections the proposition will be considered that this is not just a reconceptualisation of work in general. Modern production

---

[6]In deliberate contrast to studies that have focused on the use of functionality (eg. Summerville & Rodden, 1988; Eveland and Bikson, 1988)

[7]".... the problem of meaningful action turns on the observation that behaviour in inherently subject to indefinitely many ascriptions of meaning or intent, while meaning and intent are expressible through an indefinite number of possible behaviours." (Suchman, 1987: 3)

[8]These and other basic CSCW concepts are discussed in Robinson, 1990a.

[9]which might well be better in the plural.....

methods have evolved a new work form. Cooperation in the control of production is the second structural feature that underpins the initial corporate problematic of loyalty and staff turnover.

A dialogue about cooperation

The full debate ranges from conceptions of the market as a cooperative mechanism (Axelrod, 1990; Malone et al., 1988) to cooperation as groupwork (Greif, 1988). The focus here will be on cooperation as the reproductive principle of the production process, as postulated in Kjeld Schmidt's (1990) "Analysis of Cooperative Work"[10]. He starts by noting that work is inherently a social phenomenon. Essential but taken-for-granted skills are linguistic categories and concepts; general and domain specific knowledge acquired by socialization; ideological notions like moral and aesthetic norms, beliefs, and prejudices. This is necessary background for cooperation. Cooperative work itself is defined as pertaining to the sphere of production: to work processes related by content, the production of particular products or types of product. Cooperative work is a more specific concept than social interaction in the system of work in general.

> "Of the web of interrelated forms of interaction, one category of forms stands out as crucial, namely the forms of interaction determined by the production process itself, ie. cooperation. The form of cooperation is the *interface* between the transformation process and the social system of work. The specific configuration of cooperative work relations directly reflects the specific configuration of natural, technical, and human resources. Thus, the form of cooperation plays the mediating role of a vehicle conveying the impact of technological development on the social system of work at large. *The form of cooperation ..... is the generative mechanism of the entire edifice of the social system of work.* Therefore, the forms of cooperation may be considered the 'category of origin' of our investigation."
>
> (Schmidt, 1990: 13/14 my emphasis)

Schmidt then goes on to identify three types of cooperation, giving rise to different "edifices" of organisation, and based on different stages of development of the means of production.

augmentative cooperation

Schmidt notes this is the most primitive form of cooperation, arising because every individual is limited. By aggregating their capacities, individuals can perform a task that would have been absolutely impossible to each and every one of them individually. "As an ensemble they may, for instance, be able to remove a stone that one individual could not move one iota." In the example, and in augmentative cooperation generally, individuals are largely interchangeable. Also such cooperation is easily eroded by technical arrangements that augment individual capabilities -- eg. one individual with a bulldozer can replace dozens of individuals working with shovels.

---

[10]See also Orlikowski (1989) and Lyytinen (1990), both of whom draw on the structuration theory of Giddens (1976, 1984)

combinative cooperation

This is defined as "technique based specialization". Unlike augmentative cooperation, the allocation of different tasks to different actors is neither incidental nor temporary. Participants cannot change roles at will. The division of labour rests on skills and techniques, themselves the product of specialisation and learning. Schmidt cites "the eulogist of technique-based specialization", Adam Smith:

> 'the division of labour, by reducing every man's business to one simple operation, and by making this operation the sole employment of his life, necessarily increases very much the dexterity of the workman.'

Technique based cooperation was the ideal of the early Industrial Revolution, and is fundamental to concepts of "Scientific Management" (Taylor, 1913). Production is about combining different permanent skills, both manual and mental.

debatative cooperation

Schmidt claims that augmentative and combinative cooperation belong to pre- and proto-industrial forms of organisation. Modern forms of production and automation change industrial roles and skills, and thus the necessary form of cooperation.

> "The introduction of a machine system transfers control of the operations of tools to the machine system, leaving workers in charge of functions like planning, supervision, and fault diagnosis. Workers in modern industrial settings must cope with very complex settings where disturbances and accidents are not linear courses of events released by only one cause, and the potential ramifications of any intervention are immense. In order to cope effectively with this kind of complexity, workers in charge of operating these plants must be able to apply conceptual knowledge of the domain and the machine system. As a result of the introduction of machine systems, then, work in areas of production formerly characterised by pre-dominance of technique-based specialization is being transformed into knowledge based work and the accompanying combinative cooperation is eclipsed, and in part superceded, by the forms of cooperative decision making that characterise work in complex settings."

(ibid: 22)

Debatative cooperation is not seen as replacing augmentative and combinative cooperation, which still play a part in work in complex settings. However, it is seen as the "elemental" form in complex settings. It is necessary both for function, and for understanding what is going on. It has two major aspects: negotiation of the selection and integration of different heuristics in the construction of the work process; and "the integration of different perspectives required to match the ontological structure of the domain."

The notion of the centrality of debatative cooperation to modern production provides the second structural element to our analysis of the initial anecdote about loyalty to professional associations vs loyalty to the company. Earlier it was claimed that changes in the nature of communication media have given rise to "social fields", networks, and forms of association that are outside the possibility of management inspection and control. Schmidt's analysis implies that *the form of modern production itself (debatative cooperation) also gives rise to "social fields", networks, and forms of association that are outside the possibility of direct management inspection and control.* The outcome of negotiating different heuristics and perspectives cannot be specified in advance, anticipated, or pre-planned -- if it could be, there would be nothing to negotiate.

While agreeing with Schmidt that the form of cooperation is the basic generative mechanism of work organisation, and that forms of cooperation develop mutually with the means of production, it is possible to take a wider view of cooperation and its consequences. Schmidt's analysis concentrates on negotiation as functional within corporate boundaries and goals. The position here is that these boundaries and goals cannot be taken as given. Debatative cooperation gives rise to side effects such as the "social field", noted by Perin, and the feeling of managerial helplessness, noted by Robb. Such side effects cannot be ignored, since they spring from an essential aspect of debatative cooperation: problem structuring is agenda setting. Agenda setting, once unleashed, is difficult to contain. The limited view of "debate" gives rise to an awkward notion of cooperation. For example, Olerup (1990), referencing Nesbitt (1986) has pointed to a possible confusion between coordination and cooperation.

> "Some cases of superior and subordinate relationships are in my opinion not instances of cooperation. The boss gives the secretary a list of letters, with rough outlines, to compose and write. The secretary does this and returns the letters. Is it computer supported cooperative work, when the secretary in the morning opens her computer-mail to find this list, and having finished the job/letters sends it to the boss's computer mailbox? I have just read an article which claims this is computer supported cooperative work. To my mind this is introducing computer-means into plain old-fashioned coordination and superior subordinate relationships, but there is nothing about doing it jointly, and thus nothing cooperative. Also, it is not between two equal agents. Nevertheless, if the secretary refused to do the letters the boss would most likely say that the secretary was uncooperative, but this seems to be a very one-sided, un-symmetrical kind of cooperation (or lack of it)."

This seems a fair criticism. There is nothing in Schmidt (1990), Bannon & Schmidt (1989), Lyytinen (1990), and other proponents of the cooperative principle to exclude this situation from the classification "cooperative". On one set of distinctions, the Schmidt approach is valid. It has been pointed out by many authors (eg. Salaman, 1979; Coates & Topham, 1970) that a "work to rule" immediately shows the importance of cooperation in the functioning of enterprises -- especially in superior-subordinate working relationships. Nevertheless, there is another viewpoint, in which cooperation is associated with autonomy, equality, and agenda setting. This is not caught by the notion of debatative cooperation. There is a contradiction facing the management of the company in the initial story, reflected in Schmidt's account. Debatative cooperation is assumed to take place within a corporate agenda. It may, but it has an inherent dynamic to produce (and reproduce) its own agendas. Here lies the contradiction and potential source of new forms of conflict.

It is suggested that further distinctions are needed to augment Schmidt's categories, and to reconcile them with existing formal principles and research on cooperation as a form of management and control (Watkins, 1986; Bernstein, 1980; Rothschild & Whitt, 1986; Mellor et al, 1988; Cornforth et al., 1988; Eccles, 1981; Fairclough, 1986a,b, 1987).

functional cooperation

The Schmidt categories deal especially with levels and types of functional cooperation, with cooperative work that "pertains to the sphere of production". They do not apply to "social interaction in the system of work in general". Debatative cooperation is seen as functional cooperation because it takes place *within* a corporate agenda and within corporate boundaries. The functional analysis indicates that manual and cognitive skills are integrated in most work processes for most of the time, and this requires interpretive cooperative work from the participants whatever their status within the corporate hierarchy. The strength of Schmidt's analysis is that the cooperative aspects of work should be taken more seriously. This would help avoid re-enactment of the more disastrous system designs of the past, which ignored the needs for situated action and interpretation work.

Nevertheless, functional cooperation still assumes a dominant organisational agenda. A sensitive interpretation would not deny the existence and impact of other agendas (those of individual workers, trades unions, management, professional groups, etc.). But it would concede that, by and large, these agendas accommodate to, and operate within the dominant corporate agenda. (Hellman, 1990). In other words, an analysis exclusively in terms of functional cooperation has a tendency to assume, in common with other types of "system" thinking (see critiques by Nurminen,1988; Morgan,1986, Flood & Jackson, 1988) that organisational objectives are consensual. Such functional analysis can be augmented, and different perspectives gained by considering other forms of cooperation.

constitutional cooperation

In contrast to functional cooperation, and taking up Olerup's point, there is another perspective best exemplified in the worldwide Cooperative Movement. This is constitutional cooperation. It focuses on consumer control of retail distribution, and on worker ownership and control of enterprises. Principles of formal equality, such as those developed by the International Cooperative Alliance are applicable to both. These were an attempt to change the ground-rules of work.

It is easy to counterpose constitutional cooperation to other work forms, stressing differences of legal constitution, rather than the similarities in practice. Such counterpositions can be supported by case studies and "ideal-typical" analyses that concentrate exclusively on cooperatives. (eg. Bernstein, 1980, ICOM, 1987; Jefferis & Robinson, 1986; Rothschild & Whitt,1986). Similarities are less visible, less researched, and less dramatic. Nevertheless, they are many. Formal cooperatives take on techniques from conventional enterprises -- not just technical and financial, but managerial (Eccles,1981, Paton et al.,1989). Supposedly conventional enterprises can take on surprisingly large amount of cooperative baggage -- not just matrix management (Galbraith, 1973), consultation and participation, but even cooperative legal forms, as with ESOPS[11] (Blumenthal, 1986).

A specialisation in constitutional cooperation can under-rate the necessity for functional cooperation in production. Historically and politically this is understandable, and may be justifiable. In practice, problems with functional cooperation, whatever their source, are usually fatal (see Baumgartner et al., 1979; Landry et al., 1986 for excellent examples). Consitutional cooperation has significance as an indicator of social attitude and political movement. But as a critical variable in understanding workplace practice, and how computer support may be best deployed, it appears more a diversion than a help.

---

[11]Employee Share Ownership Plans

associative cooperation

This third form is akin to the political principle of voluntary association. It does not map exclusively onto any specific organisational form. It is an essential and explicit ingredient in the formation of a constitutional cooperative (Mellor et al., 1988) where the members collectively decide to create their own enterprise. The perpetuation of the feelings and practices of associative cooperation are viewed by many commentators as the true hallmark of a cooperative[12]. Unfortunately, there is a flawed relation between associative and constitutional cooperation. An initial common agenda (created associatively) can easily become a dominant agenda, with its "guardians" and the related paraphenalia and structures of power. The emergence of a new, hegemonic agenda -- although theoretically permissible in democratic organisations -- is discouraged and suppressed (Freeman,1973; Tynan & Thomas,1984; Paton & Lockett, 1978). Where suppression fails, a faction fight follows (McMonnies,1985; Robinson, 1983, 1987; Macfarlane, 1985), often with devastating organisational consequences.

Associative cooperation also occurs widely in ordinary work processes. People talk to each other in self selecting groups outside formal channels. Without this process, functional cooperation probably could not happen[13]. One facet of associative cooperation is of special interest here. It can and often does give rise to an autonomous agenda. This distinguishes it from functional cooperation where the purpose is to implement, through the process that Gerson and Star (1986) appropriately call "articulation work", a pre-existing dominant (corporate) agenda.

In general terms, it can be said that functional cooperation is a necessary condition of effective work. Analytically, it is not possible to account for viable organisation without this category. But functional cooperation alone is not enough. As Olerup pointed out, it may be external to the way workers experience what they are doing. Associative cooperation, in contrast, is a sufficient condition for experiencing praxis as cooperative work. It is argued here that *associative cooperation is an inevitable by-product of debatative-functional cooperation*. Here lies the problem. Associative cooperation, released by functional cooperation, is only a sufficient condition for effective work where there is a single or dominant agenda. Multiple associative cooperations may result in organisational chaos that preclude effective work. This brings us naturally to a last category of cooperation.

social cooperation

Social cooperation (by simple analogy with a society) is a process whereby multiple agendas are reconciled. This is not a place to detail, let alone advocate any particular approach to social cooperation or forms of government, only to note some recent interesting contri-

---

[12]See for instance, Yohanan Stryjan's (1987) appropriately titled "Impossible organizations: on self-management and organisational reproduction".

[13]Associative cooperation has also been picked up as a basis of some CSCW applications: for instance "Video Windows" (Fish, Kraut, & Chalfonte, 1990); "Cruiser" (Root, 1988;) COLAB (Stefik et al. 1987) and in some analysis and theory. This emphasis has often led to criticism that CSCW can be technology centred (Moran & Anderson, 1990) or that it deals with situations of artificial or contrived equality of participation (Jones & Hirst,1986).

butions (Burns & Ueberhorst, 1988; Lindblom 1990; Anderson, 1990; Funtowicz & Ravetz 1990). It can be pointed out that the concept of social cooperation is a challenge to distinctions of level and problematic between "running a society" and "running a company"[14]. At least three aspects of societal organisation, formerly thought to be only marginally relevant to "running companies" may now emerge as increasingly significant.

Societies do not have goals. They are, by and large, structured by constitutions and legal systems rather than by "objectives". Enterprises appear to be moving uncertainly away from corporate objectives -- and many have some difficulty knowing "exactly what business they are in..."

Societies find it increasingly difficult (and many claim it is undesirable) to exercise control over the movements of their members, or even over who their members are. In this latter context, de Zeeuw (1991) recently noted that that members of society "cannot be fired (at least not in any generally acceptable sense), or replaced on a reasonably short term by better specimens." The effect of cooperative technologies (such as e-mail) on the permeability of corporate boundaries may mean that companies no longer know who their members are -- at least in the sense of who it is that is influencing their "decisions".

Society's main function (without which it deservedly disintegrates) is to provide acceptable mechanisms to reconcile multiple, emerging, unpredictable, orthogonal, and often conflicting, collective agendas. In the light of the considerations earlier on the "associative" nature of e-mail, and probably of future CSCW applications generally, this latter function can be expected to take on explicit importance in corporate environments. However, it should also be pointed out that all three aspects of social cooperation have faced worker (and to some extent, consumer) cooperatives for almost three centuries. Their track record of success is not very impressive.

The interaction between types of cooperation

The interaction between types of cooperation is complex and dynamic, but some general tendencies can be sketched.

On the one hand, there are the dynamics of formal cooperatives. A political process of voluntary association gives rise to constitutional cooperation[15]. Various forms of social cooperation are then developed in order to facilitate functional cooperation. This can work well in the pre-industrial sectors, where augmentative cooperation is the main requirement. In proto-industrial sectors, where combinative cooperation is a requirement, this often violates (or makes extremely difficult) a continuation of associative cooperation whatever the form of social cooperation[16].

---

[14]It can be objected that one would not want to see a nuclear power station run in the same way as a democratic society. The answer lies, not in what we want, but in what is actually going on. The company in the anecdote at the beginning runs facilities with all the danger potential of nuclear power. The problem of associative cooperation, loyalty, and staff turnover already face it, and "Defence" industries (and thus nuclear weapons systems) in a massive way.

[15]'The system that we have here is one by which any decision at all is fully discussed, talked round about. We look at it to see if it's beneficial to us -- the whole lot of us -- and we decide for or against in that context.' " (Wajcman, 1983:50)

[16]"... both at Mondragon, and at least one of the large scale co-operatives of Britain (KME), the retention of a detailed division of labour was a source of great dissatisfaction among workers (Eaton, 1979; Clarke, 1978). It

On the other hand we find the dynamics of conventional enterprises. The evolution of the economic process of production has given rise to debatative cooperation, which in turn is giving rise to associative cooperation. There are indications that the latter is necessary for *and* conflicts with functional cooperation. This seems to indicate a need for social cooperation, and for a language in which this can be expressed.

Detailed division of labour and hierarchical organisation (whatever the constitutional form) do not generate the experience of "situational ownership". Most participants in production are not participants in the construction of the agenda of production. Even if "debatative" cooperation occurs, it can, and often does coexist with strong feelings of alienation. In contrast, modern production increasingly engenders associative cooperation that does produce and reproduce agenda setting activities[17].

Schmidt (1990) correctly points out that qualitative changes in the means of production require the application of conceptual knowledge, both the integration of heuristics and the integration of perspectives. The essential point here is that the concept of "debatative cooperation" is limited in two ways.

First, it is presented as the formulation of an agenda within a dominant corporate agenda. This is why it remains within the framework of functional cooperation. The workers and managers deal with the complexity, but not with the constraints (themselves a result of an external corporate agenda) that generate some of the complexity. Associative cooperation, arising from debatative cooperation, cannot be prevented from generating autonomous agendas. These may be necessary to resolve the "problem" in hand, but also arise spontaneously from the process of association itself.

Second, "debatative cooperation" is presented as association by groups of company personnel within company boundaries. Yet as Perin has pointed out, to repeat the previous quotation, "electronic social formations represent new sources of industrial conflict, raising questions about conventional relationships of space and time to industrial discipline and control. Dahlbom (1990: 94) has put the same theme more strongly:

> "The most revolutionary change in our world view brought upon us by computer technology is perhaps its reconstruction of space and time, the fundamental categories of a mechanistic world view, and of a modern capitalistic, industrialized society."

The full flavour of associative cooperation arises when these limits of space and time, assumed as corporate boundaries, come into question. Local agendas have always had the potential for incompatibility with corporate agendas. Increasingly, and more importantly, local agendas may arise from social fields that are external or partial to the company in question. This is the origin of Perin's legitimacy dilemma, and of Robb's feeling that organisations behave as if they have "minds of their own". Those formulating new agendas experience exhilaration. Those who thought they knew the agenda experience something else: the

---

is difficult for co-operative workers to feel they are engaging in a great co-operative experiment when their sole co-operative duty is to make several thousand spot welds each day."
Clarke (1984)

[17]The link between agenda setting and a feeling of situational ownership" is completely evident where workers decide to rescue enterprises threatened with closure (BATA-- Dubreuil, 1963; UCS- Coates 1981,;Paton et al, 1989; Hansen,G.B. & Adams,F.T. ,1987)

196

"potential for real change caused by a medium which allows widely separated people to aggregate their needs is, in fact, frightening......"

(Fanning & Raphael 1986)

Concluding Remarks

An anecdote of a large company experiencing major staff loss despite excellent wages and working conditions suggested two underlying structural factors: changes in the nature of communication media, and changes in the nature of work organisation. Both lead to informal associations, and changes in the ground on which people operate. The permeability of corporate boundaries, due to communication media, and the inevitability of informal association, due to the necessity of cooperative control of modern production, suggest a radical rethinking of the nature of companies and of management. The situation can be expressed in a simple counterposition of images. The current image, frequently seen in meetings, is of a company represented by a circle that has relationships, often represented by lines, to other companies also represented by circles. The circles are "solid". The issue, admirably served by system theories and cybernetics, is to maintain the corporate agenda and boundaries through control of inputs, outputs, and structure (cf. Beer,1975).

A more appropriate image might be to regard companies as the intersection of changing social fields. The issue would be different. How to maintain a stable intersection of fluctuating fields of independent collective actors with their own developing agendas. This is social cooperation. Unfortunately, the historical experience with social cooperation is not good. Designed constitutions prove unworkably oversimplistic. Elster (1978) has pointed out that undesigned solutions (God, "historical inevitability", or the "invisible hand" of the market) appear to lead to social and ecological disasters, similar in dynamics to Sartre's (1960) tragedy of the commons[18].

Yet the construction of social cooperation may now be the central issue. It also calls for a reconstruction of notions of cooperation. The old representation of the company as some sort of stand-alone entity often presents cooperation as an ideal to be achieved -- and "cooperative technologies" are accordingly eagerly embraced. The reality is that cooperation, especially cooperation in production, has always posed more questions than it solved. Functional cooperation is a necessary keystone for carrying out and understanding the activities of production. Its twin, associative cooperation may be with us on a large scale already, an invisible emergence from production itself. Like consumer goods, it has a deep, instinctive, and irrepressible appeal. It may have just as many side effects. Electronic mail is used despite its manifest inadequacies because it supports associative as well as debatative cooperation. The dilemmas pointed out by Perin arise because associative and functional cooperation are intertwined, both dangerous for and necessary to the survival of enterprises, and because people take to associative cooperation "like ducks to water". But *multiple associative cooperation* gives rise to *multiple collective agendas*. Neither are tractable to traditional conceptions of management.

---

[18]Each peasant seeks to obtain more land by cutting down trees. The result is general deforestation, soil erosion, and less land available to each peasant than at the outset.

It is becoming accepted wisdom that CSCW applications, and probably computer systems in general (Sorgaard,1989; Nurminen,1988), should support the associative, interpretive, debatative aspects of work. In part, and willynilly, this is also support for the formation of autonomous agendas. CSCW is the embodiment of the new structural features of communication and organisational form that have been discussed. There is every reason to anticipate a "second wave" of CSCW applicationsthat will be far more widely used than those reviewed by Greif (1988),Johansen (1988), or Schrage (1990). Perhaps this is the point at which we should be looking for "the disaster after next". The emergence of multiple, collective agendas implies a need for pluralistic political management, termed social cooperation. To date, such post-modern organisation of social cooperation is only noticeable by its absence.

REFERENCES

Anderson, W.T. 1990 Reality Isn't What It Used To Be Harper & Row, San Francisco

Axelrod, R. 1990 The Evolution of Co-operation Penguin Books. London.

Bannon, L. & Schmidt, K. 1989 "CSCW: Four Characters in Search of a Context" in Bowers, J. & Wilson,P. (eds.) EC-CSCW '89: Proc. of the First European Conference on Computer Supported Co-operative Work. Gatwick. London Sept. 13-15 1989

Bannon, L. 1989 "Computer Supported Work: Some Issues" in Proc. Mutual Uses of Science and Cybernetics Conf. Amsterdam. March 27- April 1 '89

1985 "Extending the Design Boundaries of Human-Computer Interaction" ICS Report 8505 Institute for Cognitive Science, University of California San Diego

Baumgartner,T., Burns,T.R., & Sekulic,D. 1979 "Self Management, Market, and Political Institutions in Conflict" in Work and Power Sage: London

Beer, S 1975 "Fanfare for Effective Freedom: Cybernetic Praxis in Government" in Platform for Change Wiley Chichester,UK.

Bernstein, P. 1980 Workplace Democratization: Its Internal Dynamics Transaction Books New Jersey

Bjerknes, G., Ehn,P. & Kyng,M. (eds) 1987 Computers and Democracy: A Scandinavian Challenge Avebury England

Bjerknes,G., Dahlbohm,B. et al. 1990 Organizational Competence in System Development Chartwell Bratt. Lund, Sweden.

Blumenthal, Adam 1986 Interest and Equity: Uses of Employee Ownership and Participation in the Restructuring of the U.S. Steel Industry. B.A. Thesis: Harvard College. USA

Bullen,C.V. & Bennett,J.L. 1990 "Learning from user experience with groupware" in Proc. CSCW '90 Oct. Los Angeles. CA.

Burns,T.R. & Ueberhorst 1988 Creative Democracy Praeger New York

Clarke, T. 1984 "Alternative Modes of Co-operative Production" in Economic & Industrial Democracy. Vol.5. Sage London

Clarke,T. 1978 "A Comparative Study of Three Major Workers' Co-operatives: Final Report" SSRC London

Coates, K. & Topham, T. (eds.) 1970 Workers' Control Panther London

Coates, K. 1981 Work-ins, Sit-ins and Industrial Democracy Spokesman. Nottingham. UK

Cornforth,C., Thomas,A., Lewis,J., & Speare,R. 1988 Developing Successful Worker Co-operatives Sage London

Dahlbom,B. 1990 "An Artificial World: An invitation to creative conversations on future use and design of computer technology" in Scandinavian Journal of Information Systems. Aug. Vol.2. Aalborg, Denmark.

de Zeeuw, G. 1991 "Support, Survival, and Culture" Concept Paper, Faculty of Andragology, University of Amsterdam.

Dubreuil, H. 1963 L'example de Bata: La libération des initiatives individuelles dans une entreprise géante. Grasset. Paris.

Eaton,J. 1979 "The Basque Workers Co-operatives" in Industrial Relations Journal. Vol.10 No.3

Eccles,T. 1981 Under New Management Pan. London

Elster,J. 1978 Logic and Society: Contradictions and Possible Worlds Wiley Chichester,UK

Eveland,J.D., & Bikson,T.K. 1988 "Work Group Structures and Computer Support: A Field Experiment" in Proc. Conf. on Computer Supported Co-operative Work. Portland, Oregon. Sept.26-28 '88

Fairclough, M. 1986a An Analysis of Triumph Meriden Motorcycles Ltd. 1975 - 1983 PhD Bristol University

1986b Conditional Degeneration and Producer Co-operatives: A Reappraisal of the Socialist Tradition. "The Webbs' Revenge ?" In Proc. Nat. Conf. For Research on Worker Co-operatives. Co-operatives Reseach Unit, Open University London.

1987 "Mondragon in Context" Research Report, Dept. of Sociology, University of Bristol. Bristol

Fanning,T. & Raphael,B. 1986 "Computer Teleconferencing: experience at Hewlett Packard" in Proc. Conf. CSCW '86. December. Austin. Texas.

Fish,R.S., Kraut,R.E., & Chalfonte,B.L. 1990 "The VideoWindow System in Informal Communications" in Proc. CSCW '90. Oct. Los Angeles. CA.

Flood,R.L. & Jackson,M.C. 1988 "Cybernetics and Organisation Theory: A Critical Review" in Cybernetics and Systems. Vol.19. No. 1. Hemisphere NY

Freeman, Jo 1973 "The Tyranny of Structurelessness" in Berkeley Journal of Sociology (17) 1972 - 3

Funtowicz, S. & Ravetz,J. 1990 "Post-normal science: a new science for new times" in Scientific European. Oct.

Galbraith,J.R. 1973 Designing Complex Organisations Addison Wesley: Reading, Mass.

Gerson, E. & Star, S. 1986 Analysing Due Process in the Workplace ACM Transactions on Office Information Systems. 4,3.

Giddens,A. 1976 New Rules of Sociological Method Basic Books. NY.

1984 The Constitution of Society: Outline of the Theory of Structure University of California Press. Berkeley. CA.

Greif,I. (ed.) 1988 Computer Supported Co-operative Work: A Book of Readings Morgan Kaufmann. Calif.

Grudin, J. 1988 "Why CSCW Applications Fail: Problems in the Design and Evaluation of Organisational Interfaces" in Proceedings of the Conference on Computer Supported Co-operative Work. Portland, Oregon. Sept. 26-29

Hansen,G.B. & Adams,F.T. 1987 "Saving Jobs and Putting Democracy to Work" Hum. Rel or J. of Ind & Econ. Democracy.

Hellman,R. 1990 "User Support: Illustrating computer use in collaborative work contexts" in Proc. CSCW '90. Oct. Los Angeles, CA.

Hirschheim,R.A. 1985 Office Automation -- A Social and Organisational Perspective Wiley Chichester

Hughes, Randall, and Shapiro (1991) "CSCW: Discipline or Paradigm? A sociological perspective" in Proc. 2nd. European Conference on CSCW, Amsterdam, Sept 25-27.

ICOM (Industrial Common Ownership Movement) 1987 No Single Model: Participation, Organisation, and Democracy in Larger Co-operatives ICOM: Leeds

Jefferis,K. & Robinson,M. 1986 "Social Investment in Production" in Developing Local Economic Strategies (Ed. Cochrane, A.) Open University Press. Milton Keynes.

Johansen, R. 1988 Groupware: Computer Support for Business Teams Free Press, New York

Jones,L.M. & Hirst,A.J. 1986   Visual Simulation in Hospitals: a Managerial or Political Tool? Dept. of Community Medicine, University of Edinburgh.

Kiesler,S. 1986 "The hidden messages in computer networks" in Harvard Business Review. Jan/Feb.

Kling, R. 1980 & 1988 Theoretical Perspectives in Social Analyses of Computing in Bannon,L & Pylyshyn,Z. (eds.) Perspectives on the Computer Revolution (1989), Ablex, NJ.

Landry,C., Morley,D., Southwood,R.,& Wright,P. 1986 What a Way to Run a Railroad: An Analysis of Radical Failure Comedia. London

Leroy,C.M. & Robinson,M. 1987 "Recommendations on Training Models for Development Agents and Local Development Agencies" Final Report No. 87/727. European Economic Community. Brussels.

Lindblom,C.E. 1990 Inquiry and Change Yale University Press. London & New York

Lyytinen,K. 1990 CSCW: Issues and Challenges Technical Report. Univ. of Jyväskylä, Finland

Macfarlane,R. 1985 Power and Context: Issues Raised in Co-operative Development in Britain. Richard Macfarlane London

Malone,T.W., Yates,J., & Benjamin,R.I. 1988 "Electronic Markets and Electronic Hierarchies" in Greif,I. (ed.) Computer Supported Co-operative Work: A Book of Readings Morgan Kaufmann. Calif.

McMonnies,D. 1985 "Trades Unions and Co-ops? A Merseyside Case Study: The Scott Bader -- Synthetic Resins Saga." Working Paper No. 6. Dept. of Political Theory and Institutions. The University of Liverpool: Liverpool

Mellor,M., Hannah,J., & Stirling,J. 1988 Worker Co-operatives in Theory and Practice Open University Press Milton Keynes

Moran,T.P. & Anderson,R.J. .1990.."The workaday world as a paradigm for CSCW design" in Proc. CSCW 90. Oct. Los Angeles. CA.

Morgan,G. 1986 Images of Organisation Sage Beverly Hills

Nesbit, R.A. 1986 Cooperation International Encyclopoedia of Social Science.

Norman,D. 1981 "The Trouble with UNIX" in Bannon,L.J. & Pylyshyn,Z.W. (eds.) (1989) Perspectives on the Computer Revolution, Ablex, New Jersey.

Nurminen, M. 1988 People or Computers: Three Ways of Looking at Information Systems Chartwell-Bratt. Sweden

Olerup,A. 1990 Personal Correspondence.

Orlikowski,W.J. 1989 The Duality of Technology Sloan School of Management. MIT. Cambridge MA.

Paton, R. & Lockett, M. 1978 Fairblow Dynamics CRU Monograph No.2. Open University. Milton Keynes.

Paton,R. et al. 1989 Reluctant Entrepreneurs Open University Press. Milton Keynes.

Perin, Constance 1989   "Electronic Social Fields in Bureaucracies" in American Anthropological Association, Organised Session, "Egalitarian Ideologies and Class Contradictions in American Society". Washington DC. November 1989

Reder,S. & Schwab,R.G. 1990 "The temporal structure of cooperative activity" in Proc. CSCW '90. Oct. Los Angeles. CA

Robb,F.F. 1989a "Morphostasis and Morphogenesis: Contexts of Participating Design Inquiry in the Design of Systems of Learning and Human Development" in Proc. 33rd Annual Meeting Int. Soc. for the Systems Sciences. Edinburgh. July.

1989b "The Realisation of Supra-Human Processes: The Problem ahead for Cybernetics" in Proc. 33rd Annual Meeting Int. Soc. for the Systems Sciences. Edinburgh. July.

Robinson, M. 1983 (ed.) "Size is a historic problem in all communities" Proc. of the Inaugural Meeting of the-Large Co-ops Network. Sept. '83. Kingston & Richmond Co-operative Development Agency. London.

1986 "Some Policy Implications of the Relationship between Co-operatives and New Technology" in Proc. National Co-operative Researchers Conference. CRU Open University , Milton Keynes.

1987 "Mass Conversation: An Examination of Computer Techniques for Many to Many Communication" in Proc. "Problems of (Im)possible Worlds" Conf. Univ. of Amsterdam. Spring '87

1990a 'Computer Supported Cooperative Work & Informatics for Development" in Proc. INFORMATICA '90. Havana. Feb.

1990b "Pay Bargaining in Workers' Co-operatives" in Self Referencing in Social Systems (ed. F. Geyer & J. van der Zouwen) Intersystems Publications. USA.

1991 "Double Level Languages & Co-operative Working" AI & Society, 5:34-60 Springer International.

Root,R.W. 1988 "Design of a Multi-Media Vehicle for Social Browsing" in Proceedings of the Conference on Computer Supported Co-operative Work. Portland, Oregon. Sept. 26-29 '88

Rosson,M.B. 1985 "The role of experience in editing" in Proc. INTERACT '84. Elsevier North Holland, Amsterdam. NL.

Rothschild, J. & Whitt, J. 1986 The Co-operative Workplace: Potentials and dilemmas of organizational democracy and participation Cambridge University Press. Cambridge.

Salaman,G. 1979 Work Organisations: Resistance and Control Longman London

Sartre,J.P. 1960 Critique de la Raison Dialectique Gallimard: Paris

Schrage,M. 1990 Shared Minds: The New Technologies of Collaboration Random House. New York

Schmidt,K. 1990 Analysis of Cooperative Work: A Conceptual Framework Risø National Laboratory.

Searle,J.R. 1969 Speech Acts Cambridge University Press. Cambridge. England

Sheil,B. 1983 "Coping with Complexity" in Office Technology and People, No.1. Elsevier Science Publishers. Amsterdam.

Snyders,J. 1987 "Putting zip into e-mail" Infosystems. Aug. (cited in Galagher, Kraut, & Egido 1990)

Sproul,L. & Kiesler,S. 1988 "Reducing Social Context Cues: Electronic Mail in Organizational Communication" in Greif,I. (ed.)(1988)Computer Supported Co-operative Work: A Book of Readings, Morgan Kaufmann. Calif.

Stefik,M., et al. 1987 "Beyond the Chalkboard: Computer Support for Collaboration and Problem Solving Meetings" in Communications of the ACM. Vol. 30. No.1. Jan.'87

Stryjan, Y. 1987 Impossible Organisations: On Self-Management and Organisational Reproduction University of Uppsala Uppsala, Sweden

Suchman, L.A. 1987 Plans and Situated Actions: the problem of human machine communication Cambridge University Press. New York.

Summerville,I. & Rodden,T. "Mailtrays: An Object-Oriented Approach to Message Handling" in EURINFO '88: First European Conf. on Information Technology for Organisational Systems. Ed. Bullinger,H.J. et al. North Holland Amsterdam

Sørgaard, P. 1989 Object Oriented Programming and Computerised Shared Material OOC Program. University of Amsterdam. Amsterdam. NL

Taylor, F. W. 1913 The Principles of Scientific Management, New York

Thompson,G. 1984 "Three characterizations of communications revolutions" in S. Winkler (Ed.) Computer Communication: Impacts and Implications. New York. Int. Conf. on Computer Communication.

TURN 1990 Report to Meeting: Trades Union Regional Network, Grenada, Spain. CEC Brussels

Tynan, E. & Thomas. A. 1984 KME -- Working in a Large Co-operative Co-ops Research Unit. Monograph No. 6. Open University. Milton Keynes. UK

Wajcman,J. 1983 Women in Control: Dilemmas of a Workers Co-operative The Open University Press. Milton Keynes. UK

Watkins,W.P. 1986 Co-operative Principles Today & Tomorrow Holyoake Books Manchester

HUMAN JOBS AND COMPUTER INTERFACES
M.I. Nurminen and G.R.S. Weir
Elsevier Science Publishers B.V. (North-Holland)
© 1991 IFIP. All rights reserved.

Dependencies in Research on User Controlled Information Systems Development

Siv Friis

Dept of Information and Computer Science
Lund University, Sweden
ADBSF@SELDC 52

Abstract:
In this article we focus on information systems development where the future users are in control of the development process, and the data processing experts play the role of supporters/teachers. Case studies and action research methodologies are often considered appropriate alternatives in information systems development research rather than the traditional normal science research process. With two case studies as a starting point we argue that there are dependencies in information system development models that have a user oriented/controlled perspective. These models have a structural likeness with action research methodology and, as such have dependencies similar to problems associated with action research methodologies. Here we will address two of the major problems: With problems of validation and generalization in research about information systems development. We suggest a minimal list of how to cope with these dependencies.

1 Introduction

There is a structural similarity between the normal science research process and the computer expert development of a computer based information system (CBIS) (Friis 1984, Flensburg 1986). In the research process we study some phenomena "out there" and in the systems development process we actually do the same. When doing research we use a set of predefined research methodologies and when we develop information systems we use a systems development model which has the same purpose as the research methodologies; to ensure a certain quality in the end product.

Most information system development (ISD) models in use today emanate from the old traditional Systems Design Life Cycle (SDLC) models. These are fairly well described elsewhere, and will not be elaborated further here.We will just conclude that the SDLC models are not very well suited for active user participation in the construction of the future system (Friis 1984). Traditionally, the data processing experts (DP) are here the architects of the finished CBIS. The future users are rarely involved in the development process, sometimes only as interview respondents concerning requirements.

In contrast to the SDLC model mentioned above we have tested a working model where the DP experts act as supporters / teachers and as dialogue partners in the ISD instead of interviewers. Since the main property of the model is that the users are responsible for the resulting system and they should also initiate the development. This working model has a structural similarity to the action research process which will be described next.

2 Action research

The concept of action research was brought forward by Kurt Lewin during his work among the jews in New York in the middle of the 40's, just after the second world war. According to Lewin (1947) action research consists of: analysis, fact-finding, conceptualiztion, planning, executing, more fact-finding or evaluation – and then a repetiton of the whole circle of activities until satisfaction. By doing so, you achieve a feeling for the whole.

In the perspective of William R Torbert (1987), where the researchers participate in active support in the development work, and, in collaboration with the co-researchers from a research area, they work to better a situation. It also means participation of the researchers in a constructive way in the change of the research areas as described by Kalleberg (1989).

The researcher is not only an observer, (s)he actually participates in the work. It means that the people in the research areas participate in the research and are considered co-researchers. In this perspective, the researchers have a more humane view of the research objects. They do not influence and manipulate objects, but collaborate with subjects (Torbert 1987). The latter is the perspective of the work presented here. Torbert introduces a model of social sciences based on three assumptions:
"1. that researchers are themselves active participants in the situation researched and that the researcher-situation relationship deserves to be studied,
2. that the framework and variables of study themselves change in the course of study,
3. that an important way of testing the validity and significance of social knowledge is to feed data back into the setting researched, studying how this feedback influences further action."

This is supported by Jenkins (1984) who defined action research (or participative research) as a methodology which "allows the researchers to become a part of the research – to be affected by and to affect the research". The objective is not final testing of hypothesis, but instead "realization of the human creative potential". Participation is here interpreted in a dialectic way, which means that in participative research one must also allow different perspectives in the group of actors. In much the same way Argyris and Schön (1989) discuss participatory action research (PAR) as a form of action research that involves practitioners as both subjects and co-researchers.

There are several advantages with action research in ISD research (see for examples, Wood-Harper 1984, Antill 1984) but there are also problems. One problem is the identification of the findings. Already in the beginning of the 70's Nygaard pointed out in the well known NJMF-project with the Norwegian trade unions, that the result was not the reports, but the actions undertaken by the trade union members (Nygaard, 1974). This is of course important, but we still propose that action research must to some degree be able to produce findings that to some extent can be generalised.

Therefore we propose case studies as the principal result for the research community. Case studies are in this context interpreted as descriptions of what actually happened during the action (Nygaard, 1974) according to the perspective of the researchers and participating actors. The question of generalization is then left to the reader's recognition of similarities and differences in situations where findings in cases might become applied.

Another problem is the lack of general adaptability. This means that the case study only describes what happened in the actual case and the interpretation of the actors involved.

Validation is considered of importance in traditional research. There it relates to measurement: A valid measure is one which accurately measures what it purports to measure. The notion of validity within action research must take a dialectic epistemology as a starting point. This means that we must start with people, not with methods, since, as hermeneutics teaches us (Gadamer 1975), method in itself does not lead to knowledge, it must be interpreted by human beings. This again brings us to cases comprising interpreting and acting people.

3 Empirical cases in a user controlled ISD environment

Two case studies within the PROTEVS (PROTotyping - for an EVOlutionary Systems development) program are taken as a starting point in the discussion of dependencies in user controlled ISD models. In the studies we aim to test and revise a working model for a user controlled model - the PROTEVS model. We will describe some of our experiences during this work and relate them to the above mentioned dependencies.

The fundamental idea of the model is that the problem owners (the future systems users) themselves should do the problem definitions and problem solving work in an ISD process. The concept of the model is based on the rapid prototyping model of the now classical article by Nauman and Jenkins (1982), where the DP experts are the prototype constructors. We contribute by going one step further and declare that the users themselves should be the prototype systems constructors - not the experts.

The PROTEVS model was first tested, and revised, in a case study some welfare workers in a town council 1982-1985. The revision was based on the questions and suggestions stated by the participating well-fare workers (Friis 1986). In this case all worked in true collaboration. All participants had their say in the revision of the PROTEVS model. We had no real project leader since we were all learning from one another in a 'muddling through' (Bjørn-Andersen 1974) fashion. The dependencies described in the next two cases were not, to our knowledge, present in this case.

To earn credibility and to design a fairly general model, PROTEVS is tested in other environments and in other work situations. Cases are now in progress to study how useful the working model is, e. g., in administration offices, with white collar workers, and in work shops of metal and pharmaceutical works and other industries, with blue collar workers. We shall here describe two cases: First a case in a 'wage and staff department', and then a case from the 'shop floor' of a pharmaceutical factory.

The participating actors in each case study are considered as subjects and hence co-researchers (Torbert, 1987). The data collection in each case was done as notes in diaries. Every party keeps his or her diary. The diaries are not private - more like a captain's log-book, i. e., the notes are open to all project participants. The notes are openly discussed and action is often taken in response to the notes in some log-book. The notes are also taken as evaluations of the development process in the project as well as of the research process. The co-researchers keep one log-book, and the researchers keep one each. The recollection of the two cases described below is is supported by reference to the respective log-books.

3.1 The Wage and Staff Department Case

A town council in the south-west part of Sweden was selected for one case, and we established collaboration with the 'wage and staff department' there. It was fortunate for the project that only one computer existed in this department, which was used for word processing only. In the case the future systems users were not used to computers.

After preliminary introductions of the researchers and the intended research, the department management decided upon twelve people (all clerks of some sort and status) to participate in the project. We started a project group, and planned to meet every possible Wednesday afternoon. Initially only one researcher was present at the meetings. Later on we decided it was good for the data collection in the project if more than one researcher could participate in the meetings. We also deemed it important that the model should be tested by researchers other than the creator - to test if there were any personal and/or pedagogical dependencies in the model.

At first one of the researchers was selected project leader. As in earlier cases we had the same experience with the users' quick active learning of the computers, the program system and the procedures of the working model. After only a few introductory meetings we had a 'whole day scenario' where the users, with only minor technical support from the researchers, developed three small prototype systems. After this day it was decided that the users would work on their own 'at home' with the PROTEVS model between weekly meetings. The users' working sessions should be documented in the users' log-book.

At the Wednesday meetings the researchers were to participate in the balancing of the weeks work and act as support if needed. But, it was soon realized that the users did not muster the same enthusiasm in their development work when the researchers were not present. We noticed a certain fatigue within the group.

We checked the users' log-book and found it contained no notes. We decided to act, and at an open discussion in the project group it came to attention that it was hard work for the users to do both research and ordinary daily work at the same time. Also it was mentioned that: "when Siv isn't here the sessions have no structure". Unfortunately, the researchers did not understand the undertones in this message. What the users were actually saying, which became apparent later in the project, was that:
- The users had become used to one of the researchers as 'teacher and support',
- the users were hiding behind the 'traditional user role' (Friis 1988), they did not own the project,
- the researcher did not notice this, i. e., the intentions of the PROTEVS model were not at hand.
These are serious problems in an action research project that declares the research 'objects' to be 'subjects' and problem-owners. In our case, where the researchers acted as DP experts as well as researchers, it seemed to be extra difficult to let go of the reins, and leave the development work to the 'co-researchers'.

Eventually, we learned this in another open discussion in the project group. We learned from the 'honesty of the users' when they declared: "But you don't always listen to us - you do what you think is right for us and the project. And, you are the one who knows, you are the expert, so who are we to dispute your decisions."

The project almost died at this session. Had it not been for one of the leading clerks who volunteered to become project leader, the research work would have stopped then and there, because there was a personal dependency in the PROTEVS model. The model was not explicit enough for the users.

To our dismay, we had to admit that in this case the users never really 'owned' the project. It was even said that: ".....we do this for the researchers because we like them and we know they mean well." It was apparent that we had taken on the traditional roles of researchers and DP experts (Friis 1988). We did not hear the undertones and meanings of the non-expert developers, i. e., the co-researchers. We had become 'aspect-blind'.

The concept of 'aspect-blindness' is used here in the sense as discussed by Kristen Nygaard and Pål Sørgaard (1987). They argue that the concept of perspectives is rather important for ISD. The possibility that the project leaders are suffering from aspect-blindness when dealing with the people involved in the ISD is quite common.

In the continued work and discussions in the project group we learned from this experience how to try to avoid this phenomenon. It was suggested by one of the clerks that this could be avoided if: "all involved participated in the development work, i. e., the problem definitions, solutions finding and problem solving work - both clerks and management". It was recommended by the users that we consider this for future development work with the PROTEVS model. We told the users that this was really the case with our model, but alas, we had not acted accordingly. The result of the ISD had again become our primary concern. Let us see what happened and what we learnt in our next case.

3.2 The Shop Floor Case

The pharmaceutical factory in question, which is one of five in an international concern, had financial difficulties for a long time, and had four ownership changes in the last couple of years. To stabilize the financial situation the company had considered rationalizing the factory work organization by implementing computer support in the manufacturing processes.

A negotiation meeting was set up with researchers, management, union leaders, shop stewards and other staff representatives. Management decided it was to our mutual benefit if a research team could assist in the development of the new work organization. The researchers would be able to try out the PROTEVS model on a shop floor, and the factory might gain some knowledge about computers and ISD for shop floors, and at the same time use the 'know how' of the shop floor workers in the development.

There are eight participants in this case. The main project group consists of six persons (including two shop stewards) from the shop floor and two researchers. At some of the meetings, persons from other factory departments and other researchers from other disciplines, e. g., social medicine, economic and social sciences were invited to participate. In this case study the PROTEVS model is also mostly tested by other researchers than the creator.

In this project the researchers did not start out, as in earlier cases, as teachers/supporters/DP experts in the PROTEVS model. The workers in the project group would rather discuss their present insecure work situation than discuss the PROTEVS model, because many knowledgeable workers had quit their jobs and the remaining workers were afraid that would cause the top management to close the factory. They wanted this development to give the remaining workers knowledge of new techniques such as: "computers, computer supported manufacturing and something of ISD for factories" complementary to the existing 'know how' of the workers. They wanted to test the computers first, and then analyse their present work organization.

The project meetings started in an aura of MacIntosh and HyperCard. The users did not master the computers as quickly as we had experienced in earlier cases, largely because they did not know very much about either typewriters or computers. They were insecure and looked to us for learning and support. Sorry to say, we all fell into the same trap as in the 'wage and staff department'. We stopped listening and all became teachers. We did not hear questions and suggestions - we had become 'aspect-blind' again.

After about five meetings one of the researchers noticed the same project fatigue as in the case before. We told the group members of our concern and of our earlier experiences. We suggested that they should have a meeting without the presence of the researchers, where they might discuss if and how they would like to continue the project. At the internal group meeting it was decided that they should continue the project work in the frame of the PROTEVS model, and that one of the shop stewards should act as project leader together with a researcher. All should continue to meet once every week to balance the work together. The researchers should still act as constructive and technical support, meaning that we should come to aid if called for, and we should continue to supply the group with techniques necessary for the work. The work went on. We still noticed the 'aspect-blindness', but now with the new project leaders. What we also found out was that this phenomenon actually occurred with all the group members. It was like having eight project leaders.

We also noticed that people who represented the problem area under development had difficulty in communication with the other project members even when we all tried to puncture the 'aspect-blindness'. We noticed that there were many routines and procedures the users did not think needed explaining, they were regarded as too 'obvious'. What we had was the opposite of the aspect-blindness; a 'taken-for-granted' perspective (Boughey 1978), a different kind of blindness.

We discussed this new phenomenon in the group and decided that one solution might be to let the representative of the current problem area under development act as a 'knowledge-person', and that the other members should try to do shared interpretations of the 'area of change'. The interpretations might be diagrams or drawings, or in some other descriptive technique, of the area as each had understood it. This should then be tested with the knowledge-person. All in the project group should participate in this work. Not all were interested in this ide and some of the group members dropped out occasionally.

To date we have tested this new method with one shop floor department. The findings so far, prototypes and diagrams, have been used by the workers in their negotiations with the management. The negotiations concerned possible new work organizations - if and when it is decided on computer support in the manufacturing process. During these negotiations middle management showed interest in participating in the project.

We have not quite solved the problems of aspect-blindness and/or the taken-for-granted perspectives in the current case, but we have mastered some of the problems. Together with management the project group has decided to continue the development work in other departments, with methods in the frame of the PROTEVS model. It is also decided that there should be closer cooperation with middle and top management.

What we have learnt from these and some earlier cases (Friis 1986) will now be summarized in a minimal list of validation and generalization criteria.

4 A proposed minimal list for validation and generalization criteria.

This is a short list of suggestions we think can be kept in mind in order to avoid some of the disadvantages discussed above. The list of suggested criteria is by no means exhaustive, but, applied it may make ISD research in an action research approach much more general, valid and possible to use in an open research community.

A) *Design the research in order to make all assumptions explicit.*
The validation criteria that the research should be possible to replicate in some form is quite common. In action reseach as well as in ISD this is not possible, in the sense of replication as used in normal science research. Replication can only be possible at the methodological level. One can, e g, develop a CBIS using a certain systems development model, or, one can conduct action research following a certain methodology.

Clearly, the findings of the research are dependent of how the methodology is interpreted. Since we deal with human activities the interpretations are dependent on the person conducting the research. In order to avoid misinterpretations, and in order to make as few unconscious interpretations as possible, we think it is necessary to state as many as of one's assumptions possible.

We have found an effective way of achieving this in involving other persons/ researchers/students to carry out some critical piece of research based only on written instructions. In writing the instructions for an interested layman, we force ourselves to be very explicit and in reading the result we realize how much was taken for granted. Preferrably, this should be an iterative process.

B) *Test research methods supplied by more than one person.*
As indicated above, research methods will often be very dependent on the people conducting the research. This is unavoidable and in our view not at all unfavourable. On the contrary, in letting many people use the same method, new perspectives can be applied or even developed. Letting others use the same method should not be confused with the problem discussed in A). They are two sides of the same thing.

In A) we try to make the method *per se* as explicit as possible, here in B) we use the method and compare the findings. If many people obtain the same results, then the method seems to be rather person independent. If it is the other way, where the findings are very widely dispersed, it means that the method is to a great extent dependent on people, actual problems and work situations. The nature of the dependencies must be investigated or made clear and explicit.

C) *Evaluation should not be done by the researcher alone.*
We think this is very obvious. Both findings and research process should be evaluated. Doing research is a way of living, you invest quite a lot of effort and prestige in your research project, and if under such circumstances you evaluate it yourself, you might of course be rather blind to negative aspects. Among

researchers a positive correlation between hypothesis and obtained findings is considered good and worthy of reporting.

If you should 'fail' in verifying the hypothesis, it does not mean that the research is not good. At least not in our view. On the contrary, you often learn more from projects that have failed than projects that were successful. If one tells about the mistakes and analyses the reasons, then the research can be very successful, measured in terms of impact on the research field.

D) *Present the findings in a way relevant and understandable also to practitioners other than the co-researchers of the case.*
We have seen too many research reports being published solely for some scientific community and then being hidden in a library. The findings of action research are primarily actions undertaken by the people we work with, secondarily our reports to the research communities (Nygaard, 1974). This point might hit at the heart of research, and might be a dividing point for different paradigms. We do not deny the need for 'ground research', we only mean that research, sooner or later, must be applied in some form, and this should be taken into consideration right from the beginning.

If we use a perspective like this, one may question the difference between consultancy and research. In our view the difference lies mainly in the openness of the reporting and in the level of reasoning. A good consultant make people do some actions, so do we, but we also try to describe the actions in a wider setting, e. g., why people did what they did, the reasons behind the problem, how to improve the suggested solution, etc. In acting in this way, the researcher besides the consultancy role also have a role of intermediator of some sort of empirical experience in reporting the findings of the research and in describing the research process.

E) *Field data should be open to everybody in the project*
In order to allow for different interpretations and different perspectives, field data such as diaries and/or log-books, tapes, etc., should be open and available to everbody in the project. Reporting to conferences, giving seminars and arranging user conferences is a way of achieving feed-back from the research community. As researchers often work as teachers also, it is possible that experience from field research is a good way of making lecturing more interesting.

Figure 1 shows how we currently see these action research criteria for validation and generalization hanging together with case practice.

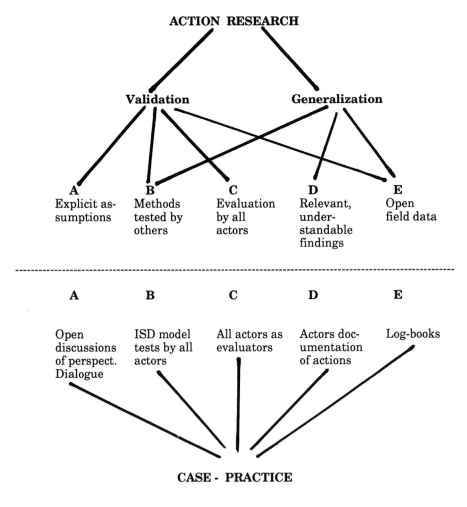

Fig. 1. Criteria for validation and generalization in action research
methodologies and practice concerning ISD research.

5 Concluding remarks

Is action research development work or research? We think it is not a matter of either doing research or consultative work, but both. In the words of Kalleberg (1989): "This kind of approach is a special blend of research activity and development work."

It is hard to do field work in accord with the action research perspectives mentioned above because: true collaboration, with users/workers, may involve continuous evaluations - which does not allow a 'complete round' of Lewin's action research model. Also, in our experience there will be continous planning and replanning in action research projects - due to the ongoing ordinary work of the actors from the research area. In a continuous user controlled working model, the development does not stop or 'freeze' - so when is it possible to achieve and measure end results?

When the users are not active enough in their development work we as researchers tend to push them, and worst of all, in the directions of our perspectives - compare the PROTEVS cases. In this way the users are not allowed to own the development (research) projects - we take over. When the users are really active in the analysis and construction work they start to push by themselves.

What we have learned in our work with the case studies so far is that there are dependencies in ISD research similar to the dependencies in action research methodologies. Hence, other interesting questions concerning dependencies are:
- How open should a researcher be to all perspectives within a project group? In our first case study (see 3.1) we had come quite far with the user prototyping (three small systems) before we noticed the phenomenon of aspect-blindness. In fact, we did not know what it was until we started the discussions and the sharing of knowledge from relevant literature: "Lack of ability to see a phenomenon in different aspects - aspect-blindness - is a common and serious cause of problems." (Nygaard & Sørgaard 1987). We argue that this problem applies to non-expert project leaders in an ISD as well as to researchers/ constructors.

- In the second case (see 3.2), we learned that not only does aspect-blindness affect researchers, but also co-researchers (users) when in control of a project. We also found the taken-for-granted perspective. Had we not had such an open and collaborative methodological approach in the case studies, we would perhaps not have noticed these phenomena. The view of the project fatigue as due only to over worked research objects might also have been accepted. This proves that an open collaborative research approach allows for more knowledge about user controlled ISD models. It both enables and forces a multi-perspective. It is also evident that case studies produce relevant knowledge that may be shared in many communities, e. g., office workers' and factory workers' communities, universities and other educational institutes.

Acknowledgement

I should like to express my appreciation to my friend and collegue Per Flensburg for ideas, suggestions and many good discussions concerning this work.

REFERENCES:

Antill L: Selection of a research method, in Mumford et al (eds): Research methods in information systems, North Holland, 1984.

Argyris C, Schön D A, Participatory Action Research and Action Science Compared, American Behavioral Scientist, Vol 32 No 5 May/June, 1989.

Bjørn-Andersen N, Informations Systemer for Beslutningstagning, Nyt Nordisk Forlag Arnold Busck, 1974.

Boughey H, The Insights of Sociology: an introduction, Allyn & Bacon, Boston, 1978.

Flensburg P: Personlig databehandling - introduktion, konsekvenser, möjligheter, Studentlitteratur, 1986, (in Swedish).

Friis, S, Användarutvecklade kravspecifikationer mha prototyping, i VÄGEN TILL BÄTTRE INFORMATIONSSYSTEM, RIKSDATAFÖRBUNDET, Stockholm 1984. (In Swedish)

Friis S, Tools for User Prototyping in Intelligent Information Systems for the Information Society, B C Brookes (ed.), Elsevier Science Publ BV (North-Holland), 1986.

Friis S, Action Research on Systems Development: Case Study of Changing Actor Roles, ACM, computers & society, Vol 18, No 1, Jan, 1988.

Gadamer H : Truth and method, The Seabury Press, New York, 1975.

Jenkins M: Research Methodologies and MIS research, in Mumford et al (eds): Research methods in information systems, North Holland, 1984.

Kalleberg R: ACTION RESEARCH AS CONSTRUCTIVE SOCIOLOGY, Institue for Social Research, University of Oslo, Norway, 1989.

Lewin K: Group decision and social change. In Newcomb T M, Hartley E L (eds): Readings in Social Psychology, Holt, Rinehart & Winston, New York, 1947.

Nauman J, Jenkins A M, "Prototyping: The New Paradigm for Systems Development", MIS Quarterly September 1982.

Nygaard K: Trade Union – a new employer in Høyet R: . over til EDB (in Norwegian), Tanum, 1974. (in Norwegian)

Nygaard K, Sørgaard P: The perspective concept in Informatics, in Bjerknes, Ehn, Kyng (eds): Computers and Democracy - a Scandinavian challenge, Avebury, 1987

Torbert W R: Empirical, behavioural, theoretical, and attentional skills necessary for collaborative inquiry, in Reason & Rowan: Human inquiry – A sourcebook of new paradigm research, Wiley & sons, 1987.

Wood-Harper T: Research Methods in Information Systems, Using Action Research, in Mumford et al (eds): Research methods in information systems, North Holland, 1984.

HUMAN JOBS AND COMPUTER INTERFACES
M.I. Nurminen and G.R.S. Weir
Elsevier Science Publishers B.V. (North-Holland)
© 1991 IFIP. All rights reserved.

Figure-Ground Reversal in Systems Development and Implementation: From HCI to OSI

David A.Buchanan

Professor of Human Resource Management, Loughborough University Business School, Human Resource and Change Management Research Unit, Loughborough, Leicestershire, LE11 3TU, United Kingdom

Abstract

This paper argues that, while we now understand the source of many information technology systems acceptability and application problems, appropriate solutions are not commonly adopted because of the way in which the development and implementation process is conceptualized. We have useful frameworks for conceptualizing the interface between user and computer (HCI); we lack models of the more complex, reflexive interface between organization and information technology system. It is further argued that the evolving nature of information technology applications in organizations, and the nature of the organizational change process itself, make Organization-System Interface (OSI) issues critical to effective implementation.
HCI frameworks present system as figure, and organization as ground. It is here argued that an OSI perspective should view the organization as figure with system as ground, and should combine the view of 'system as tool' in the domain of performance with the notion of 'system as triggering intervention' in the domain of organizational development and change, particularly in what are here defined as 'high vulnerability' contexts. In contrast with the view that the role of system designer and the boundary of HCI should be redefined to include organizational factors, this paper argues that it is the process in which system designers, managers and users engage that should be redefined.
The 'figure-ground reversal' of the title is drawn from gestalt psychology (Kohler, 1947, p.120). Perception is there discussed in terms of the distinction that can be made between the 'figure character' which is said to possess solid quality, and the more ephemeral quality of the 'ground character'. With visual images, the figure is perceived to protrude in space from the ground which is seen to be located behind, even in two-dimensional representations. Also with some visual images, it is possible to achieve a 'figure-ground reversal' where, although the overall image remains unaltered, the viewer can 'see' as figure what was once ground, and can switch from one interpretation to the other with ease. The analogy is adopted here merely to illustrate and reinforce the desirability of a change in perception with respect to the relative positions of system design and organizational development in contemporary thinking and action. All analogies quickly crumble if pursued with vigour.
The author wishes to acknowledge the invaluable comments and suggestions from colleagues on earlier drafts of this paper - notably from Linda Candy, Paul Finlay and John Storey. The author is, however, fully accountable for the gaps and errors that remain.

1   Organizational explanations for 'technical' problems

It is axiomatic that significant technological innovation generates organizational change (Boddy and Buchanan, 1986). Human performance in an information technology environment is as much a social and organizational accomplishment as a technical one. We know, from more than thirty years of research, that the application of computer technology in work organizations triggers changes in tasks and jobs, in the organization of work, in organization structure, and in organizational mission, charter or strategy (see McLoughlin and Clark, 1989, for a recent review of research).

We also know, despite the wide publicity given to the achievements of the last decade of the 'information technology revolution', that there is a high failure rate of applications and that the acceptability of some systems has been poor. We have a well-documented understanding of the causes of implementation failures. Evidence for the claim that the main problems in this context are organizational rather than technical is now overwhelming. It is not axiomatic that the organizational changes accompanying technical change will necessarily be appropriate and effective.

Miles (1990) cites a consultants' survey indicating that 30 per cent of large information technology projects in Britain run over budget and over time, mainly because of the organizational problems created by the combination of scale and complexity. Hamilton (1988) cites a survey of 68 companies in which 46 per cent of information technology applications were delivered late, and 48 per cent were delivered over budget; part of the blame lay with organizational aspects of project management and control. From a review of the North American literature, Long (1987) concluded that failures in office automation systems applications are due only 10 per cent to technical problems and 90 per cent to organizational problems such as poor planning, poor management, lack of training, and uncertainty about the problems being addressed. In recognition of this complexity, the concepts of 'information technology' and even 'computing' are now more appropriately considered as multidimensional phenomena incorporating related aspects of hardware, software, networks, communications links, systems and procedures, and management practices. McLoughlin and Clark (1989) introduce the term "engineering system" to express this multidimensionality.

A survey of 400 British and Irish companies carried out in mid-1990 revealed that only 11 per cent had been successful in their applications of information technology, on criteria concerning breadth of applications and benefits achieved, project completion on time, and return on investment (Kearney, 1990). The report concluded that this rate "must be judged unacceptably low", and also indicated that the reality may be bleaker since this was a self-selected set of respondents to a mail questionnaire which was presumably returned by the more competent and, in their own estimation, effective companies.

Among the recommendations for management action from this report were the following:

o   recognize that organization and people issues, not technical areas, are the barriers to success;

o   understand that organization and people issues are also the key contributors to success;

o   change the organization structure to capitalize on the strategic competitive advantages offered by IT;

o   appoint a user manager as project leader, not a computing or data processing specialist.

Journalistic accounts consistently confirm this pessimistic picture, with potentially damaging consequences for those professionally employed in the field. One recent account (Anonymous, 1991) describes how a large airline managed to lose £40 million in three months by running untested software, and also describes how estimates for the cost of a global computing system for a bank went from an initial £9 million to £114 million. The article offers a number of explanations for such 'horror stories'. Elegant, leading-edge systems designed in isolation may not address real business needs. Some IT departments are remote from the rest of their organizations, and have limited understanding of corporate strategies and pressures. Senior managers do not always appreciate the potential and limitations of IT. Short term problems divert attention from long term needs.

It would seem clear from this evidence that most of the problems of effective implementation lie with organizational and managerial issues, and not directly with elements of system development and design. It would appear logical, therefore, to propose that the solutions to these problems lie primarily in the domain of management action, and not of HCI.

At least two current trends reinforce the need to clarify our understanding of the relationships between organizational properties and system characteristics.

First, applications have entered a new phase characterized by transitions from one system type to another, concentrating on the exploitation of networks for competitive advantage (Earl, 1988, 1989; Friedman and Cornford, 1989). The blend of technical and organizational issues raised in the transition from one system generation to another are different from those which accompany initial applications in organizations with little or no prior experience. The issues raised by strategic changes are different from those devoted to activities not central to the 'core' activity of an organization. This may partially explain the consistent attribution of implementation problems to organizational issues in late 1980s commentary.

Second, patterns of organizational change have become more complex during the 1980s, due to a range of competitive and environmental pressures, and also to the increasingly systemic nature and impact of information technology. It is now uncommon to find an organization introducing computerization unaccompanied by other changes to manufacturing systems and administrative procedures (Peters, 1987; Preece, 1989). In addition, organizational change is increasingly 'untidy' and 'programmatic' rather than 'neat' and project driven. Programmatic change appears to be characterized by the evolutionary unfolding of interrelated, overlapping and loosely bounded projects, with shifting goals, shifting priorities, and with shifting project team memberships.

The argument of this paper is thus set in the following context:

o   systems implementation problems are explained most frequently by organizational and managerial factors;

o   organizations are increasingly seeking (not always appropriately, or effectively) to exploit the strategic implications of new systems;

o   organizational change involving information technology is likely to be programmatic rather than project driven.

2   The HCI response

Tony Gunton (1990, p.275) has recently argued with respect to the development of management information systems that:

"Somehow the technical know-how of information system specialists must be combined with an understanding of the strategic needs and the day-to-day operations of the business, in order to come up with plans for information systems that are both relevant and practical. Unfortunately, this highly desirable outcome has proved extremely difficult to achieve in practice, the main reason being that the relationship between business direction and information systems needs is not obvious."

Ernest Edmonds et al. (1989, p.1), from their research into the development of expert systems, argue that:

" . . . there is no ideal, generally applicable method for expert system development because the organizational context imposes its own imperatives within which priorities, resource allocation and deployment of personnel are decided."

It has therefore become unrealistic to contemplate organizational changes outwith the context of the computing systems that will support new structures; it has become unrealistic to contemplate systems developments outwith the organizational context in which they are to be exploited. However, much development work currently conducted under the umbrella of HCI chooses either to ignore the organizational context, or to view its attributes as merely another (albeit critical) set of design constraints to take into account.

The "Business Systems Planning" (BSP) approach developed by IBM appears to offer an effective counter to such criticisms. This approach adopts an overt "organization-wide view" and is explicitly aimed at the design of information systems geared to business strategies and objectives (see Bantleman and Jones, 1984, for a review of this and similar methodologies). However, the approach depends on the assumption of organizational stability. The BSP document states in this respect that, "information systems should be built to support the non-transient elements of the business - elements that are basic and will not change appreciably unless the basic fibre of the business itself does so". One of the advertised benefits of the approach includes, "Information systems that are relatively independent of organization structure". The benefits of such a systematic organizational approach to system design are manifest - given contexts in which the BSP assumption holds. However, there is evidence (see Peters, 1987 and 1990, for example) to suggest that in the contemporary competitive climate, the number of business elements that are 'non-transient' may be limited and the goal of creating systems that are independent of structure looks increasingly unrealistic.

Some theoretical and practical work does not go as far as BSP in addressing organizational issues. For example, Pinsonneault and Kraemer (1990) in their work on group decision and communication support systems - technologies with transparent organizational and managerial implications - present a conceptual model which explicitly excludes "the broader organizational environment" (see p.146) from their thinking, concentrating on other, narrow, "contextual variables".

It is a comparatively simple matter to demonstrate the reflexive nature of systems applications and their organizational settings; how systems properties impact on organizational parameters, and how organizational properties impact on system characteristics. A distributed management information system in an insurance company, for example, affords clear benefits in access to customer data, in speed of service response, and in management reporting. This has easily observed implications for the work of those who come into contact with the system, directly and indirectly, from branch counter staff to senior management. The properties of the organization that impact on system characteristics and on the ways in which systems are developed include, for example:

- o   the IT/DP capital budget
- o   perceived business priorities
- o   the location and distribution of relevant expertise
- o   the training budget
- o   the effectiveness of training programmes
- o   the size of the IT/DP function

o   the location of that function's staff
o   the perceived status of the function
o   the "culture" of the function
o   the status and influence of the IT/DP manager

The nature of systems development in an organization with a significant, well resourced IT function with effective training programmes, a 'computerate' user base and a board level IT manager, will be quite different from the development activity in an organization whose IT function is under-resourced with an unsophisticated and sceptical user pool resistant to training and with a function manager who does not have direct access and accountability to the chief executive officer. These are some of the main organizational properties on which the reflexive relationship with system development depends. However, we do not yet appear to have appropriate frameworks or models for dealing effectively with these relationships in practice, or a language adequate to their articulation and analysis.

The focus of HCI activity in terms of establishing user acceptability and system effectiveness is, naturally, with the 'interface' between computer systems and their human users. This is reflected in standard commentary in the field, such as Moran (1980) and Shneiderman (1987; 1989). The proceedings of HCI conferences tend to be biased towards system interface concerns. However, there has been a steady shift in the areas of task and requirements analysis and this has, in some instances, included specific contextual issues.

The goal of interface work, in Shneiderman's words, is to "create elegant systems that effectively serve the users". This is a narrow goal in at least two respects.

One problem is that computer systems, unlike other technologies, possess "autogenerative" properties (Friedman and Cornford, 1989). At least some of the innovations, in design and application, come from the users themselves, through experimentation, play and error. The original designers may thus have little control over the ultimate shape and evolution of their system given the unpredictable nature of autogenerative developments. Second, as has already been mentioned, system applications are 'systemic' in their organizational implications (Boddy and Buchanan, 1987). They can, depending on the nature of the system in use, affect the nature and scope of individual jobs, relationships between jobs, department and section management structures, the structure of the organization as a whole, and the primary task of the organization in the creation of new and improved products and services. The 'ripple effects' of many applications spread far beyond the immediate user group.

The focus on individuals interacting with computers thus tends to marginalize the issue of organizations interacting in reflexive or mutually influential ways with computing systems. These organizational issues have not gone unnoticed. Four main strands of activity (among others) are representative of the main approaches now in vogue.

First, there has been pressure for the development of human centred systems which complement, rather than replace, human capabilities in manufacturing (Rosenbrock, 1982) and in office (Matteis, 1979) contexts, and more recently in Finland with respect to human scale information systems in the Knowledge and Work project at Turku (Sorgaard, Nurminen and Forsman, 1989; Nurminen, 1987 and 1988). Much of this work has been prompted by the view that technology carries implicit social relationships in its design specifications (Noble, 1979), and that the primary - and dysfunctional - management motives for technological innovation concern systematic deskilling and management control (Braverman, 1974).

Second, there have also been developments in participative approaches to system design (e.g., Hirschheim, 1985). One well-known example of participative system design methodology is Enid Mumford's (1981; Mumford and Weir, 1979) ETHICS approach where the key ingredients include user involvement in system development and recognition of the social issues in implementation, including the socio-technical redesign of affected jobs. Tapscott's (1982) UDD (user-driven design) methodology adopts a similar phased approach to user involvement in the design of operational office systems. Wixon et al. (1990) specify an approach described as "contextual design" which is a method for "contextual inquiry" in which user needs and expectations can be more effectively understood through formally specified interview procedures. Similar approaches to "usability engineering" and to "contextual field research" are discussed by Good (1989). Although management literature provides some convincing evidence in support of participative approaches to organizational change, Ives and Olson (1984), from their review of 22 studies, conclude that the evidence to support user involvement in information system design is weak and that the benefits of such approaches remain to be demonstrated.

Third, there is now a substantial research tradition in the area of Computer Supported Cooperative Work (CSCW) which seeks to develop applications which support group collaboration in organizational settings, including remote collaboration and the use of shared multi-media databases. It is, however, interesting to note the restrictions placed on the application of CSCW - to groups working with shared goals on interdependent tasks in informal, flat organizations relatively autonomous of management control (Sorgaard, 1988, p.2); these are not features of most work groups.

It would seem that the HCI response, in terms of the development of human-centred systems, computer supported cooperative work, and participative methodologies, does not directly address the main causes of failures in system acceptability and implementation revealed by the research and experience reviewed earlier. This does not deny the significance of specific interface issues or the relevance and importance of work in this area in improving acceptability and implementation. This characterization of the HCI response is not intended to downgrade the undoubted value of that work, but highlights the closely bounded nature of the research and practical effort with respect to the organizational dimensions of the problem as it is currently understood. Put crudely, these attempts at 'getting to understand the user better' are in danger of ignoring the need to 'get to understand the organization better'. Put even more crudely, some aspects of the HCI response could be accused of concentrating on functionality at the expense of contextuality.

There is, however, a fourth perspective in which organizational issues have been explicitly addressed, through the development of formal methodologies for requirements analysis. One key representative of this work is Ken Eason, based at the Human Sciences and Advanced Technology (HUSAT) Research Centre at the University of Loughborough in England. In a text on system design and implementation (Eason, 1988), we find chapters on establishing organizational benefits, on information technology strategy, on organizational change, on socio-technical system design, and on job design. This could be seen to support the argument for, and provide a specification for, an enlarged boundary for the field of HCI.

However, what is at stake here is not the fact that organizational issues are on the HCI agenda, but their location and status on that agenda. As with the Business Systems Planning approach, Eason assumes that generic systems can be designed to support enduring organizational goals and characteristics. The requirements analysis task is conceptualized as one of matching or mapping system specifications to organizational reality. Eason (1989, p.62) claims that, "A system which accurately maps human responsibilities in this way will reinforce the social structure rather than undermining it as so often happens at present". The division of labour, and the allocation of responsibility in the organization are to be taken as given - to be considered either as constraints on the system design process, or as characteristics to be taken into account in reaching critical design decisions. Eason (1989, p.63) claims that system suppliers, "should not make assumptions about organizational role structures because they are too varied and changeable". The allocation of tasks and responsibilities in organizations change, and Eason in recognizing this recommends that systems, "will need updating to maintain the match with organizational reality" (p.64). In a subsequent elaboration of requirements analysis, Harker et al. (1990, p.296) reinforce the need for system design, "which matches the structure, objectives and characteristics of the organization".

This approach is fully sensitive to 'human centred systems' issues, and is also sensitive to change management and implementation problems and processes. But system design is still 'figure' in this perspective, with organizational issues clearly 'ground'. Organizational arrangements are accepted and the design task is to respond to these. When organizational arrangements change, design changes have to follow on to maintain compatibility.

In contrast, the position adopted in this paper is that, in some contexts, effective system design and implementation requires the undermining and change of existing social and organizational arrangements, and that this process of change can be triggered and enabled by desired system changes. For this to occur, organizational development must be 'figure', with system design issues as 'ground'.

3   Properties of the context

It is therefore appropriate to argue for a fresh perspective which seeks to locate the systems design and implementation process more adequately in an organizational context. It is necessary to identify the organizational properties - what Edmonds et al. (1989) term the "imperatives" of the context - that are significant in this respect.

From a recently completed study of the change agent's role in managing new systems implementation (Buchanan, 1990), two extreme forms of organizational context were identified for analytical purposes. The research suggested that the context facing the change agent or project team can vary between two extremes of 'vulnerability', which refers to the scale and complexity of the problems facing change agents, the degree of uncertainty and risk (personal and organizational) involved, and to the anticipated degree of contention and resistance which the change is likely to generate. The two extremes are:

high vulnerability context	low vulnerability context
strategic changes	operational changes
rapid change, quick results	slow change, slow results
significant resource commitment	few extra resources needed
disinterested top management	supportive top managers
unrealistic top management expectations	realistic top management expectations
fickle support	solid support
uncertain means	certainty of means
complex interdependencies	few interdependencies
dependent on third parties	independent
multiple 'ripples'	self contained
conflicting perceptions	shared views
multi-purpose changes	single-function systems
unstable goals	stable goals
confused responsibilities for process and outcomes	clear 'ownership' of process and outcomes

The implementation process in a low vulnerability context appears unproblematic, or less problematic. The system design and implementation lifecycle is more likely to proceed in a logically sequenced manner without significant deflection and in the comparative absence of political issues. Issues of project control are likely to be more relaxed, and effort can be effectively focused on specific user interface and ergonomic factors. This context is effectively portrayed in the 'rational-linear' accounts of the implementation life cycle which appear in many textbooks on the subject.

The implementation process in a high vulnerability context is in contrast problematic, for the project team and the organization concerned. Here the levels of risk and contention are likely to be considerably higher and the rational-linear view of the implementation process, and advice set in that frame, are less likely to be perceived relevant. Change in a high vulnerability context is a complex and untidy cocktail of rational assessment blended with differential perceptions, quests for power, visionary leadership, and the "subtle processes" of coalition building and "backstage decision making" and intrigue (Pettigrew, 1985).

In the high vulnerability organizational context, the 'truth, trust, love and collaborative approach to change' which features in the American organizational development literature, and in the literature of participative approaches to systems design, is threatened. Different managerial skills are required to operate effectively in this context; different models of and approaches to systems design and implementation are therefore also required.

It was argued earlier that the interface between organization and system is reflexive. Given earlier points about the complex, systemic, strategic nature of some information technology applications, it appears inevitable that medium to large scale systems implementations will both find themselves in, and contribute to, and reinforce the characteristics of high vulnerability contexts.

4   The problem reformulated

It may appear that improved understanding of organizational context should allow system designers to tailor applications more closely to that context, in precisely the same mode as user involvement is intended to improve the extent to which system functionality meets user needs, expectations and priorities. This, as described earlier, is the objective of requirements analysis which seeks to match or map system features to organizational reality (Eason, 1989).

This view is not supported here, for the following reasons. The task of tailoring system to organization in some kind of contingency model assumes that existing properties of the organization in question are indeed appropriate - either to the achievement of the organization's strategic aims, or to the effective exploitation of the benefits of a particular new system. That is rarely the case. This mapping approach also tends to ignore or to consider unimportant the process of implementation in which system and organizational characteristics interact, and where the context proscribes the nature of that interaction. As already established, significant technological innovation is invariably accompanied by organizational innovation; the properties of the organization thus constitute a moving target for system development and implementation, with much of that movement triggered reflexively by the system implementation itself.

There are a number of ways in which the relationship between system and organization can be conceived. First, systems can be seen, as we have already mentioned, to determine organizational design and social relationships through the explicit technological manifestation of the assumptions on which system design is based (related in particular to human strengths and failings, the desire to avoid human interference, and the perceived need for management control). Second, new systems can instead be seen to open a 'design space' for social relationships, creating fresh opportunities for the development of new forms of work organization, for skill enhancement and improvement of quality of work life (Bessant, 1982; Buchanan, 1989). Third, systems can be seen as vehicles for the legitimation of certain structural options, determined by key decision-makers in the organization. Perrow (1984), for example, argues that technological innovations are often used to reproduce existing structures of power, influence, authority and decision making.

This does not imply that organization structures are fixed or rigid. On the contrary, such structures are socially constructed and reconstructed, and the extent to which alternative organizational forms develop depends on the extent to which actors can successfully contest existing arrangements. Wilkinson (1983) convincingly demonstrates the negotiated and contested nature of management objectives and organizational design in the application of new manufacturing process technology.

Let us label these perspectives:

'technological determinism'
> systems characteristics determine social relationships and working arrangements;

'design space'
> systems characteristics open the design space for the creation of new forms of work organization;

'legitimation'
> systems characteristics are used to legitimate favoured forms of work organization;

Which of these perspectives best addresses the implementation problems identified here ? The research evidence appears to support the 'legitimation' perspective, based on a concept of organization as a socially constructed political domain characterised by contested, negotiated, ambiguous and loosely articulated goals particularly with respect to technical change. From their review, McLoughlin and Clark (1989, p.40) argue that:

> " . . . the assumption that the outcomes of technological change, rather than being determined by the logic of capitalist development, or external technical and commercial imperatives, are in fact socially chosen and negotiated within organizations by organizational actors. It therefore follows that rather than there being any uniform tendency when new technology is introduced, the changes that occur are likely to reveal considerable variation between organizations, even where the technology concerned and organizational circumstances involved are the same. This directs attention to processes of change within particular organizations and the manner in which managers, unions and workforce are able to intervene to influence outcomes."

The legitimation perspective most adequately exposes the limitations of the goal of improved user understanding. This view also exposes potential problems with attempts to 'map' system design onto existing organizational arrangements. Technological determinism denies options. The 'design space' approach denies political realities and the socially constructed and contested nature of organizational design.

The work of Edwin Hutchins with respect to distributed cognition in information technology environments indicates the importance of the ability to define reality, to specify the nature of and delimit the boundaries of operational decisions, and to impose interpretations of the situation on other members of the organization or operating group (Hutchins, 1985; 1987). Systems implementation can thus be used to support, defend and legitimate organizational arrangements that favour dominant actors and coalitions seeking to establish, maintain and enhance positions of influence and status. Different models of the design and implementation process establish different levels of exposure and challenge for legitimating attempts and strategies. Conventional 'rational-linear' models based on the concept of the implementation life cycle tend to offer little or no threat to such legitimation strategies.

Rather than attempt to map system design features to user needs or to organizational properties, it appears more appropriate, practical and realistic to tailor the system development and implementation process to properties of the organizational context in ways that allow alternative interpretations to surface for open debate. Through such a strategy, the poverty of technological determinism is revealed, and the 'design space' is more adequately discussed. This resolution could be viewed as a politically informed attempt to move legitimation tendencies into the (often more acceptable) design space mode.

In this reformulation, system is seen not just as tool for task performance, but primarily as intervention in the process of organizational change and development. Systems design and implementation processes can thus be used as a trigger, in certain contexts, to enable and empower the wider processes of organizational change and development.

5   Resolution

The problem is here characterized as one of managing the reflexive interface between organization and system in a high vulnerability context through a non-linear and quasi-rational process. The apparent intractability of this situation appears to defeat simple resolution.

Most of the prescription in this field has been concerned with the need to change the role of the system designer, to "push out the boundaries of the system under discussion" (Hutchins, 1985) by sensitizing design specialists to social and organizational issues (Perrow, 1983). Klein and Newman (1987) attribute the problem to the "splitting" of professional sub-specialisms and argue for "integrated thinking" to overcome the "human interface" problems identified earlier in this paper. The British Computer Society has recently launched an initiative designed to improve education and training for computing professionals, to increase the number of 'hybrid managers' who combine information technology expertise with business awareness and management skills (Palmer and Ottley, 1990; Earl and Skyrme, 1990).

The reader who has accepted the arguments up to this point will, it is hoped, be sympathetic to the view that merely changing the training and perception of systems designers will not adequately address the main problems. System designers sensitive to organizational and managerial issues are likely to be more effective in their work. Senior (non-computing) managers sensitive to information technology opportunities and constraints are also likely to pursue more realistic goals.

It is the process in which systems designers, organization managers and users collectively engage that must change. In this view, the role of the system designer remains unaltered and what changes are:

o   the composition and leadership of the project team;
o   the public objectives and agendas of that team;
o   the map of the terrain which they are to travel.

With respect to project team composition, those involved in change should be represented, should contribute, and should ultimately experience 'ownership' for all or a major part of what eventually happens. Boddy and Buchanan (1987) offer systematic advice for project team building. Everything we know about the management of change, in high or low vulnerability contexts, reinforces the need for participative approaches and the involvement of those affected. Nothing in the argument so far contradicts this aspect of conventional wisdom. Team composition must also take account of the recommendation concerning team objectives and agendas.

With respect to project team leadership, the argument advanced here implies that this should be vested in user management, and not necessarily in a computing 'professional'. This leadership principle serves to resolve at least two critical issues. One concerns the need to bring specific business understanding to system design decisions. The other is the need to clarify responsibility and accountability for the project during and after implementation. Hamilton (1988) supports this view by arguing that, given the importance of managing the organizational process, "computer illiterate" project managers can be effective in some circumstances. Classe (1991, p.18) points out that, " . . . ICI opted for a commercial manager rather than an IT specialist to run its IT function because the important task is to understand the impact of IT on the business. And people who are technologists are often too wrapped up in the technology to get the best results for the business". Classe also advances the argument that, with technology developing so fast, IT expertise is valuable, and the British Computer Society's 'hybridization' policy dilutes that resource.

With respect to the public agenda of the project team, in a high vulnerability context, objectives should encompass and prioritize organizational development. The project team should have the explicit goal of recommending and initiating action in this domain. Their agendas should express organizational design issues as well as system design issues. Alternative interpretations of organizational arrangements should be encouraged to surface, and should be explored, not deterred. These should not be seen as 'out of scope' or illegitimate activities; in contrast, they should be regarded as primary objectives, triggered, made possible, and legitimated by the systems implementation process, and made public throughout the organization.

The 'map' of the logically sequenced, rational-linear implementation cycle should be replaced by a 'transition management' model of the organizational development and change process which recognises the non-linearity of change, the importance of contested views and interpretations, the reality of power and influence in the organization, and the 'solution driven' nature of some technical and organizational change (see, for example, Pettigrew, 1985). The figure on this map, to borrow a term from gestalt psychology (Kohler, 1947), is organizational development; the ground is system design and development. The object of the process is organizational development; the means, or the trigger for this process, is system development. This does not imply a subordinate role for system design, or for system designers. On the contrary, this merely implies a different - enabling - role.

Klein and Newman (1987) argue that bringing such project teams together, "has proved too ephemeral". A high vulnerability organization context certainly poses difficulties for a project team, however composed, and it is not being suggested here that this prescription is problem-free. However, project team performance is a management problem and there are methods and techniques beyond the scope of this paper that can be deployed to increase the chances of success. Issues of composition, leadership, objectives, agendas and process understanding are not always explicitly addressed by project teams. Lack of attention to these issues is perhaps more prevalent in teams comprising professional technical personnel with little or no grounding in management techniques, particularly with respect to the interpersonal and social skills involved in team building, group problem solving and the management of meetings.

The 'organization-system interface' approach advocated here does, however, find support in the conclusions of Edmonds et al. (1989) who advocate an iterative design and development model for a design team with user representation. Macaulay et al. (1990) in their description of the User Skills and Task Match (USTM) methodology specifically identify support for project management as a key criterion for their approach, and seek also to 'pull through' organizational design requirements into system specification, recognizing that "the introduction of any new computer system to the users' environment will necessarily cause change to that environment" (p.114).

This argument also finds support from Gunton (1990) who is highly critical of the conventional, linear system development life cycle, and who advocates an iterative and evolutionary approach through what he calls "the four course meal principle". This argues that system development should be a gradual and mutual learning process in which design options are closed at a much later stage than is usual, giving users and designers more time to understand and to shape developments. For the "hors d'oeuvers", users are offered appetizing applications that make their lives easier in demonstrable ways. For the "main course", applications that solve real business problems are developed. Then the "cheese course" links users and their applications to other company systems and procedures. Further system enhancements and upgrades - the "sweet course" - are then used to sustain the enthusiasm of existing users and to lower barriers to wider use.

The scope for organizational transformation through the approach advocated here is significant and potentially more interesting and exciting than narrowed attempts - covert or overt - merely to reproduce and legitimate existing or similar structures. The scope for organizational performance improvement, as well as for system effectiveness and contribution, should also be enhanced through this mode of implementation.

The argument in summary, contrasting the HCI and OSI perspectives, is as follows:

The HCI Case	The OSI Case
Widen HCI boundaries to include organizational issues.	Adopt an organizational development methodology that utilises HCI - without changing the latter's boundaries
Bring organizational requirements analysis into system design methodology	Bring system design issues into the organizational development process
Consider the organizational changes that accompany or follow system implementation	Use system design and implementation systematically and opportunistically to drive organizational changes
Match system functionality to organization purpose and structure	Use system design and implementation to trigger organizational change and development
Put organizational issues on the HCI agenda	Put system development issues on the OD agenda
Design systems that will be flexible given organizational change	Use system design to initiate discussion about desired organizational change

Finally, the perspective and process of the organization-system interface agenda may look like this:

The OSI Agenda

Perspective:

o   organizational development (OD) is the goal, particularly in high vulnerability contexts
o   system development is the intervention that triggers the process
o   the relationship between organizational development and system development is reflexive

Process:

o   the project team has an OD focus
o   the project leader is a user representative
o   competing interpretations of different constituencies can be legitimately raised
o   the project team is not tied to a rigid and preconceived implementation plan

References:

Anonymous, 1991,
'Learning the secrets of the IT winners', The Sunday Times, 3 February, p.4.13.
Bantleman, J-P. and Jones, A.H., 1984,
'Systems analysis methodologies: a research project', in Th. M.A. Bemelmans (ed.), Beyond Productivity: Information Systems Development for Organizational Effectiveness, Elsevier Science Publishers, North Holland, pp.213-227.
Bessant, J., 1982,
'Management and manufacturing innovation: the case of information technology', in G. Winch (ed.), Information Technology in Manufacturing Processes, Rossendale, London, pp.14-30.
Boddy, D. and Buchanan, D.A., 1986,
Managing New Technology, Basil Blackwell, Oxford.
Boddy, D. and Buchanan, D.A., 1987,
The Technical Change Audit: Action For Results, Manpower Services Commission, Sheffield.
Braverman, H., 1974,
Labour and Monopoly Capital: The Degradation of Work in the Twentieth Century, Monthly Review Press, New York.
Buchanan, D.A., 1989,
'Principles and practice in work design', in Keith Sisson (ed.), Personnel Management in Britain, Basil Blackwell, Oxford, pp.78-100.
Buchanan, D.A., 1990,
'Vulnerability and agenda: context and process in project management', Loughborough University Management Research Series, paper 1990:19, November.

Buchanan, D.A. and Boddy, D., 1982,
   'Advanced technology and the quality of working life: the effects of word
   processing on video typists', Journal of Occupational Psychology, vol.55, no.1,
   pp.1-11.
Classe, A., 1991,
   'Top dogs', Computing, 31 January, pp.18-19.
Earl, M., 1988
   Information Management: The Strategic Dimension, Clarendon Press, Oxford.
Earl, M., 1989,
   Management Strategies for Information Technology, Prentice Hall, Hemel
   Hempstead.
Earl, M. and Skyrme, D., 1990,
   'Hybrid managers: what do we know about them ?', Oxford Institute of Information
   Management, Research and Discussion Papers, Oxford, June.
Eason, K., 1988,
   Information Technology and Organizational Change, Taylor and Francis, London.
Eason, K., 1989,
   'Designing systems to match organizational reality', in People and Computers 5,
   Proceedings of the HCI '89 Conference, Nottingham, BCS/Cambridge University
   Press, pp.57-69.
Edmonds, E.A., Candy, L., Slatter, P. and Lunn, S., 1989,
   'Issues in the design of expert systems for business', Expert systems for information
   management, vol.2, no.1, pp.1-22.
Friedman, A. and Cornford, D., 1989,
   Computer Systems Development: History, Organization and Implementation, John
   Wiley, Chichester.
Good, M., 1989,
   'Seven experiences with contextual field research', SIGCHI Bulletin, vol.20, no.4,
   pp.25-32.
Hirschheim, R., 1985,
   Office Automation: A Social and Organizational Perspective, John Wiley, New
   York.
Gunton, T., 1990,
   Inside Information Technology: A Practical Guide to Management Issues, Prentice-
   Hall, Hemel Hempstead.
Hamilton, S., 1988
   'The complex art of saying no', Computing, 13 October, pp.30-31.
Harker, S.D.P., Olphert, C.W. and Eason, K.D., 1990,
   'The development of tools to assist in organizational requirements definition for
   information technology systems', in D. Diaper et al. (eds), Human-Computer
   Interaction - INTERACT '90, Elsevier Science Publishers, North Holland, pp.295-
   300.
Hutchins, E., 1985,
   'The social organization of distributed cognition', Intelligent Systems Group,
   Institute for Cognitive Sciences, University of California San Diego, Working
   Paper, November.
Huchins, E., 1987,
   'Learning to navigate in context', paper presented to the Workshop on Context,
   Cognition and Activity, Stenungsund, Sweden, August.
Ives, B. and Olson, M.H., 1984,
   'User involvement and MIS success: a review of research', Management Science,
   vol.30, no.5, pp.586-603.

Kanter, R.M., 1983,
    The Change Masters: Corporate Entrepreneurs at Work, Unwin, London.
Kanter, R.M., 1989
    When Giants Learn to Dance: Mastering the Challenge of Strategy, Management
    and Careers in the 1990s, Simon and Schuster, London.
Kearney, A.T., 1990,
    Barriers to the Successful Application of Information Technology, A.T. Kearney,
    Department of Trade and Industry and CIMA, November, London.
Klein, L. and Newmann, W., 1987,
    'A strategy for integrating human-computer interface considerations into Alvey-2
    application projects: action version and working papers', mimeo, September.
Kohler, W., 1947,
    Gestalt Psychology, Mentor Books, New York.
Long, R., 1987
    New Office Information Technology: Human and Managerial Implications, Croom
    Helm, London.
Macaulay, L., Fowler, C., Kirby, M. and Hutt, A., 1990,
    'USTM: a new approach to requirements specification', Interacting With Computers,
    vol.2, no.1, pp.92-118.
McLoughlin, I. and Clark, J., 1989
    Technological Change at Work, The Open University Press, Milton Keynes.
Matteis, R.J., 1979,
    'The new back office focuses on customer service', Harvard Business Review,
    vol.57, March-April, pp.146-59.
Miles, R., 1990
    'A stitch in time', Computing, 11 October, pp.22-3/
Moran, T., 1980,
    'A framework for studying human-computer interaction', in Guedj et al., eds,
    Methdology of Interaction, North Holland Publishing, pp.293-301.
Mumford, E., 1981,
    'Participative system design: structure and method', Systems, Objectives, Solutions,
    vol.1, no.1, pp.5-19.
Mumford, E. and Weir, M., 1979,
    Computer Systems in Work Design - The ETHICS Method, Associated Business
    Press, London.
Noble, D.F., 1979,
    'Social choice in machine design: the case of automatically controlled machine
    tools', in A. Zimbalist (ed.), Case Studies on the Labour Process, Monthly Review
    Press, New York, pp.18-50.
Nurminen, M., 1987,
    'How to work with paradigms', paper presented to the IRIS X conference, August,
    Vaskivesi, Finland.
Nurminen, M., 1988,
    People or Computers: Three Ways of Looking at Information Systems,
    Studentlitteratur, Lund, Sweden.
Palmer, C. and Ottley, S., 1990,
    From Potential to Reality: 'Hybrids' - A Critical Force in the Application of
    Information Technology in the 1990s, British Computer Society, London.
Peters, T., 1987,
    Thriving on Chaos: Handbook for a Managerial Revolution,
Peters, T., 1990,
    Towards Entrepreneurial and Empowering Organizations, TPG
    Europe/3i/Economist Intelligence Unit, London.

Pettigrew, A.M., 1985,
   The Awakening Giant: Continuity and Change in Imperial Chemical Industries,
   Basil Blackwell, Oxford.
Pinsonneault, A. and Kraemer, K.L., 1990,
   'The effects of electronic meetings on group processes and outcomes: an assessment
   of the empirical research', European Journal of Operational Research, vol.46,
   pp.143-61.
Preece, D.A., 1989
   Managing the Adoption of New Technology, Routledge, London.
Rosenbrock, H.H., 1982,
   'Technology policies and options', in N. Bjorn Andersen, M. Earl, O. Holst and E.
   Mumford (eds), Information Society: For Richer, For Poorer, North Holland,
   Amsterdam.
Shneiderman, B., 1987,
   Designing the User Interface, Addison-Wesley, Reading MA.
Shneiderman, B., 1989,
   'Designing the user interface' in Tom Forester (ed), Computer in the Human
   Context, Blackwell, Oxford, pp.166-73.
Sorgaard, P., 1988,
   'A framework for computer supported cooperative work', Aarhus University
   Computer Science Department, May.
Sorgaard, P., Nurminen, M. and Forsmann, U., 1989,
   'System maintenance and organizational change research programme', Department
   of Computer Science, Abo Akademi University, Turku, April.
Tapscott, D., 1982,
   Office Automation: A User-Driven Method, Plenum Press, New York.
Wilkinson, B., 1983,
   The Shopfloor Politics of New Technology, Heinemann, London.
Wixon, D., Holtzblatt, K. and Knox, S., 1990,
   'Contextual design: an emergent view of system design', CHI '90 Proceedings,
   Association of Computing Machinery, April, pp.329-36.

Section 7

Learning and Hypermedia

HUMAN JOBS AND COMPUTER INTERFACES
M.I. Nurminen and G.R.S. Weir
Elsevier Science Publishers B.V. (North-Holland)
© 1991 IFIP. All rights reserved.

As We May Learn: Training With Multimedia

Arja Vainio-Larsson

Dpt. of Computer Science, Linköping University, S-581 83 Linköping, Sweden

email (Internet): ava@IDA.LIU.SE
phone: +46 13281477
fax: +46 13142231

Abstract
In order to obtain an understanding of the different needs for users and enterprises in multimedia learning environments the introduction, organization and planning of education utilizing multimedia technology has been evaluated. Two different interactive video training packages were tested. Evaluation methods comprised a combination of seminars, questionnaires, video recordings and interviews. In total 131 users participated in the study. The results show that direct manipulation in terms of point-and-click is limiting and may confuse the users' interaction with a system. Usually the combination of text, graphics, audio and video is highly appreciated by most users. However it may impose cognitive passivity on some users. For applications where the multiple linkages of information are important, the combination of insufficient possibilities for users to navigate freely and the lack of effective guide-lines is particularly negative. Different learning methods affect users' self-esteem and hence their learning behaviour. The mere possibility of obtaining feedback from a system and not from another person (e.g. a teacher) may positively influence users' willingness to try different parts of a system. Self-instructive courseware needs to offer a learner-driven system that provides both a teacher- and a learner-directed interaction. For training to be successful it also has to become a natural part of peoples' working environment.

1. BACKGROUND AND INTRODUCTION

This paper presents a case study where multimedia training has been used in the workplace. The study was carried out as a joint project between Telepedagogik (within Swedish Telecom), British Telecom and the Department of Computer Science, Linköping University. A main purpose of this study was to evaluate the different needs for users and enterprises in multimedia

232

learning environments. Another but minor aim was to assist in the specification of the EPOS[1] user environment.

Two different interactive video training packages were tested. Evaluation methods comprised a combination of seminars, questionnaires, video recordings and interviews. In total 131 users participated in the study.

The paper opens with a brief presentation of the different evaluation methods used in this study. Some facts about the equipment and the users' background and previous experiences of computer supported learning are described. The results are presented and commented before the paper ends with a summary and a discussion of multimedia-based learning in relation to hypermedia.

2. EVALUATION METHODS

Ten local training departments within Swedish Telecom were included in the study, one of which withdrew during the course of the evaluation. The number of users at each training department varied from 5 up to 47 users. In total 131 users participated in the study. Of these 43% (56 users) were female.

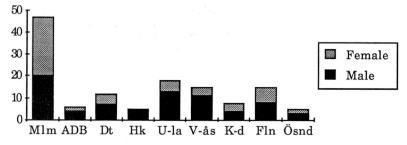

Figure 1: Number of participants by district and sex

2.1. Seminars

Of the departments' training staff in total nineteen participated in a two day start-up seminar and a one day follow-up seminar.

Since the evaluation study involved several districts from all over Sweden, the co-operating training staff had an important role both in providing information about the study locally, as well as in their support of the on-going evaluation (for example, in distributing and collecting questionnaires).

---

[1] EPOS stands for European PTT Open Learning Service and is part of the European DELTA program (Developing European Learning through Technological Advance).

2.2. Questionnaires

Questionnaires were distributed to all users and a second questionnaire was also distributed to the participating training staff. Of a total of 131 questionnaires, 123 (94%) were completed and returned. The participants did not represent a random sample since they were explicitly chosen on account of their familiarity with the English language and their post of employment. Consequently, the compilation and the analysis of data gathered could not be carried out with any major statistical refinement.

The questionnaires included quantitative, as well as qualitative questions, i.e. questions regarding position, length of employment, as well as attitudes, opinions, etc. For easy identification users were asked to fill in their names on the questionnaires. Each questionnaire was then checked against a booking list and a manual log. In this way it was possible both to register every user of a system (even those who were not actually part of the study) and to collect events, data not anticipated for in the questionnaire.

2.3. Video recordings

Video recordings were made of both the user and the screen. In total 23 sessions were videotaped and over 46 hours of video recordings were generated. A protocol had been created in order to facilitate the analysis of these tapes. The categories used were partly generated in order to complement the questionnaire.

2.4. Interviews

Users were asked to 'think aloud' while they were interacting with the system. Supplementary informal interviews were carried out with those users who found it difficult to act and reflect simultaneously.

Interviews with the participating staff from the training departments were also undertaken, when so was possible. In order to obtain more comparable data, these interviews were supplemented with a questionnaire.

3. USERS' BACKGROUND

Nearly one third of the users (31.5%) have worked for Swedish Telecom between 0,5 and 5 years, 57% of the users have been employed by Swedish Telecom between 5,5 and 25 years. The remaining users (11.5%) have been at Swedish Telecom for more than 25 years, of these 2% have been within the company 43 years.

The current level of employment was specified by 97% of the respondents. Of these 23% have some kind of managing position where a part of their duties is to appraise other people. Nearly 8.5% of the respondents have a position within the personnel office of the company. Approximately 18.5% of the users have positions that directly relate to training and educational tasks. There are minor overlaps between some subgroups, e.g. there are respondents that are managers at the personnel office.

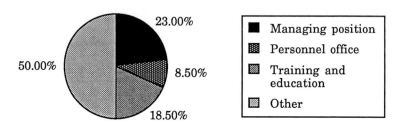

Figure 2: The users' current position.

3.1. Previous Experience of Computers

All users have previous experience of computers (though 26% characterized their experience as limited). They do not have access to a personal computer or a workstation of their own, but interact with a central computer via terminals. The tasks they perform are in general simple read and updating functions. Nearly three quarters of the users (74%) have experience of various computer environments such as PC, Macintosh and VAX computers.

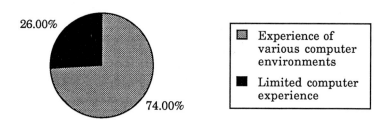

Figure 3: The users' previous experience of computers

3.2. Previous Experience of Interactive Video

Although one could expect interactive video to be common only 6% of the users had some previous experience of interactive video, 4% of these had only had a demonstration of the technique. The remaining users (2%) had actually used interactive video (one while she was a trainee at British Telecom).

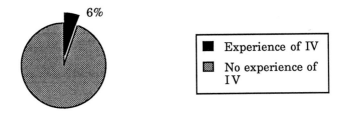

Figure 4: The users' previous experiences of IV

The users were also asked about their previous experience of computer supported training in general. Nearly 84% had no such experience at all. About 16% of the users had used computer-based training packages for linguistic exercises, programming, word processing, etc.

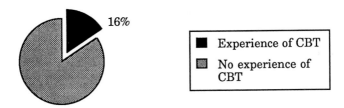

Figure 5: The users' previous experiences of CBT.

4. USERS' TRAINING

The training departments were provided with either of the two interactive video courses, 'Appraisal and Counselling' and 'Effective Questioning'. The 'Effective Questioning' course ran at five of the departments and was tested by 66% of the users, and the 'Appraisal and Counselling' course was tested by four departments (i.e. by 34% of the users). Generally, the courses were appreciated by all users. Most users considered them to be relevant or highly relevant for their duties within the company.

Each training department had access to at least one workstation of its own. The work station was made up of a personal computer, a monitor, a keyboard, a two-button mouse, and a laser vision disc drive (including the necessary software and video discs). The user dialogue was mainly specified on a point-and-click bases, by means of the two-button mouse. The keyboard was used for interaction only to a minor degree.

The equipment was not always located in the same building in which the users normally worked. No difference was, however, registered between the use of these systems compared to the use of the systems which were located in the same building as their users.

Most users (about 75.5%) spent between one and two hours working with the system: 14% spent less than one hour, 8.5% spent between 2 and 4 hours, and only 1% spent more than 6 hours working with the system.

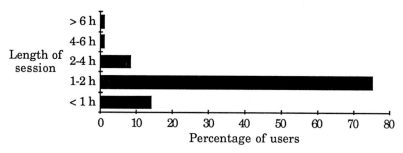

Figure 6: Length of users' training sessions.

4.1. The Course Packages

Both the courses are divided into learning modules and further subdivided into learning sections. Within these video sequences are interweaved with computer generated frames. Nearly all users found the quality of the images produced to be satisfactory though there was a noticeable qualitative difference between digitized and analog based pictures (in favour of the latter). The sound quality was experienced as somewhat muffled. The equipment in itself also emits minor noise. This was, however, usually not perceived by the users.

4.1.1. Appraisal and Counselling

This course package is designed to assist managers to effectively appraise and counsel their staff. It comprises a video disc in two parts (Part 1: Appraisal and Part 2: Counselling). Each part consists of eight learning modules. It is up to the user to choose in what order these are to be studied and if a module is to be omitted or reviewed. Each module is divided into learning sections consisting of one or several video sequences and computer-based displays. A video sequence can always be interrupted by the user. In order to continue the interaction the user has to choose one of five alternatives from a menu displayed at the bottom of the display (Restart; Review; Play; Cue; Exit). The computer generated frames are either in the form of questions to be answered or summary displays.

The Tutorial mode is a special part of the course where the users can deepen their understanding of a subject. User options within this section are all variously coloured. This was a source of confusion to many users who tried to interpret the proper meaning of each colour. The strong effect that colours have on users may be illustrated by the following comment: *"I thought that the different colours had a special meaning, red for clarifying options; green for tutorial comments, etc.".*

4.1.2. Effective Questioning

The purpose of this training package is to provide easily accessible training on various questioning strategies. This course is divided into three main learning modules:

(1) *A Training Department,* which provides a tutorial on different question types and strategies, together with examples on their use.

(2) *An Interview Room,* where users are provided the opportunity to interview a person with or without interactive guidance and to directly observe the effect of their questioning technique. Before the actual interview takes place the user is provided a resumé of the person to be interviewed and from this a preparation plan for the interview is to be outlined.

(3) *A Press Conference Department,* where the users can test their ability to recognize different question types and strategies, and their effects. Twelve different questions are to be categorized and their use is further explained by a special 'Why' option.

To obtain a general assessment on how you are doing the 'Editor's Notepad' may be consulted. It is a simple log on the departments visited and, based on the user's result hitherto, guidance on what to do next.

5. RESULTS

Since most users had no previous experience of computer- or video-based learning the users spontaneously compared interactive video (IV) to traditional teacher-driven learning and learning by books.

5.1. Benefits of IV

In open case studies as this (with no control groups, no regular use of the equipment, etc) the Hawthorne effect[2] has to be considered. Since it was impossible in this particular study to estimate this effect the figures presented have to be interpreted with caution.

A large majority of the users (90%) assessed interactive video to be effective in learning tasks. The main benefits reported were that:

- not all users have to be on course simultaneously, IV was believed to positively complement conventional learning methods,
- users may work on a course in a fairly flexible manner, at their own pace and at a convenient time,
- training becomes more vivid due to the possibilities of simulation and animation provided by this technique,

---

[2] The mere fact that people participate in something new and special tend to affect their opinions and behaviour, this is denoted the Hawthorne effect.

- when well produced, interactive video arouses users' enthusiasm, and
- IV decreases users' feelings of inferiority.

None of these statements uniquely identify the benefits of using IV-technique in learning. Instead they may be valid for also other forms of learning.

Several users reported that they sometimes found it difficult to combine training and work; too often too many emplyees are abscent. This have a negative effect on the planning and organization of working tasks. The users would prefer training to be an integral part of the working environment so that it was successfully supported while working.

A persons self-esteem and success or failure in learning often are strongly associated. Some users felt that a major drawback in teacher-driven learning is the risk to lose face. For these users the mere possibility of obtaining feedback from a system and not from another person was highly appreciated and positively influenced their willingness to try different parts of the system. This study also revealed the importance of proper feedback. Unsure learners often demand extensive feedback; not only need their incorrect decisions or actions to be commented, but also their correct actions need to be verified properly by the system.

Some crucial issues in learning are thus emphasized by these statements: flexibility in time and space, compatibility, and the importance of emotional impact.

5.2. Modifications to IV

Modifications were also suggested, such as:

- access to the equipment should be carefully planned and adapted to the overall structure of a course package (the users also thought that IV needs to be supplemented with printed material),
- these systems must support cooperative work since learning is part of a social context,
- both the physical and the logical portability of these systems need to be developed further.

The three statements all focus on the social qualities of learning and the necessity of a proper infra structure for learning. Free access to the equipment was not considered to be neccessary, instead the learning and the organizational context should control access.

The fact that there were no printed material supplied with the course had the effect that suprisingly many users tried to write down actually everything (even the course of interaction). Since users were supposed to operate the mouse with their right hand, righ-handed users had to move their hand between mouse and pencil. This resulted in problems of locating the mouse or the pen and, due to the bulky equipment, there was sometimes not enough space for manual editing tasks.

Many users recognized the fact that what they are trained to do are strongly related to the work of other collegues and they felt that this relation must be supported by these systems.

Users can not always be expected to be able to generalize properly from training to practice. So, when practice is a major part of the tasks being trained, on-line training needs to be combined with off-line practice (for a more thorough discussion of the integration of practice and instructions see [1]). In another study, by the Open University, interactive video was combined with follow-up workshops in order to provide an opportunity to discuss the material and to practise the skills of appraisal and counselling [2].

5.3. Problems of Interaction

Both the programs adopted a form of case-based learning. When this learning strategy was combined with role playing it was possible for users both to observe and to take direct part in a case. However, due to insufficient modelling capabilities and navigational support (see section 5.3.2.) users were unable to work through and to examine several cases within one session. In Effective Questioning, for example, the users had difficulty pursuing an interview according to their own initial plan. Instead they had to adapt to the system's underlying model in order to avoid dead ends. Several crucial mechanisms were lacking:

- There were no easy way for users to survey the contents of the question bank other than clicking the 'Next' button in order to see one question at a time. This made it difficult for them both to remember each question and to recognize its type, as well as to find out the structure of the question bank which is crucial if you are supposed to make strategic decisions.
- There was no way for users to return to and to modify their initial plan of interview while interviewing (the users had thus no possibility to compare the outcome of an interview with its plan).
- Multiple plans were not supported (different interview situations could hence not be modelled and compared within a session).

5.3.1. Point-and-Click

About 53% of the users had never used a mouse and 26% of the users had only minor experience of using a mouse. The remaining users (21%) have all more extensive experience of using a mouse as input device. (However, their experiences were limited to one-button mouses.)

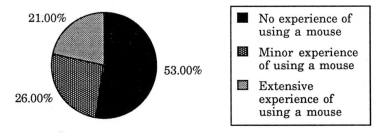

Figure 7: The users' previous experience of the mouse as input device

A mouse-based interaction technique and a point-and-click dialogue certainly simplify the users' interaction with a system, but they also make it easier for users to make mistakes. In this study users encountered difficulties both in undoing an erroneous operation (a simple press on the wrong mouse button sometimes required several corrective steps in order to be undone) and in interpreting the proper meaning of a simple click operation. A click always implies a select operation, however, its meaning varies depending on what has been selected and the context where the selection was made.

Although about 53% of the users had never previously used a mouse their confidence in operating a mouse increased during a 1 to 2 hours' training session. The users' spontaneous strategies to operate the pointer were:

- to use the mouse as a unit of remote control,
- to place the mouse directly on the display, or
- to click the two mouse buttons.

The mouse only caused minor problems for left handed users. Not yet confident mouse users had great problems in moving the mouse on the surface of the desk in a comfortable manner. Other common problems were:

- the synchronization of mouse and pointer movements,
- the synchronous clicking of the two mouse buttons (e.g. when issuing the command 'Exit'), and
- the selection of mouse buttons.

Some users reported that they would have preferred a keyboard oriented interaction due to their problems of effectively controlling the pointer via the mouse and the fact that only a minor part of the screen was mouse sensitive. Users who were experienced typists seemed to have greater difficulty accepting the mouse as sole input device. The keyboard not only caused these users frustration, but also took up a lot of space.

Several users were not aware of the fact that the input device was labelled 'mouse'. This hindered them to make a linking between mouse symbols on the display and the input device. Neither did they observe that these mouse symbols pointed either to the right or to the left in order to symbolize right and left mouse button, respectively.

5.3.2. Navigation and Orientation

The users general overview of the programs was obstructed due to insufficient navigational support for rapid and arbitrary jumps as well as insufficient support for browsing. Navigational aids such as overview diagrams were not supplied, nor could the users browse back and forth through the course in order to survey its contents. They had instead to navigate section by section (sometimes even frame by frame) by means of several successive clicks on the mouse button.

The importance of an effective backtracking facility when navigating is commented on in [2]. In our IV-system user were able to backtrack only by selecting the 'Exit' command. However its function confused several users. All users certainly understood that 'Exit' means a jump from a situation to another, but 'Exit' sometimes meant 'jump to the Main Menu', in this case the users felt it to be conceptually synonymous to a 'return'. Sometimes, however, 'Exit' actually meant 'jump to next section', for users this was conceptually *opposite* to a 'return'. There were hence occasions when users thought they were backtracking the dialogue when they actually was doing the opposite. The users also felt uncertain about if 'Exit' implied 'exit from session' or 'exit from section'.

5.3.2.1. Order as a Means for Orientation

Some users disliked the omission of clear guide-lines as to what order the different modules should be worked through. Only a rough structure into Part 1 and Part 2 (where the numbers signal a suggested order between these two parts) was provided. Within each part the different modules were presented without any numbering or further instructions as to what order they should be taken in. The users did not know how to interpret this freedom of order. Questions were raised such as: are the modules on top of the menu also to be seen as higher level modules; should you hence start with the top module and then successively progress down the menu; and does the physical layout also indicate a logical relation, i.e. do modules close to each other also have closely related contents.

5.3.3. Cognitive Control

In a discussion of users' cognitive abilities and disabilities it is important to remember that most users in this study (75%) spent only about 1 to 2 hours working with the system, and for a majority of users, this was also their first experience of interactive video.

Nevertheless 62% of the users considered that they had a high degree of control over their own learning situation, 36% considered their control to be of a minor degree and 2% stated that they felt no control at all. Consequently, 62% reported that they actually worked through the course in their own order.

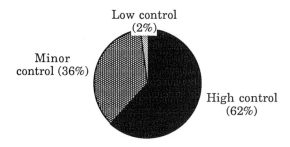

Figure 8: The users' control over their learning

As could be expected, the combination of text, graphics, audio and video was highly appreciated by most of the users. However, some users reported that interactive video may have a negative effect, in that it, as they felt: *"blocks the mind"*. Instead of being in control these users felt conceptually controlled (cf.

[3]). They expressed a fear of being unable to reflect adequately upon material presented.

In spite of the fact that users sometimes found the video sequences too lengthy the users were unwilling to use the video control facility and interrupt or to browse a too lengthy sequence due to a fear of skipping something that later on would turn out to be essential. According to these users the contents of a video are sometimes too complex to be grasped by browsing. The more explicit structure of a text supports browsing whilst the browsing of a video film is harder since it is a dynamic sequences of images.

5.3.4. Linguistic Considerations

More than half of the users (54%) ignored the fact that the packages were in English. The remaining 46% reported that a major cognitive effort had to be put into their comprehension of the language. This severely affected their understanding of the subject taught in that they often both had difficulties in perceiving (or reading) what was said (or written) as well as correctly understanding the things said or read. This was still more accentuated if the subject or context was unknown to the user.

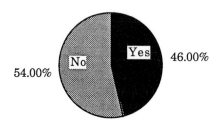

54.00% No Yes 46.00%

Figure 9: Did the fact that the course was in Englich affect your understanding?

Also users with a great interest in the English language run the risk of losing the contextual connectivity since they concentrated too much on the linguistic aspects of the course.

6. SUMMARY AND DISCUSSION

Important user demands reported in this study were: support for arbitrary jumps within and between different learning modules, enhanced support for browsing, and global overviews. The users tried to compensate the lack of these by means of step-by-step navigation.

Particularly negative was the *combination* of insufficient possibilities for users to navigate freely within and between the different learning modules and the lack of effective guide-lines as to what order these modules should be worked through. In order to avoid placing additional responsibilities and cognitive requirements on users (for accessing, sequencing and deriving meaning from information) every arrangement of data has to make sense. This is a highly critical property of applications where multiple linkages are important, [4].

Sometimes users avoided interrupting the dialogue since they had no way of easily controlling the things overlooked. Especially the contents of a video sequence was felt too complex to be grasped by browsing. Interactive video was reported to 'block the mind', in that pictures stick to the mind in a way that texts do not. Whilst training becomes more vivid due to the possibilities provided by interactive video, some users also felt that this technique may impose cognitive passivity.

Direct manipulation in terms of point-and-click tends to become semantically overloaded, confusing the users' interaction with the system. Rapid transfers and shortcuts are crucial in order for an interactive dialogue to be successful. All too often interactivity is presupposed to be something intrinsic positive. However, interaction usually takes time and when (as in this study) users need to specify every step of the dialogue on a point-and-click bases the system's interactivity tend to become a boring property.

If a system, as in this case, utilizes more than one interaction technique, users should be allowed to choose the interaction technique they prefer themselves and not be forced to use the one or the other exclusively.

6.1. Multimedia as a Teaching and a Learning Environment

Even if the degree of learner control varies between different multi- and hypermedia systems users are expected to be able to take on functions conventionally carried out by teachers.

Teachers are expected to make clear the conceptual dependencies (i.e. relations, connections) within and between materials. From a learning perspective, however, you have to free yourself from a material so that it can be reused in a way that profits your own needs and skills. In this study the dependencies that existed within the material were not always clearly visualized, this hindered the users' understanding of the material both from a teaching perspective, as well as from a learning perspective.

When designing self-instructive courseware one needs to take both these perspectives into account and offer users both a 'teaching mode' where the information's logical connections are obvious, and a 'learning mode' where users are allowed to use the material in a highly flexible although purposeful manner. In order to avoid designing systems that work well for overachievers and less well for average and below-average learners a *learner-driven* system need to be designed, that provides both a teacher-directed and a learner-directed interaction.

6.2. Multimedia as Part of a Hypermedia Environment

One of the benefits using IV for training is that users do not have to be away 'on course'. It is very common that people attend different courses as part of their work. Although this opportunity to acquire new knowledge is often needed and is also appreciated, some people find it difficult to combine learning (in terms of education) and work. Instead they would prefer learning to be arranged so that it was successfully supported while working. For interactive video alone to become a natural part of the working environment it requires users that are able to make the necessary connections between training and actual practice.

It is the linking functionality between different systems that makes the difference between multi- and hypermedia. The definition below discriminates hypermedia and multimedia:

Hypermedia is multimedia. However, whilst multimedia combine different sorts of audio-visual information, hypermedia integrate these within a computer-based system.

On a technical level it has been possible in a fairly flexible way to combine texts, pictures and sounds. When this information also is digitally coded then we really have taken a technological step towards true hypermedia environments.

Multimedia acknowledge the fact that, in many cases, learning is more effective if different types of information (motoric, audio, visual, lingustic, etc.) may be integrated conceptually. However, the mere combination of different information within the framework of an integrated system does not *per se* benefit learning (or users' understanding in general). It can instead be a hindrance for effective learning (due to added cognitive processing load In this study, for example, simply the use of colours increased the cognitive complexity experienced by the users). Further designing hypermedia increases the design complexity considerably and requires designers that understand:

- the pragmatics of learning,
- the target domain,
- the use of static (e.g. pictures) as well as dynamic data (e.g. video), and
- the design of truly interactive systems.

"Fall down on any of these and the hypermedia base suffers as a whole" [6].

ACKNOWLEDGEMENT

A special thanks to the members of the training department staff that took part in this study. Without your fine support this study could not have been realized. Thanks also to all those users who so very kindly contributed with their experiences and opinions.

LIST OF REFERENCES

1 Baggett Patricia (1988): "The Role of Practice in Videodisc-Based Procedural Instructions", *IEEE Transactions on Systems, Man and Cybernetics*, vol. 18, no. 4, p. 487-496.

2 Kirkwood Adrian (1988): *"Report on the Evaluation of the British Telecom 'Appraisal and Counselling' Training Package"*, Institute of Educational Technology, Open University, p. 1-62.

3 Nielsen Jacob (1990): Through Hypertext. *Communications of the ACM*, vol. 33, nr. 3, p. 297-310.

4 Salomon G.(1984): "Television is 'easy' and print is 'tough': The differences in investment of mental effort in learning as a function of perceptions and attributions", *Journal of Educational Psychology*, vol. 76, no. 4, p, 647-658.

5 Jonassen David and Heinz Mandl (1990) : *Designing Hypermedia for Learning*. Edited by D, Jonassen and H. Mandl, NATO ASI Series F: Computer and Systems Science, vol. 67.

6 Russel Daniel (1990): "Hypermedia and Education: A tutorial on the uses, roles, development, & creation of hypermedia for education", presented at the 1st European Conference on Hypertext, ECHT '90, 27-30 November, Versailles, France.

HUMAN JOBS AND COMPUTER INTERFACES
M.I. Nurminen and G.R.S. Weir
Elsevier Science Publishers B.V. (North-Holland)
© 1991 IFIP. All rights reserved.

An environment for evaluating browsing in hypermedia systems

P.L. Loo and T.M. Chung

Institute of Systems Science, National University of Singapore, Heng Mui Keng Terrace, 0511, Republic of Singapore

ISSLPL@NUSVM.BITNET and ISSCTM@NUSVM.BITNET

Abstract

Hypermedia systems encourage exploratory information acquisition. Browsing, an exploratory behaviour, is therefore crucial in navigating in such systems. The study of browsing can help designers to create systems which are compatible with users navigation pattern. However, browsing behaviour is very difficult to measure because the experimenter cannot foretell where in an information space a user will browse and no two users browse the same material the same way. In this paper, we report the creation of an environment in which browsing can be studied efficiently. In this environment, three tools were implemented: An automatic logging tool to record in log files how and where users browse, a visualisation tool to scan these files and plot useful charts automatically, and a dynamic questionnaire customisation mechanism to retrieve questions from a question bank according to location browsed and time spent on each location. With this environment, browsing patterns and knowledge retention can be assessed effectively.

1. INTRODUCTION

In only a few decades, computers have increased information available to us by many orders of magnitude. To access and present complex information, a new technology is required. The development of hypertext systems is to extend the traditional 'flat' or 'linear' information structures to a nonlinear one so that a large amount of information can be read efficiently [5]. The concept of hypertext is to provide links between associated objects [5]. Users can navigate in an information base by selecting links to jump between related objects. In hypermedia systems, the presentation of information can be in different media: text, graphics, images, sound, and animation. The hypertext technology has created much excitement and recently, it has become the standard in information presentation in many software applications. The next generation of youth will probably grow up in the hypertext culture.

2. INFORMATION ACCESS IN HYPERTEXT SYSTEMS

With a hypertext system, the information base can be accessed in three ways: browsing, search and directed navigation. Browsing is "an exploratory, information-seeking strategy that depends on serendipity" (Marchionini and Shneiderman, 1988). It encourages exploration into an uncharted domain or fuzzily-defined problem areas. There is no specific intention on what to look for. As a result, the information acquired after browsing is incidental. Users can browse either by following links to examine the contents of a subject or by using a map as an aid. The map displays the information structure in a graph so that users can orient themselves when they navigate. A map is an important component in large hypertext systems because as information becomes complex, it is very easy to lose one's way in a huge system [5].

On the other hand, if one wants to retrieve something specific, it requires more than casual browsing, or, incidental learning. Browsing alone is not enough for information retrieval. When retrieving information, search becomes a necessary tool: database retrieval technology like searching for a string, keyword, or values is used.

Directed navigation [6,8] lies between browsing and search. It is not as specific as search but it is more specific than browsing. Directed navigation is dictated by a general purpose in mind. For example, when looking for references to support one's argument a user is likely to look up material in different places in the information base. The information thus acquired is not incidental, it is intentional.

The navigation strategy a user employs is influenced by his or her intention in navigation and familiarity with the system. If a user only wants to leisurely explore an information base like navigating through a system in the museum, browsing is preferred [12]. If a user wishes to compare data, opinions, or write about a topic area, directed navigation comes into play. If a user requires a specific chunk of information, search will be efficient. Also, as a user becomes more familiar with a system and its information base, the navigation pattern will gradually migrate from browse to search [11].

Search is a relatively well-defined area of study with considerable past and on-going research. Also, there is significant research done on directed navigation in both hypertext and linear systems. Browsing, however, is a new area of research which arises out of hypertext systems. This paper reviews experimental studies on browsing and introduces an environment in which browsing can be studied efficiently.

3. BROWSING

Hypermedia systems can be very complex, especially for new users. These systems have varying user-interfaces such as different number of windows used in different systems, and unique functionalities such as the capability to associate concepts easily. Therefore, navigation patterns on these systems could be different from other linear systems. Discovering these patterns is crucial in developing useful hypermedia systems [2]. Since browsing is an important component in traversing a hypermedia system, experimental studies of browsing are needed to guide hypermedia system user-interface design. The following discusses experimental methods that can be employed in the study of browsing and measures used to evaluate browsing.

3.1. Methodologies and measures

In general, there are five methods to evaluate a user-interface [10]:

1. expert commentary: getting comments about the design from human factors specialists;

2. survey: getting user opinions, testing for memory retention, asking for free recall after navigation, or asking users to look for answers while navigating;

3. customer interview: talking to potential customers to find out whether the system provides functionalities and design needed for them to perform efficiently;

4. protocols: video-taping user-testing sessions and then analyse them to find out problems of the interface;

5. audit trail logs: putting code in programs to monitor how the system is used. Audit trails such as keystrokes, mouse movements, and errors can be time-stamped and stored in log files. By analysing the audit trail, the pattern of system usage like how

often certain buttons are pressed, and how often users asked for help can be revealed. This method can be used to study complex pattern of usage and "there is no limit to the sophistication of analysis" [10].

To evaluate browsing, measures are needed. The usual measures are: the time spent to acquire an answer, the number of errors made, the amount of information remembered during free-recall and question probes, data collected from usage logs like the number of key presses, the type of buttons pressed, the location of mouse clicks, the number of screens viewed, and so on. The following section reviews the methodologies of experimental studies on browsing and the measures used.

3.2. Experimental studies on browsing

In a study [6] which aimed at evaluating and analysing navigation pattern on a hypertext system called SuperBook, behaviour like search, directed navigation, and browsing are investigated. The information base contains a statistics text. To assess browsing, free-recall was used: users were asked to recall as many chapter headings, commands, and datasets they would remember. They were also asked to describe the operation of system commands. The measure for evaluating browsing behaviour was the number of items correctly recalled.

In the study [7] on the effects of hypertext on reader knowledge representation, the survey method was employed. Half of the users were asked to browse the system for casual reading and the other half read technical articles with instructions to learn. Both groups were asked to read two articles, one in hypertext format and the other, linear format. Questions were developed to map out users' knowledge structures constructed during the period in which they work on the system. First, each of the articles was transformed into a hierarchical tree of concepts. Then, questions were created according to the relations of concepts and the organisation framework of the article. For example, "when people have very similar attitudes and behavioural characteristics" is a child concept of "commonality". The question probe would be "what is commonality?" From user responses, the experimenter could be able to assess a user's newly formed knowledge structure

After the user had worked on the system, they were given a free-recall test followed by a question probe. The measure used to evaluate memory retention in the free recall test was the total number of words generated and the contents of the organisation framework. The measure used in the question probe test was whether answers were semantically similar to that in the information base.

In a similar study [13], the performance of users browsing a computer program using a hypertext browser is compared to two other sequential browsers, namely, scrolling and folding. The survey method and a simple audit trail capturing device were used to study navigation pattern. Users were asked to obtain answers to fifteen questions by browsing the program with one of the three browsers provided. Once the user had obtained an answer, he or she would tell the experimenter and the amount of time spent would be recorded automatically by the audit trail capturing device. Measures used to evaluate the efficiency of the browsers were the time taken to arrive at an answer, the number of correct answers, and the number of correct items recalled. In addition, data collected in the usage logs were analysed: whether users tend to use a sequential expository structure or hyperlinks.

In another study of browsing [8], the authors investigated the effects of browsing with different browsers like bare hyperlinks, hyperlinks with maps, index, or tour, and a combination of the above. Both the survey and the audit trail capturing methods were employed to study navigation behaviour. Half of the subjects was assigned to the browsing situation where they were told to study the information for a subsequent test. The other half was assigned to the directed navigation condition in which subjects were given a list of questions to answer when studying the information base. The subjects were further divided into five groups differing in the browsers available.

Measures used in evaluating navigation patterns were data from usage logs and the accuracy in tasks completed. From the analysis of usage logs, it is possible for the experimenter to identify navigation patterns and browser performance. In terms of navigation conditions, subjects with exploratory intention might view the most number of screens as compared to the directed navigation or search conditions. In terms of browser performance, the experimenter could identify whether there were differences in the usage of available browsers in the five groups. For example, whether map and index were more useful in directed task condition while the tour facility was beneficial to the browsing condition. To identify the differences, usage log records on browsers employed to transfer from one screen to another were analysed. If users employed a particular browser to transfer from one screen to another significantly more than the rest in certain conditions, the authors would conclude that that browser was effective under the condition tested. In addition, analysing usage logs would reveal the number of screens viewed and the type of browser employed. For example, whether subjects with bare hyperlinks view the least number of screens as compared to subjects using other browsers.

In the task performance measure, accuracy of tasks completed would indicate whether there were differences in performance between the use of different browsers. Task accuracies between navigation strategies employed (browse vs directed navigation) were compared to find out whether different strategies influence task performance. Task accuracy could also be analysed in conjunction with data collected from the usage log to find out the effectiveness of different browsers. For example, whether subjects who employed a certain browser browsed significantly different number of screens and whether there were correlated differences in task performance.

Another interesting study was carried out by Nielsen and Lyngbæk [14]. In the study, navigation behaviour of kindergarten children were investigated to find out whether they could read hyperstories. To study children of three, four, or five years of age, the use of the questionnaire survey method would not be effective. Therefore, data had to be captured solely by the use of audit trail. The measure used was mouse-clicks required to continue with the story. According to the authors, the usage logs could be used for statistical analysis but they believe that graphs summarising the log files help experimenters gain the best insights into children's navigation behaviour.

3.3. Findings

In studies discussed above, we found that the survey method and the audit trail capturing method are most widely employed in the study of navigation in hypermedia systems. In addition, we also found that these two methods are best suited for the study of different navigation strategies. If a study on directed navigation is needed, the survey method is adequate because the target information can be assessed by task performance during or after navigation. If users perform successfully on most tasks, that is, correctly answer most of the questions, we can conclude that the system is useful for that kind of tasks.

On the other hand, when the study of browsing is needed, the survey method would not be sufficient. Audit trail is required to achieve best insights in navigation behaviour: In the study of exploratory behaviour, navigation should be dictated by users' interests, not by directed navigation. Thus, the experimenter cannot create a standard questionnaire for users to fill out during or after browsing the system. The experimenter simply could not foretell where users would travel to in the information base. Furthermore, no two users would travel to same places so the questions cannot be identical across users. It would not be a fair measure if a user is asked questions about places he or she has never browsed. In addition, certain users might spent a large amount of time reading a portion of the information base in detail where others might just browse widely to get a general impression of the subject matter. Again, it would not be a fair measure if the questionnaire cannot reflect such behaviour.

To create a customised questionnaire without the audit trail mechanism, the experimenter would have to record every screen browsed, every button pressed, and the time spent on each interaction. Even if this is made possible by employing a few assistants, the data would not be as accurate as those captured by the computer and the concentration of the users will also be affected. Moreover, the data collected manually have to be tabulated before appropriate questions can be selected. To study browsing effectively, the system has to have the ability to customise questions dynamically. Therefore, audit trail is a necessary tool in the study of browsing. In fact, in Perlman's paper on Asynchronous Design/Evaluation Methods for Hypertext Technology Development [11], usage log was listed as a method for collecting data. In the hypertext interface (SAM) to the Smith/Mosier Guidelines he built, he has actually incorporated the auditing mechanism as a standard functionality of the system. By analysing the audit trail, he can find out how users make use of the guidelines. "With the auditing capabilities of SAM, I will be able to see what capabilities are used, by which users, and in what contexts (early in a session, in particular windows). This information, although simple, goes beyond the usage evaluation of most systems" [9].

In the following section, we will discuss the experimentation of creating a browsing evaluation environment. In this environment, we have built a mechanism to capture navigation patterns in a hypermedia system built for the National Museum of Singapore. Furthermore, we agree with Nielsen & Lyngbæk [14] that to achieve insights in navigation behaviour, graphical representations of the data are needed. Therefore, in our browsing evaluation environment, we have built a visualisation tool that can automatically scan the log files and plot charts with pre-specified variables. To extend the functionalities of the usage log, we have created a tool to customise questionnaires according to the time spent on the portion of information base browsed by each user. We will discuss this interesting environment in the following sections.

4. THE ENVIRONMENT

The environment consists of the hypermedia system proper, the usage log and the dynamic questionnaire.

4.1. The Hypermedia System

The hypermedia system illustrates the life and music of the author of Singapore's national anthem, Zubir Said. It consists of text, graphics, animation, sound, images as well as links that users can follow to read detailed information on a particular topic. The whole system consists of twenty-one pages and it is divided into six chapters, namely, Introduction, Youth, Career, Family, Music, Awards [3].

The user interface of the system consists of two parts (figure 1):

- The *Display Area* is for displaying the title of the page, digitised images, textual description for that page, embedded links (figure 2) for users to travel to places that contain related information, pop-up text (figure 3), animation, and recording play-back buttons.
- The *Control Panel* consists of buttons of all kinds, that is, the auto-pilot button, the help button, sequentially paging buttons, the index button, chapter buttons, the jukebox button, and the end button. Users can navigate the system by selecting these buttons.

There are two other pop-up windows that supplement the user interface:

- The *Musical Jukebox* is a menu of Zubir Said's compositions. It allows random selection of musical pieces and provides a volume control knob for adjusting the play-back volume (figure 4).
- The *Index Window* is an index to the application. It allows random selection by the user so that any of the twenty-one pages is just one keypress away (figure 5).

252

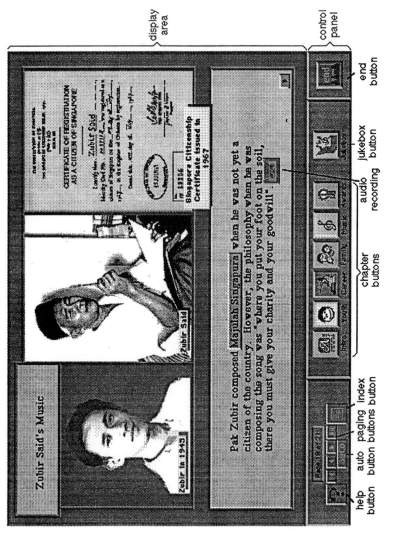

Figure 1. The User-interface

link button
popup buttons
The composer of our National Anthem Majulah Singapura, Zubir Said, is a great artist who lived and loved his times. His music was aired through the mass media and heard as much in offical buildings as in entertainment venues.

Figure 2. Embedded links

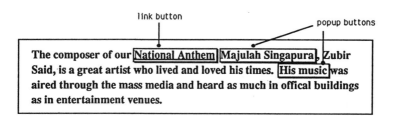

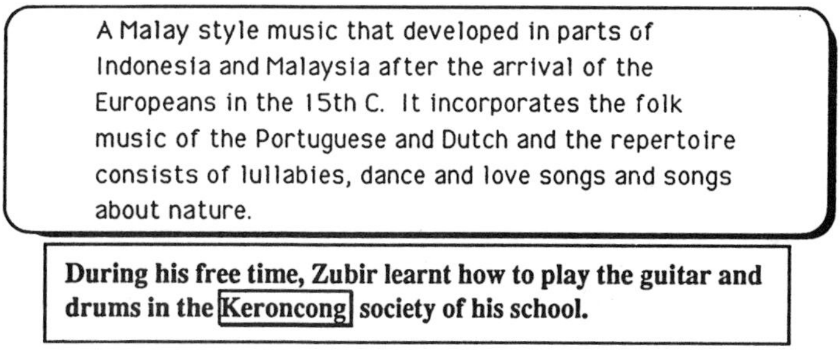

A Malay style music that developed in parts of Indonesia and Malaysia after the arrival of the Europeans in the 15th C. It incorporates the folk music of the Portuguese and Dutch and the repertoire consists of lullabies, dance and love songs and songs about nature.
During his free time, Zubir learnt how to play the guitar and drums in the Keroncong society of his school.

Figure 3. Popup text

Close
Bunga Dan Budi
Majulah Singapura
Dayung Kolek
Desa Permai-m
Bunga Dan Budi
Chantek Menijau
Ikan Besar
Apek Kong Kong
7
Volume
1

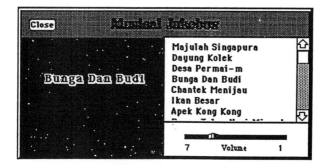

Figure 4. The musical Jukebox

Figure 5. The index window

4.2. The Audit Trail Mechanism

4.2.1. The anatomy of the usage log

Users tend to browse museum systems to acquire general information. Since browsing is very difficult to study without an audit trail mechanism, an audit trail mechanism was installed to capture user responses. Key press patterns, the time spent in navigation, and objects selected can be recorded and stored in files known as *usage logs* for analysis. The system will create a usage log for each user. A keypress is treated as an interaction. Each interaction recorded in the usage log takes up a line and it has four parts:

1. the interaction number
2. the time the interaction occurs,
3. the page the interaction occurs (an asterisk '*' indicates that the interaction occurs in either the index or jukebox window), and
4. a description of the interaction.

An interaction could be one of the followings:

1. begin <logNum> <time> <date>: This indicates the identity of the log, the time of day and the date the usage begins. This is the first item of every user log and it only occurs once in the entire log.
2. end <time>: This indicates the time of day the usage ends. This is the last item of every user log and it also occurs only once in the user log.
3. button <buttonName>: This indicates a special button is selected; <buttonName> can be one of the followings: jukebox, help, index and auto.
4. tape <tapeName>: This indicates a tape is activated.
5. chapter <chapterName>: This indicates a chapter button is selected.
6. go <type>: This indicates one of the paging buttons has been selected. There are four paging buttons indicated by <type>: first, next, previous and last.
7. more: This indicates that the `more' button on a page has been selected.

8. popUp <popupName>: This indicates that a button embedded in the text which leads to a pop-up text has been selected.

9. link <linkName>: This indicates that a button embedded in the text which leads to another page (ie. reference link) has been selected.

10. error <xPos>,<yPos>: This indicates that a non-selectable point on the screen is selected; ie. an error. The numbers <xPos> and <yPos> are the x and y coordinates where the error was committed.

A typical user log looks like this:

```
0     0      1    begin 776 1:45:46 PM 10/25/90
1     25     1    chapter career
2     36     8    more
3     50     9    tape violin
4     97     9    go next
5     106    10   chapter music
6     118    16   more
7     126    17   more
8     140    18   tape soil
9     171    18   more
10    181    19   link National Anthem
11    192    17   more
12    200    18   chapter awards
13    225    21   chapter youth
14    230    2    more
15    237    3    tape flute
16    309    3    more
17    316    4    popUp number notations system
18    330    4    error 375,280
19    334    4    error 332,332
20    337    4    popUp number notations system
21    342    4    link retired in 1964
22    354    14   tape last wish
23    383    14   go next
24    389    15   go next
25    394    16   go next
26    401    17   go first
27    413    1    button index
28    425    *    index pages "10   10    pay"
29    431    *    index pages "19   19    inspiration"
30    433    19   error 190,432
31    437    *    index close
32    443    19   end 1:53 PM
```

4.2.2. Measures derived from the usage log

Some interesting measures on how a user browse through the system can be derived automatically by incorporating a device to scan and tabulate data from the log.

1. The total time of usage: 443 seconds, reflected by the time of the end' item.

2. The respective elapse time between two consecutive interactions: 25, 11, 14, 47 ... seconds, which were the differences between consecutive pairs of interactions.

3. The number of errors (occur when the user clicked non-selectable objects): 3.

4. The number of times the index window was used: 2.

5. The pages visited: page 1, 2, 3, 4, 8, 9, 10 etc; that is, 14 out of 21 pages.

With further program instructions, we can measure facts such as: average time spent on each page, rate of error and the rates of utilisation for paging buttons, chapter buttons, index pages, more buttons and so on. From analysis of user navigation patterns, one can find out the navigation strategies employed, for example, whether users differ significantly in the use of sequential paging, links, or indices; whether there is a particular strategy that users overwhelmingly prefer over others; whether there is a learning effect, for example, is it likely that users change strategy after extensive use of the system?

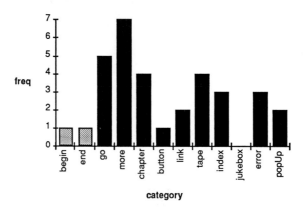

Figure 6. Categories of interaction

4.2.3. Visualisation tools

Visualisation of data is more revealing than displaying a long list of measures. In our dynamic browsing evaluation environment, there is a built-in automatic visualisation functionality. This function is customisable, that is, the variables used in plotting charts are specifiable. Two examples are shown in figure 6 and 7:

In figure 6, a bar chart is automatically plotted to show the frequency of different interactions, for example, how often the index function was activated. In figure 7, the rate of interaction is depicted. For example, within the first hundred seconds, five interactions occurred. The gradient of the curve is the rate of interaction: a steeper curve means less interactions.

If aggregation of data is desired, the visualisation tool can be customised to scan all usage logs, find the total amount for each measure and plot charts using these new values.

4.2.4. Expandibility

If subtle reactions of the users are needed for analysis, for example, we might want to track users' eye-movements, facial expressions while they are not selecting any objects, video-taping can be used in conjunction with the audit trail mechanism. Moreover, mouse movements can be recorded so that the session can be recreated on screen with minimum programming effort. During the play-back, the experimenter can even pause and then resume the play-back on the computer screen at a later time. In fact, our system is able to capture mouse movements but they are not recorded in usage log files.

The data obtained can be written to ASCII files and piped to statistical packages like SAS and SPSS for analysis. Therefore, tedious procedures like using stop watches to time interactions, video-recording testing sessions, manually analysing video tapes, keying in hundreds of pieces of data, cross-referencing between tapes and data on papers and so on can be avoided. With the use of the audit trail device, the experimenter can save much time and effort on routine chores. He or she can concentrate on analysing the results.

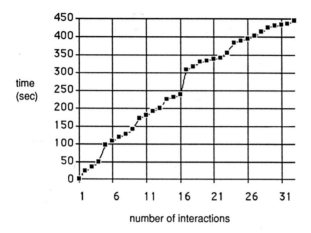

Figure 7. Rate of interaction

4.3. The dynamic questionnaire

An important measure used to evaluate browsing is successful task completion rate, that is, whether user can find correct answers during navigation or recall correct information after navigation. However, in studying exploratory behaviour where navigation is dictated by user interests, it would be inappropriate to ask users to find answers to questions during navigation. Furthermore, it would not be efficient to create a standard questionnaire for users to answer after navigation. It is because not all users browse the same pages so some answers could be missed by some users.

Although one can use conventional free recall to supplement the task performance measure, a problem still exists: Users' attention would not be directed to the same objects in the same pages and they would not spent the same amount of effort on the same objects. For example, some might listen to a recording play-back in a page while others only read the text on the same page. A user cannot recall or recognise information he or she has not seen or heard before. Therefore, the experimenter cannot simply conclude that the interface or the browser is problematic from the material recalled, or rather, not recalled. It could be that we need a more sensitive method to study browsing. We *need* a method which can reveal the portion of the information base browsed and test users based on the material browsed. The dynamic questionnaire customisation tool is created with such flexibility in mind.

4.3.1. The Question Bank

In the dynamic browsing evaluation environment, the usage log is scanned after a user has explored the information base. Since every interaction (mouse click) is time stamped, questions can be retrieved from a question bank according to the information browsed such as where does an interaction occur, how long does the interaction last, and what kind of interactions have taken place (figure 8).

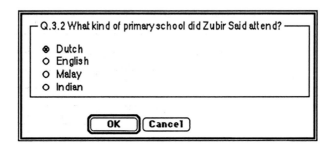

Figure 8. A dynamically generated question

To create such an environment, the experimenter needs to generate a large set of questions on information in the information base. From the creation of the question bank of the Zubir Said system, some guidelines were derived: In the question bank, categorise questions according to their logical grouping, for example, questions belonging to a page, a concept, a window, or a sound track. Furthermore, it would be easier to generate questions from general to specific, for example, from a probe on the general idea of a concept to detailed information about that concept. Questions should also be able to 'standalone', that is, a user need not recall information in other pages to be able to answer a question about the present page. If additional information is needed, the experimenter should provide it in the question. Questions can be created in such a way that they assess the parent-child relationship of information in the information base so that the newly formed knowledge structure of a user can be reflected [7]. Preferably, answer options should be provided so users do not need to recall information: Recognition is relatively effortless and more fruitful [15]. Furthermore, answer options should also be 'standalone', that is, do not include many incorrect options taken from the vicinity of the correct option in the information base. Of course, questions and answer options need not be limited to text. They can be sound, images, animation, or video clips. They are also not restricted to the semantic meaning of the information. They can include a wide range of attributes like the sex of the speaker, style of the music, memory of colour coding and so on. The questions generated will make up the question bank from which questions can be retrieved according to criteria set by the experimenter.

4.3.2. Criteria for question retrieval

After the question bank was created, the experimenter then specified the criteria for question retrieval. In our system, the criteria were derived from past usage log records.

1. Threshold time:

- For a page: In general, users took 12 seconds to glance through the text and images displayed on the screen. If a user stayed in a page for 12 seconds, the system would retrieve a question pertaining to the text of this page. If the user stayed in that page for more than 12 seconds, additional questions would be asked. The assumption is that the longer a user takes to browse a page, the more in-depth knowledge will be gained, and therefore, more specific questions should be asked.
- For a piece of pop-up text: users took about 12 seconds to glance through the pop-up text so a threshold of 12 seconds was set.
- For a sound track: user took longer to process sound because it is strictly sequential. In our case, about 30 seconds were required for users to fully grasp the gist of a piece of recording. The longer a user listened to a piece of tape, the more questions would be asked on that tape.

2. Types of questions retrieved: General questions were retrieved first. Question that required specific answer like dates of birth were retrieved only if the user had spent long enough time on that page.

4.3.3. Measure

With criteria specified, the system would scan a usage log with a keypress and appropriate questions would be retrieved. User responses would be recorded and values of measures would be automatically generated. In this environment, a useful measure called retention can be obtained.

$$\text{Retention} = \frac{\text{number of successful attempts}}{\text{total questions probed}}$$

At a glance, the retention rate is similar to the successful task completion rate used in the conventional survey method. In the survey method, users are given a list of questions to answer and the successful attempts are tabulated. However, this value is based on the assumption that users have navigated, or learned, specific information in the information base. This value is not a very good measure for browsing behaviour.

In our measure of retention, the value obtained is based on the amount of information browsed. Although it is not the best measure for evaluating browsing because of other uncontrolled factors like subject motivation, it is an adequate indicator. With this measure, an experimenter can find out how much information a user has acquired in relation to places he or she has visited and the time spent on each location.

With the usage log analysis and the retention value obtained from the adaptive questionnaire, the experimenter will have a very clear idea of how users browse the system, where they like to visit, where the problem areas are, how much information they have acquired, and what information structure they have constructed during browsing.

4.4. Implementation

The hypermedia system, *The Life and Music of Zubir Said*, was implemented on a Macintosh II computer using SuperCard and the underlying scripting language was SuperTalk [1]. The usage log was also generated with scripts written in SuperTalk.

Microsoft Excel [4] was the tool used for scanning and analysing usage logs. Excel is a spreadsheet program with a sophisticated macro language. Macro programs were written to automatically read in usage logs so that scanning and analysis could be performed. Charting is a functionality of Excel; macros programs were also written to automatically plot charts. Excel was also used to hold the question bank and program the logic for retrieving questionnaire dynamically. Simple dialog boxes are provided in Excel; these were used to display questions with multiple choices. User responses were recorded and analysed by Excel.

5. FUTURE RESEARCH

The dynamic browsing evaluation environment is likely to lead to new areas for future research.

The analysis of patterns in usage logs is important to user interface design. We hope to study patterns captured to answer questions such as: what are the patterns which correspond to the different degrees of interest experienced by various users? what are the patterns which indicate novice, experienced or expert users? what are the patterns exhibited by users when they are lost in a hypermedia system?

The ability to associate user's states with browsing patterns enables us to build systems with adaptive helps and user interfaces. Tailored information can be presented to users with the knowledge provided by the analysis of browsing patterns.

The use of Artificial Intelligence in the analysis of usage log and the generation of dynamic questionnaire is also an interesting research topic. Currently, we have used simple guidelines for the customisation of questionnaire. More sophisticated methods such as the use of a rule-based expert system could be used.

Browsing changes the way systems are evaluated: browsing is a personal activity with which the user selects information to view according to his own interests. We can extend this viewpoint to the more general process of human learning. This process, in the future, could become very personal as the ability of computers to store information increases. For example, when the world's knowledge can be accessed at a key press, the learning process and the evaluation process could be changed fundamentally. Conventional methods of instructing and evaluating human learners are usually based on standardised material and standardised tests across learners. These methods could be inadequate for a personal learning process based on free exploration.

The use of the dynamic questionnaire or more generally, the dynamic browsing evaluation environment, ensures that learners are evaluated based on individual learning characteristics. Furthermore, we can infer, according to the knowledge captured by the environment, the different interests and strengths of learners. This will tremendously impact future courseware research.

6. REFERENCES

1. Burns, T. and Gaffney, J. (1989). *SuperTalk: The SuperCard Language Guide.* San Diego, CA: Silicon Beach Software.
2. Chung, T. (1990). "Browse and Search in Non-Linear Systems". Technical Report: Institute of Systems Science, National University of Singapore.
3. Chung, T. and Loo, J. (1990). "Navigation, User Interface Design, Methodology for Behavioral Studies of a Museum System". Technical Report: Institute of Systems Science, National University of Singapore.
4. Cobb, D. (1985). *Excel in Business.* Redmond, Washington: Microsoft Press.
5. Conklin, J. (1987). "Hypertext: An Introduction and Survey". *IEEE Computer,* 20, 17-41.
6. Egan, D., Remde, J., Landauer, T., Lochbaum, C. and Gomez, L. (1989). "Behavioral evaluation and analysis of a hypertext browser". *CHI'89 Proceedings,* 205-210.
7. Gordon, S., Gustavel, J.,Moore, J.; and Hankey, J. (1988). "The Effects of Hypertext on Reader Knowledge Representation". *Proc. Human Factors Society,* 296-300.
8. Hammond, N. and Allinson, L. (1989). "Extending Hypertext for Learning: An Investigation of Access and Guidance Tools". *Proc. BCS HCI'89.*
9. Perlman, G. (1987). "An Overview of SAM: A Hypertext Interface to Smith & Mosier's Guidelines for Designing User Interface Software". TR-87-09: Wang Institute.
10. Perlman, G. (1989). "Evaluating How Your User Interfaces are Used". *IEEE Software,* 6, 112-113.
11. Perlman, G. (1989). "Asynchronous Design/Evaluation Methods for Hypertext Technology Development". *Hypertext '89 Proceedings,* 61-81.
12. Marchionini, G. & Shneiderman, B. (1988). "Finding Facts vs. Browsing Knowledge in Hypertext Systems". *IEEE Computer,* 21, 70-80.
13. Monk, A., Walsh, P. and Dix, A. (1988). "A Comparison of Hypertext, Scrolling and Folding as Mechanisms for Program Browsing". In D. Jones and R. Winder (eds.): *People and Computers IV,* Cambridge University Press, 421-435.
14. Nielsen, J. and Lyngbæk, U. (1989). "Two Field Studies of Hypermedia Unsability". *Hypertext'2 Proceedings.*
15. Zechmeister, E. and Nyberg, S. (1982). *Human Memory.* Monterey, CA: Brooks/Cole Publishing Company.

HUMAN JOBS AND COMPUTER INTERFACES
M.I. Nurminen and G.R.S. Weir
Elsevier Science Publishers B.V. (North-Holland)
© 1991 IFIP. All rights reserved.

Learning and Hypermedia: Discussant's Note

Pentti Hietala

Department of Computer Science, University of Tampere
P.O.Box 607, SF-33101 Tampere, Finland

1. INTRODUCTION

Hypermedia can be defined as a collection of nodes, each possibly containing text, picture, video, sound, or computational elements, all organised into a linked structure which can be explored in a nonlinear fashion [1]. It seems rather evident that this kind of structure offers huge possibilities for the designer of educational software and it is now possible to create interesting and earlier unreachable learning environments. The uses of hypermedia in learning are many, for example, Russell [1] identifies five styles of hypermedia: learning resource, conventional computer-assisted instruction (CAI) program, participatory world, construction kit, and passive media.

One dimension in which the uses of hypermedia in learning differ is the degree how engaged the learners will be while working for example with one of the above styles. In my opinion, this is one of the key questions. Browsing aimlessly in the hypermaterial is not enough, regardless of how many selection possibilities are offered to the user who goes on clicking and clicking. What matters is whether the learner is in deep interaction with the semantic content of the material, not how many clicks he/she has performed. Indeed, hypermedia favours associative and impulsive moving around, but as Kibby [2] has put it, "serendipity - scorprire qualcosa per fortuna - is not usually recommended as a prime method of learning". In order to establish lasting, high-quality and in practice useful knowledge structures the learner must have a goal and work systematically for that, not barely follow one's impulses.

There are also other problems in the use of hypermedia - Hammond [3] gives the following list related closely to learning from hypermedia: getting lost in hyperspace, difficulties in gaining an overview of the material, difficulties in locating material even if one knows it is there, and, finally, users (particularly non-experts) may ramble through the hyperspace in an unmotivated and inefficient fashion. Problems related with browsing have been augmented by adding maps, footprints, landmarks, overview diagrams etc. However, the system should also be able to assist the navigation in the conceptual space of the subject to be learned, not only in the more or less syntactic hyperspace [2].

Although hypermedia seems to offer utmost interesting new avenues to pursue, several researchers have noted (see e.g. Jonassen and Grabinger [4]) that current hypermedia systems favour the over-achievers, that is, learners who already are good readers, experienced problem solvers or experts in the area. Unfortunately, in my opinion, these students are not the main target of computer-assisted instruction. The average or poor learners should be especially taken into account when designing better educational software.

To sum up, one must be very careful when constructing educational applications of hypermedia. Hypermedia may not be equally good in each and every learning situation: classroom education in schools, self-study, different training situations, say, or, throughout various subject matter areas, e.g. science, languages, art, or social science. To determine whether an application is suited for hypertext we can, for example, turn to "the three golden rules" proposed by Shneiderman [5]: a large body of information is organized into numerous fragments, the fragments relate to each other, and the user needs only a small fraction at any time. These criteria provide a good starting point for decisions if one considers presenting educational material through hypermedia technology.

The two papers that my discussant's note concerns (namely, a paper by Vainio-Larsson: "As we may learn (Training with multimedia - A case study)" and a paper by Loo & Chung: "An environment for evaluating browsing in hypermedia systems") address the theme "Learning and Hypermedia" from two different angles. The first paper is closer to training with traditional educational software, but, contains clear implications to hypermedia, while the second paper is a more technically oriented paper on hypermedia, but, on the other hand, contains potential for learning applications. However, I think that it is possible to find also another common denominator for these papers, namely the user interfaces for educational software. This is an important issue often neglected in practice and research. For example, Frye and Soloway [6] argue that the user interface is particularly important for educational software because, firstly, it must provide an entry to the content domain of the program rather than vice versa and, secondly, it must be sensitive to the general skill and/or developmental level of the user. Thus all contributions in the area are very welcome.

2. COMMENTS ON THE PAPERS

If one tries to place the two papers in the session "Learning and Hypermedia" into the spectrum of hypermedia applications in learning, the first paper quite naturally falls into the area of video as part of hypermedia. It brings new empirical data on how video as a media should and could be integrated into educational applications of hypermedia. The second paper introduces a tool for evaluating browsing. Thus it offers a new possibility to adjust the level of browsing, hopefully nearer to that of the conceptual space than to that of "physical" hyperspace.

2.1. The first paper: Vainio-Larsson - As we may learn (Training with multimedia - A case study)

The goal of the paper is to evaluate the interfaces of two Interactive Video training packages in order to get ideas for a system for PTTs (a new system called EPOS - a DELTA project). The evaluation is entirely based on questionnaires and observations, so that it seems more of a 'look-and-feel' evaluation than a complete evaluation of a educational software package which, I think, includes also evaluating the learning outcomes. On the other hand, the evaluation carried out in the paper fits well into a conference focussing mainly on interfaces. Moreover, I must admit that finding appropriate situations to test the learning outcomes here might have been difficult. Personally I have doubts concerning an evaluation of educational software without any remarks on the actual learning effects, even in the training of adults. Finally, I must say that evaluation of hypermedia-based learning is even more problematic: see e.g. Marchionini [7] for more details. However, also here measurable (quantitative) learning outcomes are usually expected, although now in more informal settings.

The paper spends a great deal of space describing data that was gathered of the participants: sex, length of employment, current position, previous experience with computers, previous experience with Interactive Video, previous experience with computer-based training. However, this information is very scarcely made use of when presenting the results. The data could and should have been used more extensively, because for example the names of participants were insisted on quizzes, thus making usage logs identified. As an aside I would like to note that this might not be a good policy to insist on names on answer sheets because it might influence the answers. Anyway, because the opportunities for further analysis were not fully utilized (at least in this paper), the results presented obtain a flavour of being just observations.

There is surprisingly little information in the paper concerning the targets of the evaluation, namely the Interactive Video courses. Inclusion of this (e.g. screen layouts) would have assisted the reader of the paper. Moreover, no differentiation between the courses is made when presenting the results (from the description one has in the paper one gets the impression that they are a bit different: 'Appraisal and Questioning' and 'Effective Questioning' - but both for managers). Because the participant job profiles were rather varied (e.g. less than 25% were in managing position) it leads the reader to ask whether these programs were really interesting and motivating for all the participants and relevant to their everyday jobs. Furthermore, because the ultimate goal of the study is not clearly identified, that is, its effect to the EPOS system to be built upon these experiences, the selection criteria for these two example programs is left unclear.

In the paper, hypermedia is mentioned only as one possible path in the future for integrating different materials, e.g. the study distinguishes a need for arbitrary jumps within and between various learning modules. This, of course, points clearly to the direction of applyng hypermedia techniques when building similar instructional programs, although the difficulties mentioned earlier still remain unsolved.

To sum up, the paper by Vainio-Larsson is interesting in the respect that it shows that combining Interactive Video to hypermaterials might not automatically be advantageous. Similar kind of results were found in another study [8], where video was used as a part of a media integration project providing navigational agents in multimedia documents. Laurel et al. [8] note that "the responses to video were both paradoxical and illuminating." Users were engaged by the video, but also questioned its validity. As in the case of Vainio-Larsson, video might serve best in educational settings as a participatory world, two of the best examples so far being the Palenque system [9] for exploring ancient Maya ruins in Mexico and the intelligent interactive video simulation of program code inspection at Software Engineering Institute [10].

2.2. The second paper: Loo & Chung - An environment for evaluating browsing in hypermedia systems

The goal of this paper is to build an environment for studying browsing efficiently (however, mainly from the human-computer interaction point of view, not specifically from the learning point of view). The environment comprises an automatic logging tool, a visualization tool, and a dynamic questionnaire customization tool.

The paper begins with an in-depth review of experimental studies on browsing (some of which are concerned with learning). Drawing upon this review an environment for studying browsing is outlined and an implementation is discussed (a small example hypermedia system called "The Life and Times of Zubir Said, a museum system implemented in SuperCard in 21 cards). The degree of automation in the "automatic logging" in this first prototype means just injecting the logging scripts by hand into appropriate places in the stacks. More "automatic" facilities for the designer of hypermedia should and I think can be developed. Also, it seems possible to implement a similar environment using other card-based hypertext tools, such as HyperCard and ToolBook.

In my opinion, the dynamic questionnaire customization tool is the most interesting from the point of view of educational software design. However, I do not hold as positive opinions concerning its usefulness as the authors do. They state that it "ensures that learners are evaluated on their individual learning characteristics. Furthermore, we can even infer, according to the knowledge captured by the environment, strengths of learners. This will have a tremendous impact in future courseware research". The individualization of course materials has been the goal of CAI from the early 1950's, but it is not an easy task (see e.g. the problems encountered in student modelling in the area of Intelligent Tutoring Systems [11]). A tool enabling a student to obtain questions only concerning the parts of the material he/she has seen might not be a good idea in all educational situations, in some areas the questions definitely should cover the whole material. Also, the student might skip some material because

264

he/she already feels confident with it, but according to this of "seen - mastered" philosophy that material would be classified as "not known" and no questions would be posed to test it.

The authors state that "Questions should be able to be stand-alone questions, e.g. related to one card only". This may be valid for checking the recognition of units in a museum system, but generally in learning I think we should move away from fragmentary knowledge, i.e. if there are questions, they should mainly focus on more general concepts than those on one card. Relations between concepts on different cards should be the goal to be strived for in questionnaires. The authors state that other techniques besides the threshold time (i.e. the fact that a question associated with a card will be in the questionnaire if that specific card has been visited for more than 12 seconds) might be applicable. If one had some kind of "higher-level rules" to guide the selection of questions, it might lead towards the direction of more general questions pointed out above. It remains to be shown in further experiments how these more "non-fragmentary" questions could be achieved with the dynamic questionnaire technique.

Finally, I must say that I have doubts on the usefulness of questionnaires after browsing hypermaterials. I myself would rather like to see a facility to activate students during their browsing, e.g. notebooks or "bags" where they collect items useful for their assignment. Thus, the ultimate value of the tools described in this paper might be more in the area of providing us building blocks for better and more "cognitive" browsing tools for hypermedia than in the area of providing us building blocks for designing better courseware.

References

1   Russell, D.M. Hypermedia and Education: A tutorial on the uses, roles, development and creation of hypermedia for education. First European Conference on Hypertext, November 27 - 30, 1990, Versailles, France.
2   Kibby, M.R. Intelligent hypermedia for learning. In Bottino, R.M., Forcheri, P., Molfino, M.T. (eds.), *Knowledge Based Environments for Teaching and Learning: Proc. Sixth International PEG Conference,* May 31 - June 2, 1991, Rapallo, Italy, 3-12.
3   Hammond, N. Hypermedia and learning: who guides whom? In Mandl, H., (ed.), Proc. ICCAL'89: International Conference on Computer Assisted Learning, *Lecture Notes in Computer Science 360*, Springer-Verlag, Berlin, 1989, 167-181.
4   Jonassen, D.H., Grabinger, R.S. Problems and issues in designing hypertext/hypermedia for learning. In Jonassen, D.H., Mandl, H., (eds.), *Designing hypermedia for learning.* Springer Verlag, Berlin, 1990, 3-25.
5   Shneiderman, B. Reflections on authoring, editing, and managing hypertext. In Barrett, E. (ed.), *The Society of Text*, The MIT Press, Cambridge, MA, 1989, 115-131.
6   Frye, D., Soloway, E. Interface design: a neglected issue in educational software. In Carroll, J.M., Tanner, P.P. (eds.), *Proc. CHI+GI 1987: Human Factors in Computing Systems and Graphics Interface*, April 5-9, 1987, Toronto, Canada, 93-97.
7   Marchionini, G. Evaluation of hypermedia-based learning. In Jonassen, D.H., Mandl, H., (eds.), *Designing hypermedia for learning.* Springer Verlag, Berlin, 1990, 355-373.
8   Laurel, B., Oren, T., Don, A. Issues in multimedia interface design: media integration and interface agents. In Carrasco Chew, J., Whiteside, J. (eds.), *Proc. CHI'90 Human Factors in Computing Systems*, April 1-5, 1990, Seattle, WA, 133-139.
9   Wilson, K.S. Palenque: an interactive multimedia digital video interactive prototype for children. In Soloway, E., Frye, D., Sheppard, S.B. (eds.), *Proc. CHI'88 Human Factors in Computing Systems*, April 1-5, 1988, Washington, DC, 275-279.
10 Stevens, S.M. Intelligent interactive video simulation of a code inspection. *Comm. ACM* 32, 7, July 1987, 832-843.
11 Self, J.A. Bypassing the intractable problem of student modelling. *Proc. ITS-88: Intelligent Tutoring Systems*, Montreal, June 1-3, 1988, 18-24.

HUMAN JOBS AND COMPUTER INTERFACES
M.I. Nurminen and G.R.S. Weir
Elsevier Science Publishers B.V. (North-Holland)
© 1991 IFIP. All rights reserved.

DEVELOPMENTAL WORK RESEARCH: RECONSTRUCTING EXPERTISE THROUGH EXPANSIVE LEARNING

Yrjö Engeström
Laboratory of Comparative Human Cognition, University of California, San Diego

INTRODUCTION: AT THE LIMITS OF CARTESIAN APPROACHES

In his recent book on human errors, James Reason (1990) differentiates between *active errors* that have almost immediate effects and *latent errors* whose consequences may lie dormant with the system for a long time. The former are associated with the performance of 'front-line' operators while the latter are typically associated with design, decision-making, construction, management and maintenance.

Detailed analyses of recent accidents (...) have made it increasingly apparent that latent errors pose the greatest threat to the safety of a complex system. In the past, reliability analyses and accident investigations have focused primarily upon active operator errors and equipment failures. While operators can, and frequently do, make errors in their attempts to recover from an out-of-tolerance system state, many of the root causes of the emergency were usually present within the system long before these active errors were committed. (Reason, 1990, p. 173)

Reason offers an analogy between latent failures in complex systems and 'resident pathogens' in the human body. Complex systems contain built-in weaknesses or potentially destructive agencies.

The resident pathogen notion directs attention to the indicators of 'system morbidity' that are present prior to a catastrophic breakdown. These, in principle, are more open to detection than the often bizarre and unforeseeable nature of the local triggering events. (Reason, 1990, p. 198)

These ideas take human error research close to its limits. The focus is shifted from individual operators and equipment components to entire organizations and systems of production. However, the notion of resident pathogens is only an analogy, borrowed from medicine. It is not yet a conceptual tool suited for analyses of latent failures. An exciting new vision is opened - but the lack of adequate theoretical instruments leaves the reader in a state of mild disappointment.

In a new paper, Rob Kling (in press) asks why applications of computer-supported cooperative work (CSCW), or 'groupware', have been so slow to be adopted. He points out that a key dilemma lies in the CSCW movement's reliance on positively loaded terms, like 'cooperation' and 'collaboration,' to characterize work - and an effective taboo in examining conflict, control, coercion, and contradiction in work settings. This taboo makes many CSCW analyses unable to understand the actual uses of groupware.

Kling demonstrates that the dominant latent theory of CSCW researchers depicts work as "the integration and harmonious adjustment of individual work efforts towards the accomplishment of a larger goal" (Ellis & al., 1991, p. 43). Kling suggests that researchers should examine a variety of social relationships in workplaces - cooperative, conflictual, competitive, etc. - in order to create more realistic images of the likely uses of the CSCW systems.

Kling's analysis takes CSCW research close to its limits. The focus is shifted from groupware technologies and idealized collaborative groups to the social relationships and structures of entire organizations. But again, the conceptual tools are not yet there.

Without stating it explicitly, both Reason and Kling point toward the need to overcome the confines of Cartesianism in the study and development of human work. Even the CSCW movement, in spite of its emphasis on cooperation, is still largely a prisoner of the Cartesian idea of the individual mind as the fundamental unit of analysis, regarding cooperation simply as 'harmonious adjustment of individual work efforts.' Not accidentally, Cartesianism goes hand in hand with technocentrism. After all, the Cartesian root metaphor depicts the mind as a clockwork (see Markova, 1982, for a critical analysis of Cartesianism in the study of cognition).

In this paper, I will present one attempt to formulate and apply a non-Cartesian theoretical framework, called Developmental Work Research. I will first characterize three crucial theoretical principles of this approach. After that, I will discuss and illustrate the key steps of a prototypical project of Developmental Work Research. I will use data from a study conducted in a Finnish health center during a period extending from 1986 to 1990 (see Engeström, 1990).

THREE THEORETICAL PRINCIPLES OF DEVELOPMENTAL WORK RESEARCH

Cartesian approaches take it for granted that expertise resides under the individual's skin, in the form of explicit or tacit knowledge, skills and cognitive properties (e.g., mental models). Thus, performing a discrete task alone and without external aids is seen as the proper unit of analysis. This definition contains three interrelated aspects: the object-related aspect of discrete tasks, the social aspect of loneliness, and the artifact- and tool-related aspect of single-handed, unaided performance.

The larger context of expert performance leaks into mainstream discussions chiefly in two forms. Firstly, there is always the issue of 'external constraints' or 'environmental constraints', such as time, amount and quality of information available, and the like. Secondly, there is the issue of motivation. It is somewhat disturbing to realize that the dominant traditions say practically nothing about the factors that make experts learn and perform their discrete tasks in the first place.

According to Glaser and Chi (1988, p. xix), when experts face and analyze a task, they 'add constraints to the problem'. Reducing the search space - or reducing the context of thinking - seems to work fine in stable conditions where tasks are standardized and problems have predetermined 'correct solutions.' In changing or otherwise unpredictable conditions, narrowing down the search space may actually lead to a cognitive tunnel where dysfunctional conventional solutions are repeated. Charles Perrow (1984) analyzes a series of cases where unexpected and intertwined multiple failures in complex technological systems were met with narrowing down the search space by the experts - with catastrophic results, like in the Three Mile Island nuclear power plant.

In novel situations of uncertainty, the lonely, unaided and task-oriented expert appears helpless and sometimes dangerous. Non-standard problems and disturbances seem to be outside his or her field of control. The unit of analysis adopted by the dominant approaches to expertise supports and reproduces this helplessness.

Drawing on the cultural-historical theory of activity initiated by Vygotsky (1978) and Leont'ev (1978; 1981), Developmental Work Research uses the *socially distributed activity system as the unit of analysis*. An activity system comprises the individual practitioner, the colleagues and co-workers of the workplace community, the conceptual and practical tools, and the shared objects as a unified dynamic whole. A model of an activity system is presented in Figure 1.

The model reveals the decisive feature of *multiple mediations* in activity. The subject and the object, or the actor and the environment, are mediated by instruments, including symbols and representations of various kinds. This triangle, however, is but 'the tip of an iceberg'. The less visible social mediators of activity - rules, community, and division of labor - are depicted at the bottom of the model. Between the components of the system, there are continuous transformations. The activity system incessantly reconstructs itself.

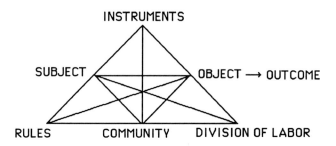

Figure 1. Model of the socially distributed activity system (Engeström, 1987, p. 78)

An activity system is much more competent and robust than any of its individual expert members. The individual expert would quickly perish if divorced from the activity system. Similar views of work, cognition and expertise as artifact-mediated, socially distributed activity have recently been discussed by Bodker & Gronbaek (in press), Bowers & Middleton (1991), Goodwin & Goodwin (in press), Hutchins (1990), Hutchins & Klausen (in press), Raeithel (in press), Star (in press), Suchman (in press), and others, although usually without explicating the generic structure of activity in such detail as in Figure 1 above.

The activity system contains a variety of different viewpoints or 'voices', as well as layers of historically accumulated artifacts, rules and patterns of division of labor. This multi-voiced and multi-layered nature of activity systems is both a resource for collective achievement and a source of compartmentalization and conflict.

A conceptual model of the activity system is particularly useful when one wants to make sense of the seemingly individual and accidental disturbances, deviations and innovations occurring in the daily practice of workplaces. What motivates the actions taken by practitioners in these problematic situations? In more general terms, what makes activity systems change and develop?

These questions lead to the second crucial theoretical principle of Developmental Work Research - that of self-organizing, *systemic causality* and *inner contradictions*.

An activity system does not exist in a vacuum. It interacts with a network of other activity systems. For example, it receives rules and instruments from certain activity systems (e.g., management), and produces outcomes for certain other activity systems (e.g., clients). Thus, influences from outside 'intrude' into the activity systems. However, such external forces are not a sufficient explanation for surprising events and changes in the activity. Direct mechanical causation cannot be identified. The outside influences are first appropriated by the activity system, turned and modified into internal factors. Actual causation occurs as the alien element becomes internal to the activity. This happens in the form of imbalance. The activity system is constantly working through tensions and contradictions within and between its elements. In this sense, an activity system is a virtual disturbance- and innovation-producing machine.

Obviously the changes are not only incremental and piecemeal. There are also crises and qualitative reorganizations of the overall activity system - processes that lead to the solution of existing contradictions and to the emergence of new ones. The third theoretical principle of Developmental Work Research has to do with the explanation of time and change in activity systems.

The evolution and change of activity systems may be depicted as *cycles of expansive reorganization*. Such cycles typically extend over periods of several years. In an expansive cycle, the activity system moves from 'business as usual' to an unarticulated 'need state' and then to a stage of increasingly aggravated inner tensions (double bind; see Bateson & al., 1972) which eventually threaten the very continuity of the activity. Parallel to the failures, conflicts and tensions, there are individual innovative attempts to overcome the limitations of the present organization. At some point, efforts are made to analyze the situation, which often further sharpens the double bind. In the midst of regressive and evasive attempts, there emerges a novel 'germ cell' idea for the reorganization of the activity in order to solve its aggravated inner contradictions. This idea gains momentum and is turned into a model. The model is enriched by designing corresponding tools and patterns of interaction. The new model is implemented in practice, producing new conflicts between designed new ways and customary old ways of working. By working through these conflicts, the designed or *given new* model is replaced by the *created new* model, firmly grounded in practice.

These idealized steps of the expansive cycle are depicted in Figure 2. The expansion in the cycle has several facets. First, through the expansive cycle the activity system reconceptualizes its object and outcome, putting the in a new, wider context. In other words, the practitioners ask what they are doing and why, not just how they are doing it. Secondly, the expansive cycle starts out with a few individuals acting as spearheads of change, but leads to a movement or a bandwagon that involves the entire community and eventually affects several related activity systems (on movements and bandwagons, see Kling & Iacono, 1988; Fujimura, 1988; Zald & Berger, 1978). Finally expansion implies diversification of the initial model into various applications and modifications, often substantially different from and critical toward the initial model.

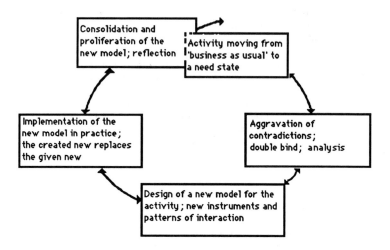

Figure 2. The expansive cycle (Engeström, 1987, p. 189)

The expansive cycle is above all a process of learning. Cartesian approaches describe expert learning in the form of a continuum from novice to expert. Apprenticeship-like acquisition of experience under the guidance of masters is offered as the basic form of learning.

However, the very same masters, with their insistence on conformity and orthodoxy, are a major source of trouble. This observation leaks into mainstream discussions of expertise through findings from studies based on behavioral decision theory.

In many studies, experts do not perform impressively at all. For example, many expert judges fail to do significantly better than novices who, at best, have slight familiarity with the task at hand. (Johnson, 1988, p. 209; see also Brehmer, 1980.)

The studies Johnson refers to deal with probabilistic judgment and decision-making under uncertainty. There is also evidence that novices may be superior to experts in dealing with sudden changes in the task (Hendrick, 1983). Our own research on novice and expert janitorial cleaners (Engeström & Engeström, 1986) suggests that established mastery is questionable yet in another respect. The novice cleaners performed better than expert cleaners in tasks requiring reasoning about the goals and structure of the entire activity system and organization. The experts outperformed the novices in discrete routine tasks.

For Developmental Work Research, the crucial learning in expert activity systems is *learning what is not yet there*. An activity system deeply involved in its inner contradictions will not find relief by looking for established masters who could tell the practitioners what model to adopt for the future. There are no such masters. When this is realized, learning becomes a question of joint creation of a zone of proximal development (Vygotsky, 1978) for the activity system. The needed new model must be internalized in the very process of generating and externalizing it. In other words, learning becomes a venture of designing, implementing and mastering the next developmental stage of the activity system itself. A similar view of learning as 'progressive problem solving' and 'working at the edge of one's competence' has recently been suggested by Bereiter and Scardamalia (in press), although still limited to the level of an individual subject.

To understand an expansive cycle, following it and analyzing it *ex post facto* may not be enough. In fact, following and recording the cycle inevitably means that the researcher also intervenes in it. Developmental Work Research capitalizes on the interventionist nature of longitudinal research. The researcher formulates hypotheses and conducts quasi-experiments in strategic phases of the cycle, thus pushing the process forward and sharpening its contradictions. In Figure 3, typical steps of research and intervention are placed in appropriate phases of the expansive cycle.

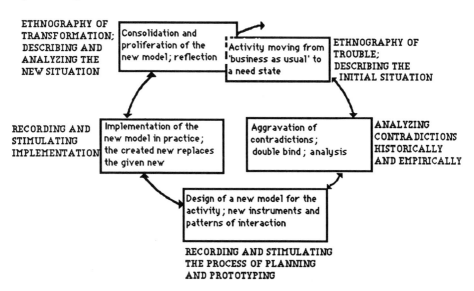

Figure 3. Steps of developmental work research

Like the cycle itself, the research steps depicted in Figure 3 are an ideal-typical sequence, not necessarily something done in every concrete project of Developmental Work Research. In the following sections, I will elaborate and illustrate the initial steps the cycle with the help of data from a project which actually went through the cycle quite systematically. I will focus on two particular aspects of the transformation of the work in the health center: the nature of doctor-patient communication in consultations, and the use of computers as instruments of problem solving and communication by the practitioners.

ETHNOGRAPHY OF TROUBLE

If inner contradictions are the moving force behind expansive cycles, one needs to identify concrete manifestations of such contradictions. Symptomatically enough, in studies of work, mistakes, disturbances, failures and disasters have attracted the attention of researchers for quite a while.

One of the pioneers was the sociologist Everett Hughes (1951) who took up the significance of mistakes at work. Continuing Hughes' lead, Riemer (1976) showed that many mistakes in construction work are quite inevitable in the given structural conditions (see also Strauss & al., 1985). This structural or, more appropriately, contextual and cultural-historical embeddedness of seemingly arbitrary and irrational troubles at work has subsequently been analyzed from various viewpoints (e.g., Turner, 1978; Perrow, 1984; Hargrove & Glidewell, 1990; Reason, 1990).

Along with studies of major disasters, an increasing amount of research is being done on less spectacular 'everyday troubles', misunderstandings and conflicts, particularly in work settings requiring intensive communication between experts and clients (e.g., West, 1984; Grimshaw, 1990; Conley & O'Barr, 1990; Coupland, Giles & Wiemann, 1991). In the Finnish health center setting, we found that troubles of this kind were indeed extremely common.

In Finland, each municipality is legally required to organize a health center which provides primary health care services to the local population free of charge. Our study took place in the district of Leppävaara in the mid-sized city of Espoo, located next to the capital Helsinki. During the first year of our health center study, we videotaped 85 doctor-patient consultations, four or five from each of the 16 general practitioners employed by the two health stations in the district. After the consultation, both the physician and the patient separately viewed the videotape and gave their interpretations of the events in the consultation; these interviews were audiotaped. In addition to this material, we had access to the cumulative computerized medical records of the patients.

Below I will present two condensed descriptions of doctor-patient encounters from this first stage of the research. The first case is a single consultation, the second case consists of two successive consultations a patient had with two different doctors (for a more detailed analysis of the second case, see Engeström, Engeström & Saarelma, 1988).

Case #1

A female patient in her 40's comes as an acute case without appointment to see a male doctor. In 1986, the patient had 11 visits to six different doctors in the health center. Her current complaint is a cold with fever which has lasted more than a week. Four days ago she initially came to the walk-in urgent care at the station where another doctor saw her. Two days ago she visited a nurse at the station; the nurse took a routine blood sample and noticed that the level of leucocytes was unusually high, therefore recommending that the patient contact a doctor. The patient came yesterday again to the walk-in urgent care where she was first seen by yet another doctor who sent her to medical tests; after the tests that doctor was not available anymore and the present doctor saw her for the first time. Today, the patient comes to hear the rest of the test results and to get the doctor's diagnosis and recommendations. Thus, this the third doctor and fourth caregiver she sees and the fourth visit she makes regarding this illness episode.

In the consultation, the doctor focuses entirely on the acute biomedical symptom. He asks no questions concerning the patient's social background and life situation. In the post-consultation interview he justifies this approach by pointing out that "it was kind of a typical acute consultation ... one focused only on the matter itself, nothing else." In her post-consultation interview, the patient mentions that she has stress at home. Her mother had a stroke and was paralyzed a year ago, being now hospitalized. The patient takes care of her mother at home during weekends.

The test results indicate that the patient has some sort of an infection. The patient has previously had myocarditis, but this time tests show no indication of that. The doctor is unable to diagnose the reason for the infection and refers the patient to a specialist of internal medicine in the city hospital. The patient mentions that she has also lost 17 kilos of weight during the past year. The doctor states that looking into that and other possible problems would prolong the examinations and repeats his recommendation that the patient should see a specialist. That is the end of the very short consultation. In his interview the doctor explains that the acute fever and the patient's weight loss are two different matters. The latter "must be looked into at some later point"; discussing it now would have iappropriately prolonged the acute consultation for which "we have a certain routine which steers these things."

In his interview the doctor also explains that "if one referred [to specialists] only cases in which something serious is found, one would perhaps work too extensively here." One refers patients "even when one is almost sure that nothing serious will be found." In her interview, the patient tells that "one always gets such a strange feeling if one gets a referral to hospital; one gets the feeling that this is more serious than I thought." She says that she is "a bit used to it", having got so many referrals before in other matters. "I guess that they kind of want to transfer the responsibility forward."

One more detail is worth mentioning. For this consultation, the doctor only checked the preceding consultation in the medical record. During the consultation the doctor mentions in passing that the patient had the myocarditis "a year ago"; the patient does not contradict the statement. The doctor also writes this piece of information into the medical record. Later we found out in earlier records that the myocarditis occurred in fact about three years ago.

Case #2

A male patient in his early 20's comes as an acute case to see a female doctor whom he has not seen before. The patient complains of a cold and cough. The doctor examines the patient and gives him a sick leave for two days. She then suggests to the patient that the current symptoms might have something to do with the patient's previous chest pains and hyperventilation problems of which she learned from the patient's computerized medical record. The patient denies the connection. In the post-consultation interview the doctor explains that from the patient's multiple previous recorded visits she got an impression of "a young man who may react sensitively with his body."

This doctor is unusual in that she takes a quite careful look at the past record of a patient with a common cold, even if the patient makes it clear that the symptoms has emerged only yesterday. The doctor makes a hypothesis linking the cold and the patient's frequent visits to his history of frequent colds, chest pains and hyperventilation for which he has been treated in a hospital. Considering the fact that the doctor has never seen the patient before and that she hasn't had a chance to discuss the patient with her colleagues, the computerized record functions here in quite a remarkable manner as a diagnostic aid. The artifact provides a bridge between the past recorded by others and the present faced by the first-timer.

The same patient returns to the health center about three months later. He comes to another female doctor whom he has not seen before, again as an acute case without appointment. Again, the complaint is rather commonplace: "when I breathe out or cough or laugh, it hurts here kind of like in the lung..." The doctor examines the patient physically. She then asks whether the patient has ever before had "anything in his lungs." The patient denies. The doctor gives the patient a two day sick leave. She then sends the patient to X-rays to make sure that there is no organic abnormality in the lungs. She enters the referral to X-rays into the computer.

All in all, this doctor takes an approach very different from the previous one. Instead of studying the record to make a hypothesis based on the patient's history, this doctor acts on the basis of the patient's explicit statements and physical examination. In the post-consultation interview, she justifies her approach by referring to the acute nature of the case. She states that had the patient had a similar problem previously, she would have suspected anxiety or related psychic reasons. But since the patient denied having similar lung or chest problems previously, she went ahead on purely biomedical basis.

In other words, the first doctor's hypothesis about a connection between the patient's repeated colds, previous chest pains, hyperventilation and possible underlying psychic problems was not followed up by the second doctor. The two consultations happened as if with two different patients. Ostensibly this break occurred because the second doctor did not check the patient's previous records.

In his post-consultation interview, the patient expressed no dissatisfaction with such a discontinuity and compartmentalization. Rather, it seemed to fit and reinforce his own way of drifting through the events of life - and from one doctor to another.

The two cases demonstrate interesting variations of everyday trouble in this activity system. It might be tempting to dismiss these two cases as medically insignificant and too vague to be taken seriously. However, both patients used a lot of health care services by drifting or being randomly pushed from one doctor and one variation of symptoms to another. They thus significantly contributed to the production pressure felt by practitioners in the activity system.

ANALYSIS OF CONTRADICTIONS

How can one analyze such everyday troubles as the two examples given above? What might be their more general significance?

Developmental Work Research does not attack ethnographic data directly. It takes a strategic detour through an historical analysis of the evolution of the activity system, using documents and oral history interviews as data. Space doesn't permit here a detailed presentation of our analyses of the evolution of the work of general practitioners in Finland (Engeström & al., 1987) and of the primary health care services in district of Leppävaara (Engeström & al., 1990). The main historical phases of the evolution of general practitioners' work may be summarized as follows (Table 1).

Table 1
Historical phases in the evolution of general practitioners' work in Finland

----

Historical phase	Period	Type of work
District doctor	1749-1882	Pre-professional craft
Municipal doctor	1882-1972	Craft professionalism
Health center doctor	1972-	Rationalized-bureaucratic
Personal doctor	1990(?)-	?

In 1985, the Finnish government made a decision to start preparations for
the introduction of the personal doctor system which would assign a
certain population to each health center doctor. The new system was
characterized very vaguely, and it was left largely to the municipalities to
design the actual organization and contents of the personal doctors' work.
Our project was the first one where this task was tackled by the
practitioners themselves.

As an outcome of the historical analysis, we formulated a hypothesis
concerning the crucial inner contradictions of the present health center
work. In Figure 4, this historical hypothesis is depicted with the help of the
triangle model of activity, using the physician's vantage point.

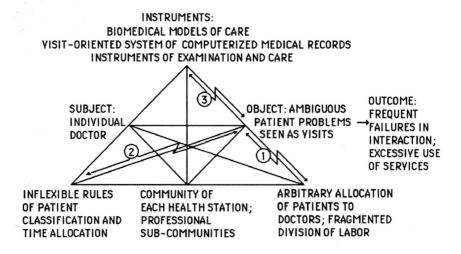

Figure 4. Hypothesis of the inner contradictions of health center work

To test and elaborate the hypothesis with data from the ongoing activity,
such as the two case descriptions presented above, one needs intermediate

concepts and theoretical instruments. One such intermediate conceptual tool is a distinction between open *discoordinations* of interaction, latent or hidden *ruptures* of intersubjective understanding, and clearcut *mistakes.* In addition, there are *innovations,* situations and action sequences where actors attempt to go beyond the normal scripted precedure in order to achieve something more than the routine outcome of the encounter.

By discoordinations I mean deviations from the normal scripted course of events in the work process, normal being defined by plans, explicit rules, or tacitly assumed traditions. A discoordination may occur between two or more people, or between people and instruments, appearing in the form of an obstacle, difficulty, failure or conflict. To analyze the communicative discoordinations between doctors and patients, we developed and employed the framework depicted in Figure 5 (for details, see Engeström, 1990, p. 85-93; for a striking example of such discoordinations, see Whalen, Zimmerman & Whalen, 1988).

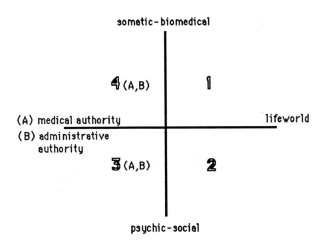

Figure 5. Framework of analyzing discoordinations in doctor-patient communication (Engeström, 1990, p. 86)

The four fields in Figure 5 represent the different 'voices' (Mishler, 1984) the doctor and the patient may employ. For example, in field 1 the speaker talks about somatic-biomedical issues using the terminology and evaluative criteria of the patient's experiential lifeworld. Discoordinations occur when the doctor and the patient talk with different voices in the same topical phase of their discourse.

In the first doctor-patient encounter described above, an open discoordination occurs when the patient mentions her weight loss and the doctor rejects it as a legitimate topic in the present consultation.

Patient: [With a low voice] What I also have wondered about is that I've lost 17 kilos of weight during a year.

Doctor: Yes, there would of course be many things... I, too, could begin to investigate. But since there is that fever phase going on now, otherwise it will be prolonged so much. That is, the test results. It will easily be two more weeks before they are here. If nothing is found, it will lead there anyway, so I think it would speed up things. I think you could just go in there as an acute case without appointment. I thought that you need not go today, but during the day tomorrow, if you have a chance to go. ... So let's do that. I'll write down the test results, and you visit them. Then we'll see after that...

Here the patient's initiative (voice 1) is countered by the doctor's rather administrative rejection (voice 4B), softened by formulations like 'if you have a chance to go.'

By ruptures I mean blocks, breaks or gaps in the intersubjective understanding and flow of information between two or more participants of the the activity. Ruptures don't ostensibly disturb the flow of the work process, although they may lead to actual discoordinations or mistakes. Ruptures are thus found by interviewing and observing the participants outside or after the performance of work actions.

In the first case described above, there is a rupture between the doctor's and the patient's understanding of the referral to the specialist. This is manifested in the patient's *increased insecurity* ("strange feeling ... that this is more serious than I thought"), as contrasted with the doctor's *increased security* ("even when one is almost sure that nothing serious will be found"). This rupture is extended into the different interpretations of the general function of referrals: patient's guess that "they want to transfer the responsibility forward" versus the doctor's belief that without frequent referrals "one would perhaps work too extensively here."

Finally, in the first case we also find a clearcut mistake when the doctor states and records the time of the myocarditis inaccurately. In his interview, the doctor is asked whether he felt uncertain about anything in the consultation. His only uncertainty was that "if the patient herself had not mentioned the myocarditis that occurred a year ago ... I would probably have evaluated the situation quite differently." In spite of the importance of this particular piece of information, the doctor relied only on the patients oral communication regarding the previous myocarditis. He did not check the previous records in the computer. While that particular mistake itself had no significant consequences, it reflects the more general condition of avoiding the use of computerized records in acute consultations in order to save time.

In the second case, the communicative rupture between the two consultations and the respective doctors remained latent and unnoticed. It did not surface as an open discoordination - although such situations sometimes eventually do. It would be easy to blame the second doctor's superficial approach or the technical shortcomings of the computerized records systems for the rupture. But that would not help us understand the recurrent features of the activity system which make such ruptures commonplace. Actually the second doctor acted according to the rules of the system. It was the first doctor who violated the rule which required that in acute cases attention is supposed to be paid only to the current acute symptom.

In this activity system there were structural features that explain such ruptures better than mere technical aspects of the medical record system or the so called psychological resistance of the doctors toward computers and communication. The existing division of labor distributed patients arbitrarily to physicians, each compartmentalized and effectively separated from the others. Patients were categorized according to consultation types. Especially in the category of acute consultations without appointment, a tacit rule demanded very speedy examination focusing on the acute chief complaint only. The ensuing production pressure reinforced a compartmentalized approach on the doctors' part. The medical record then easily served as only a minimal administrative device, especially since the computerized record system was indeed difficult to use for the purpose of getting a condensed holistic overview of the patient's history and problems. Such a compartmentalized approach in turn reinforced drifting on the patients' part. Unhappy with the results of speedy and impersonal consultations, many patients returned again and again - thus further increasing production pressure and making it increasingly difficult to get an appointment - which further reinforced the tendency to use the acute walk-in services. A vicious circle was established.

In the second case, the first doctor actually tried to transcend the routine way of dealing with acute cases - an attempted innovation. This attempt was not successful: the patient did not respond to the offer made by the doctor. This is a good example of how an innovation may lead to a discoordination. This example also shows that the traditional narrow procedure is not only something imposed on clients by the professional experts. Like all aspects of the activity, it is jointly constructed by the participants.

The *discoordination* in the first case can be seen as a manifestation of the contradiction between ambiguous patient problems and inflexible rules of classification and time allocation (marked as number 2 in Figure 4). The doctor justified his actions by referring directly to the rule of acute consultations. The *rupture* in the first case may be understood partly as a manifestation of the same contradiction, partly as a manifestation of the contradiction between ambiguous patient problems and the fragmented division of labor (marked as number 1 in Figure 4). The structural lack of collaboration and communication between practitioners caused a situation where doctors routinely referred even mildly problematic patients to specialists, instead of consulting each other. The *mistake* in the first case may be understood partly again as a manifestation of contradiction number 2, partly as a manifestation of the contradiction between ambiguous patient problems and the visit-oriented medical record system which made it clumsy and frustrating for the doctors to try and reconstruct overall summaries of patients' past problems (marked as number 3 in Figure 4).

In the second case, the *rupture* may be regarded as a manifestation of all three contradictions. The division of labor enabled and perhaps forced the patient to shift doctors arbitrarily; the time pressure associated with acute consultations made the second doctor operate without studying the previous records; and the visit-oriented character of the computerized record system itself reinforced this tendency.

In our health center study, analyses of this type were repeatedly carried out jointly with the practitioners. Looking at and discussing videotaped and transcribed troubles from one's own work produces strong stimuli for personal involvement. The double bind for the practitioners emerged as a pressing tension between the realization that things cannot go on as they are - and the deepseated belief that the organization of work cannot be changed from below. At the same time, the double bind began to take shape in a very material form: several doctors were planning to leave the health center and some actually left for the private sector in order to escape the unsatisfactory nature of their work. This emerging flight threatened the very continuity of the activity system: when there are too few doctors, lines and waiting times become longer and the remaining doctors have an increasingly impossible job; this in turn affects the image of the health center and makes it increasingly difficult to hire new doctors.

THE NEW MODEL

The new model for the activity system was designed by the practitioners (primarily doctors, nurses, and health center assistants) during the second year of the project. Essential features of the new model are depicted in Figure 6 (persistent features of the old model, such as the existing centralized system of computerized medical records, are not depicted in the model for the sake of clarity).

The initial 'germ cell' of this new model was the idea of the multi-professional *team* as the new subject of the work activity. The idea of the team made it possible to envision the personal doctor principle without falling back to the individualism of traditional craft professionalism (Engeström, Brown, Engeström & Koistinen, 1990). The designed new division of labor radically alters the conditions for exploiting the distributed cognitive resources of the activity system. Each physician was assigned a geographical area with a population of 2000 to 2500 inhabitants for whose primary health services the physician is responsible. Four physicians, two to three health center assistants and a nurse responsible for adjoining areas constitute a team.

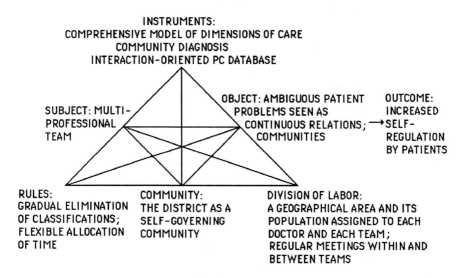

INSTRUMENTS:
COMPREHENSIVE MODEL OF DIMENSIONS OF CARE
COMMUNITY DIAGNOSIS
INTERACTION-ORIENTED PC DATABASE

SUBJECT: MULTI-
PROFESSIONAL
TEAM

OBJECT: AMBIGUOUS PATIENT
PROBLEMS SEEN AS
CONTINUOUS RELATIONS;
COMMUNITIES

OUTCOME:
INCREASED
→SELF-
REGULATION
BY PATIENTS

RULES:
GRADUAL ELIMINATION
OF CLASSIFICATIONS;
FLEXIBLE ALLOCATION
OF TIME

COMMUNITY:
THE DISTRICT AS A
SELF-GOVERNING
COMMUNITY

DIVISION OF LABOR:
A GEOGRAPHICAL AREA AND ITS
POPULATION ASSIGNED TO EACH
DOCTOR AND EACH TEAM;
REGULAR MEETINGS WITHIN AND
BETWEEN TEAMS

Figure 6. The designed new model for the health center activity system

Team members help each other. For example if a doctor is ill, others in the team make sure that an excessive patient backlog will not be generated for that doctor. Each team has its own designated physical space and patient registration within a health station. In that way, the large health stations were effectively decentralized. The teams meet regularly to organize, plan and evaluate their work. Teams are responsible for analyzing the health-related needs of their target populations (community diagnosis). Health center assistants are drawn into direct interaction with patients, giving guidance and participating in actual care. As full-fledged team members, they also take responsibility for the overall functioning of the team.

The three contradictions of the existing activity were addressed by means of the following solutions. First, the arbitrary allocation of patients to doctors was to be replaced by assigning a fixed geographical area and its population to each doctor and team. This would enable the object - the patients' problems - to be redefined as continuous relationships of care and also as entire communities.

Secondly, the strict classification of visits (acute walk-in; appointment) was to be gradually eliminated, and the practitioners and teams were to be given free hands with regard to the use and distribution of their time. Thirdly, the existing instruments were to be gradually complemented by new PC-based work stations and interaction-oriented databases for the teams, as well as by conceptual tools for community diagnosis and comprehensive evaluation of the qualitative dimensions of care.

IMPLEMENTATION IN PRACTICE

The implementation of the new model had some dramatic aspects. In 1987 and 1988, the crisis of health center began to deepen rapidly and several doctors left the activity system. It was extremely difficult to recruit new doctors. The new model required that for each carefully formed population area there is a designated doctor. By the summer of 1988, the two health stations where the project was carried out were increasingly anxious to start implementing their new model in practice - but the lack of doctors threatened to postpone the implementation. The postponement would allow the crisis to deepen, thus making the implementation ever more improbable. In other words, an aggravated form of the double bind was emerging.

After an initial two-month postponement, a series of crisis meetings were held among the personnel of the stations. The personnel of the smaller station came up with an expansive solution. They proposed that they would lend some of their doctors temporarily to the bigger station, so that the implementation could proceed in the population areas of that station. The smaller station would operate with utterly minimal personnel resources, as if on an emergency basis, until the new model's beneficial impact in the bigger station would attract a sufficient number of new physicians to the system. This proposal was accepted. In the fall of 1988, inhabitants of the areas designated to the teams of the bigger station got a letter telling them who is their personal physician and what is their designated team.

The implementation was in fact so successful that by the summer of 1989, all the vacancies were filled and the two stations started to operate jointly on the basis of the new model. The new model has dramatically changed the availability and accessibility of care. The long waiting times and queues have all but disappeared, and there is no more a shortage of physicians willing to work in the stations. For example, in October 1988 (the last month before the implementation of the new model), the average waiting time for patients coming to the walk-in urgent care was 103 minutes; a year later it was 27.5 minutes. In 1988, a patient had to wait three to four weeks for an appointment. In 1990, all doctors had appointments available within one to three days. These changes are reflected in the distribution of different types of visits to the doctors (Table 2).

Table 2
Distribution of visits to doctors before and after the implementation of the new model

	1/1 to 6/30/1988	1/1/ to 6/30/1990	Change in %
With appointment	14724	20192	+37
Without appointment during daytime	8023	4973	-38
Walk-in urgent care in the evenings	4946	3895	-21
Telephone contacts	3600	5277	+47

The deeper effects of the transition on the quality of interaction between patients, doctors, and health center assistants, as well as on the cognitive processes and tools used by them, are currently under analysis (Engeström, forthcoming).

As presented in Figure 6, the model is of course a strong idealization. Different parts of the model were and are still being designed with different time tables. The relatively autonomous teams as well as the assigned areas and population responsibilities were the cornerstones operating from the beginning. Today, all components of the new model are being implemented, at least in limited forms by some of the teams. There is an agreed-upon division of labor between the teams regarding experimentation with and implementation of selected aspects of the overall model.

But have the actual contents of work and quality of services changed? The patient whose consultation from 1986 I discussed above as case #1 may serve as a partial answer. She visited her personal doctor and assigned team for the first time in August 1988 and we videotaped her consultation.

The patient comes because of a fever that had lasted more than two weeks. Thus, the complaint is quite similar to the one she had in 1986. She called her assigned team yesterday and got an appointment for this morning. In her interview, she expresses her surprise concerning the speedy access: "if I had come through the walk-in urgent care, I wouldn't be anywhere yet, still out there."

In the consultation, the doctor spends several minutes asking questions concerning the patient's background: work, family, smoking, past illnesses, etc. Before the consultation the doctor took a quick look at the patient's previous history in the computerized record. During the consultation, the doctor asks the health center assistant to bring the patient's old hospital reports and EKG films which he reads and discusses during the consultation.

In the interview the doctor justifies his approach: "In this new model of work, it makes sense to treat this type of a patient, who has a prolonged problem, actively from the beginning. You can't deal with it shortsightedly, like here is medicine and come back if it continues - because the patient comes back to you yourself. It's better to spend a bit more time at the first time, you'll get the benefit when it continues. I mean, do it properly right away. Previously we were tempted to do it more superficially and we hoped that the patient will go to someone else if the problem continues."

The doctor dicusses the patient's previous myocarditis. He is frustrated because the original EKG film on which the myocarditis diagnosis was based cannot be found. From the hospital reports, the doctor sees that the patient has also had a breast inflammation about three years ago. He actively asks the patient about it and finds out that the patient is currently undergoing examinations in the hospital because of bleeding in the breast. The doctor asks whether the situation worries the patient. In the post-consultation interview, the doctor states he tried to find possible connections between the patient's frequent fevers and other problems - but the hospital documents were unsatisfactory and vague: "it was a similar confusing situation, the patient does not bring out her problems clearly, they hide behind the mask of fever."

In her post-consultation interview, the patient reflects on her experiences: "I thought that when I've visited the walk-in urgent care, particularly because of the these colds and such, they just look you up in the computer terminal, they ask for your name and complaint. But they don't take a person as a human being. This time I got a quite different experience. It seemed clear that he tried to get to know me more broadly. (...) Perhaps I even thought that since this is a personal doctor, he knows that I surely will come another time."

On the other hand, the patient is also slightly confused: "I was surprised, of course, when he started to ask so broadly. All other illnesses and such... I came as a patient with a cold. If I had come for some other reason, I would have understood..."

Obviously this consultation does not correspond to the narrow script of a traditional acute consultation. The doctor consciously breaks the confines of that routine and constructs a broad initial knowledge base for a continuing relationship of care. In fact, the patient subsequently visited the station seven times during 1989, each time seeing the same doctor.

The doctor did not rely on the patient's answers only. He actively used previous hospital records. However, the computerized record system was not actively used. The doctor stated that using it more comprehensively "would have taken a lot of time." This is the same argument we found three years earlier. In the meantime, analyses of the computerized record system (called FINSTAR, a modification of the old American COSTAR system) had shown that the system itself was indeed very difficult to use interactively and for the creation of holistic summaries (Engeström & al., 1990).

In part it is experiences like these that have prompted the practitioners to develop a prototype of a PC based interactive database for the teams. The prototype is built using the AskSam database program. Its main purpose was to enhance the ability of the teams to retrieve for themselves and to give patients information on illnesses and treatments, as well as on various aspects of the community. The prototype was arranged to enable the team to produce quick printouts for patients on relevant topics. In addition to the above mentioned information, the prototype included a computerized version of a new handbook for general practitioners which contains a large quantity of biomedical knowledge easily retrievable for practical diagnostic and other needs. The prototype replaced the regular FINSTAR terminal. The PC was connected to the FINSTAR by the Crosstalk Mk.4 terminal program. Thus, information from medical records could also be transmitted to the database and printed out for patients. The Desqview interface program was used to provide for easy transitions from one program to another (for details, see Saarelma & al., 1991).

The main menu of the prototype looks as follows (Table 3).

Table 3
The main menu of the prototype interactive database (Saarelma & al., 1991)

(SELECT:)

COMMUNITY	(Database on community)
CERTIFICATE	(Instructions on certificates and benefits)
PATIENT INSTR	(Care instructions for patients)
CONDITIONS	(Information on conditions of employment etc.)
MANUAL	(Handbooks, users' own notes)

The prototype was tested in the winter of 1990/91 in one team which had five PCs for the purpose, four in the doctors' offices and one in the team office. During a ten-day period, the users registered in a diary all actions in which the prototype was used. There were altogether 42 such actions during those 10 days. Interestingly enough, the four doctors registered 18 actions and one single health center assistant working in the team office registered 24 actions.

Out of the actions performed by the assistant, four were done to serve colleague; others were done to serve patients coming from consultations with the doctors. An example of the latter situations is an elderly patient who asked the assistant: "Would that computer of yours know any good pedicurist?" In 15 out of the 42 actions, a printout was given to the patient. Roughly half of the printouts concerned medical problems, another half concerned services and community information.

During the testing period, the practitioners developed certain new ideas to improve the database. These include adding components on side effects of medications and on health education. Most importantly, the new tool stimulated the practitioners to adopt new forms of interaction in work. One doctor actually stated that he preferred to use the PC in the team office rather than in his own office because that provided for more social interaction. At the end of the testing period, four of the five PCs had to be returned. The team decided to keep the remaining PC in the team office.

CONCLUSION

Developmental Work Research projects like the one briefly described above have been initiated and carried out in a number of workplaces and organizations in Finland and also in Sweden. My task here is not to prove the 'goodness' of the results of those projects. The robustness and validity of the approach can eventually only be tested pragmatically, by using it and following its impact over time.

Theoretically Developmental Work Research challenges a number of deepseated notions about work and learning. Work and expertise are seen neither as individual performances nor as purely structural formations dictated from above, by anonymous societal forces. Expansive learning means that not only the individual participants change in the process; they also change their collective practice and its institutional frames. Facilitating, recording and analyzing such transformations of expertise in historical light is to transcend traditional dichotomies between the psychological and the sociological, between research and development, between acquisition and creation.

REFERENCES

Bateson, G., Jackson, D. D., Haley, J. & Weakland, J. H. (1972). Toward a theory of schizophrenia. In G. Bateson, Steps to an ecology of mind. New York: Ballantine Books.

Bereiter, C. & Scardamalia, M. (in press). Expertise as process.

Bodker, S. & Gronbaek, K. (in press). Cooperative prototyping: Users and designers in mutual activity. International Journal of Man-Machine Studies (Special issue on CSCW).

Bowers, J. & Middleton, D. (1991). Distributed organizational cognition: An innovative idea? Paper presented at the Franco-British Seminar 'Information and Innovation: The Management of Intellectual Resources', Paris, April 1991.

Brehmer, B. (1980). In one word: Not from experience. Acta Psychologica 45, 223-241.

Conley, J. M. & O'Barr, W. M. (1990). Rules versus relationships: The ethnography of legal discourse. Chicago: The University of Chicago Press.

Coupland, N., Giles, H. & Wiemann, J. M. (Eds.) (1991). Miscommunication and problematic talk. Newbury Park: Sage.

Ellis, C., Gibbs, S. J. & Rein, G. L. (1991). Groupware: Some issues and experiences. Communications of the ACM 34(1), 38-58.

Engeström, Y. (1987). Learning by expanding: An activity-theoretical approach to developmental research. Helsinki: Orienta-Konsultit.

Engeström, Y. (1990). Learning, working and imagining: Twelve studies in activity theory. Helsinki: Orienta-Konsultit.

Engeström, Y. (forthcoming). Expertise in transition: Expansive learning in the workplace. Cambridge: Cambridge University Press.

Engeström, Y. & al. (1987). Terveyskeskuslääkäreiden työn kehittämistutkimus. LEVIKE-projektin I väliraportti (Developmental study of health center physicians' work. Interim report I of Project LEVIKE). Espoo: Espoon kaupungin terveysvirasto (in Finnish).

Engeström, Y. & al. (1990). Terveyskeskuslääkäreiden työn kehittämistutkimus. LEVIKE-projektin II väliraportti: Kunnanlääkäri, terveyskeskuslääkäri, omalääkäri (Developmental study of health center physicians' work. Interim report II of Project LEVIKE: Municipal doctor, health center doctor, personal doctor). Espoo: Espoon kaupungin terveysvirasto (in Finnish).

Engeström, Y., Brown, K., Engeström, R. & Koistinen, K. (1990). Organizational forgetting: An activity-theoretical perspective. In D. Middleton & D. Edwards (Eds.), Collective remembering. London: Sage.

Engeström, Y. & Engeström, R. (1986). Developmental work research: The approach and an application in cleaning work. Nordisk Pedagogik 6:1, 2-15.

Engeström, Y., Engeström, R. & Saarelma, O. (1988). Computerized medical records, production pressure and compartmentalization in the work activity of health center physicians. In Proceedings of the Conference on Computer Supported Collaborative Work, Sept. 1988, Portland, Oregon.

Fujimura, J. H. (1988). The molecular biological bandwagon in cancer research: Where social worlds meet. Social Problems 35, 261-283.

Glaser, R. & Chi, M. T. H. (1988). Overview. In M. T. H. Chi, R. Glaser & M. J. Farr (Eds.), The nature of expertise. Hillsdale, NJ: Lawrence Erlbaum.

Goodwin, C. & Goodwin, M. H. (in press). Formulating planes: Seeing as a situated activity. In Y. Engeström & D. Middleton (Eds.), Cognition and communication at work.

Grimshaw, A. D. (Ed.)(1990). Conflict talk: Sociolinguistic investigations of arguments in conversations. Cambridge: Cambridge University Press.

Hargrove, E. C. & Glidewell, J. C. (Eds.)(1990). Impossible jobs in public management. Lawrence: University Press of Kansas.

Hendrick, H. W. (1983). Pilot performance under reversed control stick conditions. Journal of Occupational Psychology 56, 297-301.

Hughes, E. C. (1951). Mistakes at work. Canadian Journal of Economics and Political Science 17, 320-327.

Hutchins, E. (1990). The technology of team navigation. In J. Galegher, R. E. Kraut & C. Egido (Eds.), Intellectual teamwork: Social and technological foundations of cooperative work. Hillsdale, NJ: Lawrence Erlbaum.

Hutchins, E. & Klausen, T. (in press). Distributed cognition in an airline cockpit. In Y. Engeström & D. Middleton (Eds.), Cognition and communication at work.

Johnson, E. J. (1988). Expertise and decision under uncertainty: Performance and process. In M. T. H. Chi, R. Glaser & M. J. Farr (Eds.), The nature of expertise. Hillsdale, NJ: Lawrence Erlbaum.

Kling, R. (in press). Cooperation and control in computer supported work. Communications of the ACM 34 (special issue on CSCW).

Kling, R. & Iacono, S. (1988). The mobilization of support for computerization: The role of computerization movements. Social Problems 35, 226-243.

Leont'ev, A. N. (1978). Activity, consciousness, and personality. Englewood Cliffs: Prentice-Hall.

Leont'ev, A. N. (1981). Problems of the development of the mind. Moscow: Progress.

Markova, I. (1982). Paradigms, thought and language. Chichester: Wiley.

Mishler, E. G. (1984). The discourse of medicine: Dialectics of medical interviews. Norwood: Ablex.

Perrow, C. (1984). Normal accidents: Living with high-risk technologies. New York: Basic Books.

Raeithel, A. (in press). Activity theory as a foundation for design. In R. Budde, C. Floyd, R. Keil-Slawik & H. Züllighoven (Eds.), Software development and reality construction. Berlin: Springer.

Reason, J. (1990). Human error. Cambridge: Cambridge University Press.

Riemer, J. (1976). Hard hats' mistakes at work: The social organization of error in building construction work. Social Problems 23, 255-267.

Saarelma, O., Iltanen, H., Hopsu, J., Seppänen, O. & Valle, S-M. (1991). Yhteiödiagnoosi ja väestövastuinen toimintamalli: Raportti tietojärjestelmäkokeilusta Espoon terveyskeskuksessa [Community diagnosis and the population responsibility model: Report on an information system experiment in the health center of Espoo]. Manuscript, in Finnish.

Star, S. L. (in press). Working together: Symbolic interactionism, activity theory and distributed artificial intelligence. In Y. Engeström & D. Middleton (Eds.), Cognition and communication at work.

Suchman, L. (in press). Constituting shared workspaces. In Y. Engeström & D. Middleton (Eds.), Cognition and communication at work.

Turner, B. A. (1978). Man-made disaster. London: Wykeham.

Vygotsky, L. S. (1978). Mind in society. Cambridge: Harvard University Press.

West, C. (1984). Routine complications: Troubles with talk between doctors and patients. Bloomington: Indiana University Press.

Whalen, J., Zimmerman, D. H. & Whalen, M. R. (1988). When words fail: A single case analysis. Social Problems 35, 335-362.

Zald, M. & Berger, M. (1978). Social movements in organizations: Coup d'etat, insurgency, and mass movements. American Journal of Sociology 83, 823-861.